MORAL DILEMM
MEDIEVAL THO

The history of moral dilemma theory often ignores the medieval period, overlooking the sophisticated theorizing by several thinkers who debated the existence of moral dilemmas from around 1150 to 1450. In this book, M. V. Dougherty offers a rich and fascinating overview of the debates which were pursued by medieval philosophers, theologians, and canon lawyers, illustrating his discussion with a diverse range of examples of the moral dilemmas which they considered. He shows that much of what seems particular to twentieth-century moral theory was well known long ago – especially the view of some medieval thinkers that some forms of wrongdoing are inescapable, and their emphasis on the principle 'choose the lesser of two evils'. His book will be valuable not only to advanced students and specialists of medieval thought, but also to those interested in the history of ethics.

M. V. DOUGHERTY is Associate Professor of Philosophy at Ohio Dominican University. He is the editor of *Pico della Mirandola: New Essays* (Cambridge, 2008).

MORAL DILEMMAS IN MEDIEVAL THOUGHT

From Gratian to Aquinas

M. V. DOUGHERTY

Ohio Dominican University

CAMBRIDGE UNIVERSITY PRESS

CAMBRIDGE UNIVERSITY PRESS
Cambridge, New York, Melbourne, Madrid, Cape Town,
Singapore, São Paulo, Delhi, Mexico City

Cambridge University Press
The Edinburgh Building, Cambridge CB2 8RU, UK

Published in the United States of America by Cambridge University Press, New York

www.cambridge.org
Information on this title: www.cambridge.org/9781107683891

First published 2011
First paperback edition 2013

A catalogue record for this publication is available from the British Library

Library of Congress Cataloguing in Publication data
Dougherty, M. V., 1973–
Moral dilemmas in medieval thought : from Gratian to
Aquinas / M. V. Dougherty.
p. cm.
Includes bibliographical references and index.
ISBN 978-1-107-00707-9 (hardback)
1. Ethics – History – To 1500. 2. Ethical problems. I. Title.
BJ231.D68 2011
170.94′0902 – dc22 2010054275

ISBN 978-1-107-00707-9 Hardback
ISBN 978-1-107-68389-1 Paperback

For Michelle

A man swears to keep secrets in silence. Afterwards the one to whom he swore reveals both adultery and a plan to kill his adulteress's husband. It seems that the swearer is in a dilemma, because if he is silent he becomes an accomplice to homicide, and if he reveals the secret, he becomes guilty of perjury.

Gregory the Great, Moralia

It seems that someone can be in a dilemma between minor sins. For example, a man promises to drink more than he is able. If he drinks that much, he sins. If he breaks his promise, he also sins.

Glossa ordinaria on Gratian's Decretum

Sometimes it happens that a fly, or a spider, or some other poisonous creature falls into the chalice after the priest has said the words of consecration at Mass. If the priest drinks from the chalice, he appears to sin by killing himself or by tempting God. If he does not drink, he sins by acting against the statute of the church. Consequently, the priest seems to be in a dilemma and unable to avoid sinning.

Thomas Aquinas, Summa theologiae

Contents

Preface

It is a pleasant task to thank those who have assisted me along the way. At Cambridge University Press, Beatrice Rehl first expressed interest in the project and Hilary Gaskin carefully guided the manuscript through the review process. Joanna Garbutt helpfully answered many queries, and Jodie Barnes and Anna Zaranko expertly oversaw the production and copyediting phases of this book. The two anonymous reviewers for the Press gave valuable comments.

My home institution provided material support in the form of a 2007 summer research grant and a 2010 fall sabbatical. Colleagues Lawrence Masek, Matthew Ponesse, and Perry Cahall read chapter drafts and offered insightful criticisms in addition to welcome company. On various occasions I have presented versions of chapters, and I am grateful to audience members for their questions and comments. In this regard I owe thanks to William Starr, Gregory LaNave, Carl Still, Brian Shanley, OP, John Knasas, Ed Houser, Mary Catherine Sommers, Christopher Martin, John Hittinger, Michael Waddell, John Finnis, James Jacobs, Nicholas Rescher, Michael Ross, Joseph Murphy, SJ, Jeffery Nicholas, W. Matthews Grant, John Simmons, Timothy Yoder, and Michael Henry.

The librarians at Ohio Dominican University's Spangler Library have been quite helpful, especially Jim Layden, Cathy Kellum, Evelyn Burns, and Joshua Alvarez. I am also grateful to Peter Veracka and Michelle Brown at the Wehrle Library of the Pontifical College Josephinum.

The Philosophy Documentation Center granted permission to incorporate revised excerpts of three previously published articles into the fourth and fifth chapters of this book. The original publications were: "Perplexity *simpliciter* and perplexity *secundum quid*: a look at some contemporary appeals to St. Thomas Aquinas," *International Philosophical Quarterly* 41 (2001), 469–80; "Thomas Aquinas and divine command theory," *Proceedings of the American Catholic Philosophical Association* 76 (2002), 153–64; "Moral dilemmas and moral luck: reckoning with the Thomistic ethical tradition," *Proceedings of the American Catholic Philosophical Association* 78 (2004), 233–46.

Kurt Pritzl, OP, Richard Taylor, and John Jones have provided helpful guidance to me over the years, and I am pleased to mention my gratitude to them. My parents, Mike and Gilda, have been a continuous source of support in all of my studies. My two young sons, Thomas and Benedict, have managed to extract their father from the Middle Ages on many occasions, and they are a source of great joy. This book is dedicated to my wife, Michelle Ruggaber Dougherty, whose careful comments have improved its content, and whose love has improved its author.

Introduction

Is moral wrongdoing ever genuinely unavoidable? That is, will anyone ever experience real conflicting obligations at a given moment and thereby be compelled to act wrongly? This study considers several medieval theorists who dealt with the question of whether moral dilemmas are part of the moral life. As it is often assumed that serious theorizing about moral dilemmas was first achieved in modern philosophy, only to be refined further by contemporary thinkers, this book analyzes a rather neglected part of the history of Western ethical thought. The common view assumes that during the medieval period all moral theorists adhered to the maxim "ought implies can." In contrast to that view, this book identifies medieval adherents to "ought but cannot." Several medieval thinkers not only wrestled with the problem of reconciling the experience of moral conflict with the widespread assumption that no one should ever be forced to do wrong, but they also propounded their solutions with a level of sophistication that may be surprising to present-day philosophers. In light of these overlooked medieval contributions, the history of moral dilemma theory must be re-written. This book discloses that much of what seems particular to twentieth-century moral theorizing was quite well known long ago.

The present volume offers a sampling of these medieval debates, with particular attention to the diversity of examples of moral dilemmas central to those discussions. Many of them are surprisingly vivid, extraordinary, and at times quite shocking. As shall be seen in the chapters that follow, collectively they depict an exotic cast of agents oftentimes in unusual circumstances. While it should be expected from medieval thinkers that we hear of situations involving monks, priests, and heretics, we also hear of murderers, adulterers, thieves, and lovers (some of whom are monks, priests, and heretics). These moral dilemmas involve a full range of human activities: sex, commerce, friendship, promises, political maneuvering, crimes, secrets, and religious observances. We hear of curious unwitting individuals tricked by powerful demons, as well as everyday individuals whose consciences issue contradictory commands. Since these cases were proposed by some of the best teachers of philosophy and theology in the Middle Ages, undoubtedly a pedagogical concern accounts for many of the more unusual examples, as students often take a greater interest in entertaining and memorable situations. Some of these cases even developed a quasi-canonical status in the Middle Ages, becoming stock examples revisited by later generations of medieval theorists.

The strongest defenders of moral dilemmas in the medieval period tethered their arguments to an ancient moral principle: that of the lesser evil. While the principle of the lesser evil was understood in a variety of ways, it was generally invoked to counsel individuals caught in moral dilemmas to strive to minimize wrongdoing when its complete avoidance is impossible. Even though the principle of the lesser evil is proverbial today and appeals to it are not difficult to find in politics and in law, its long ancestry is not well known. In the medieval period, the history of appeals to the principle of the lesser evil is inseparable from the history of moral dilemma theory.

That this book could be written will be a surprise in some quarters of philosophy, as historians of the discipline have too often assumed that the medieval period has little to offer on the question of moral dilemmas. The present volume attempts to overturn this prevalent assumption. Plato's brief but well-known mention of a moral dilemma in the *Republic* – featuring an agent who wonders whether he should fulfill a promise to return a weapon to an owner who has suddenly become insane – is largely regarded as the beginning of the history of moral dilemma theory. This history then traditionally continues with Immanuel Kant's succinct denial that a strict conflict of duties is possible, followed thereafter by John Stuart Mill's contention that all moral dilemmas can be solved simply by appealing to the notion of utility.[1] While at times this leap from ancient Greek philosophy to the modern period is shortened with a passing footnote to Thomas Aquinas, it is generally assumed that medieval thinkers were not concerned with the issue of moral dilemmas in any substantive way, if at all.[2] The high point of the history of moral dilemma theorizing is usually

---

[1] These classic texts are: Plato, *Republic* I, 331e–332a; Immanuel Kant, *The Metaphysics of Morals*, trans. Mary Gregor (Cambridge University Press, 1996), 16: "a *collision of duties* and obligations is inconceivable (*obligationes non colliduntur*)"; John Stuart Mill, *Utilitarianism*, in *Collected Works of John Stuart Mill*, ed. J. M. Robson, 33 vols. (University of Toronto Press), x: 226: "If utility is the ultimate source of moral obligations, utility may be invoked to decide between them when their demands are incompatible."

[2] For an overview, see Christopher W. Gowans, "The Debate on Moral Dilemmas," in *Moral Dilemmas*, ed. Christopher W. Gowans (New York: Oxford University Press, 1987), 3–33, esp. 4–12, and

considered to be the latter half of the twentieth century, when the topic becomes one of the key issues of the period's philosophical ethics.[3] It can be said that the medieval period either gets a footnote (at best) or is entirely ignored (at worst) in the history of moral dilemma theory. The present work challenges that history.

DEFINING MORAL DILEMMAS

The procedure of this book is historical and exegetical, yet it seeks to consider moral dilemmas in terms that are consistent with contemporary philosophical discussions. To this end, the notion of a moral dilemma assumed throughout is the following:

A moral dilemma is any situation in which an agent cannot fulfill all genuine impending moral obligations.

This definition is intentionally general to cover all situations in which, whatever one does, one will commit a moral wrong. More specifically, it applies to at least two classes of moral conflict examined by contemporary theorists.[4] The first consists of situations where an agent is obliged to perform more than one action, can perform each one singly, but cannot perform all of them jointly. In these cases, an agent is bound to perform actions $\{a, b, c \ldots\}$ but due to some accidental feature of the world cannot do all of them, as the performance of one obligatory action precludes the performance of at least one of the remaining obligatory actions. An agent experiencing such a situation might say, "I should do a, I should do b, and I should do c, but I cannot do all of them together." As the simultaneous performance of all the obligatory actions is impossible, the agent is thereby judged to be in a moral dilemma. By extending the term *dilemma* to

---

P. S. Greenspan, *Practical Guilt: Moral Dilemmas, Emotions, and Social Norms* (New York: Oxford University Press, 1995), 11–23.

[3] After Gowans's *Moral Dilemmas*, a second anthology of contemporary articles is *Moral Dilemmas and Moral Theory*, ed. H. E. Mason (New York: Oxford University Press, 1996). Significant monographs on the problem of moral dilemmas include: Daniel Statman, *Moral Dilemmas* (Amsterdam: Rodopi, 1995); Christopher W. Gowans, *Innocence Lost: An Examination of Inescapable Moral Wrongdoing* (New York: Oxford University Press, 1994); Walter Sinnott-Armstrong, *Moral Dilemmas* (Oxford: Blackwell, 1988); Edmund N. Santurri, *Perplexity in the Moral Life: Philosophical and Theological Considerations* (Charlottesville: University Press of Virginia, 1987). See also Daniel McInerny, *The Difficult Good: A Thomistic Approach to Moral Conflict and Human Happiness* (New York: Fordham University Press, 2006).

[4] For the distinction between these two types of moral dilemma, see Bernard Williams, "Ethical Consistency," in *Problems of the Self: Philosophical Papers 1956–1972* (Cambridge University Press, 1973), 166–86, at 171.

cover these situations where more than two jointly unfulfillable obligations impend for an agent, this book follows contemporary theorists who have used the term beyond its etymological sense of a *double-proposition*. In the analyses that follow, the term *dilemma* will be used in this wider sense, rather than using *trilemma, tetralemma,* or similar terms to refer to situations where an agent encounters several obligations that cannot be simultaneously fulfilled.[5]

The second class of moral conflict covered by the aforementioned definition consists of situations where an agent is simultaneously obliged to perform an action and not perform that very action.[6] In such situations, an agent discovers equally compelling moral reasons to perform and to desist from an action, and these compelling moral reasons cannot be voided. Most of the medieval theorists treated in this volume examine situations falling under this second kind of moral conflict, as they often consider moral dilemmas to be a set of contradictories, where an act and its omission are simultaneously obligatory. In these cases, an agent fails by acting or not acting, since at least one prong of the dilemma will not be fulfilled with the selection of the other prong. The notion of moral dilemma adopted here accounts for such moral dilemmas composed of contradictory prongs, as well as situations where an agent is subject to

---

[5] Some philosophers define moral dilemmas in a way that offers the possibility of more than two obligations in conflict. See, for instance, Thomas Nagel, "The Fragmentation of Value," in *Mortal Questions* (Cambridge University Press, 1979), 128–41, at 128: "The strongest cases of conflict are genuine dilemmas, where there is decisive support for two or more incompatible courses of action or inaction"; Greenspan, *Practical Guilt*, 9: "cases in which all of the agent's alternatives, through no fault of his own, turn out to be morally wrong"; and Santurri, *Perplexity in the Moral Life*, 2: "a moral dilemma is a situation in which it actually *is* the case (rather than merely *seems* to be the case) that a moral transgression is unavoidable." Other theorists offer definitions that highlight situations consisting of simply two prongs. Consider Terrance C. McConnell, "Moral Residue and Dilemmas," in *Moral Dilemmas and Moral Theory*, 36–47, at 36: "A moral dilemma is a situation in which each of two things ought to be done but both cannot be done"; Ruth Barcan Marcus, "Moral Dilemmas and Consistency," *The Journal of Philosophy* 77 (1980), 121–36, at 122: "In the one-person case there are principles in accordance with which one ought to do *x* and one ought to do *y*, where doing *y* requires that one refrain from doing *x*"; and Earl Conee, "Why Moral Dilemmas are Impossible," *American Philosophical Quarterly* 26 (1989), 133–41, at 134: "There is a moral dilemma just if someone morally ought to take each of two incompatible alternatives . . . This is the sort of moral dilemma that philosophers have argued about."

[6] Many contemporary theorists frame their discussions with this type of moral dilemma in mind. See, for instance, E. J. Lemmon, "Moral Dilemmas," *The Philosophical Review* 70 (1962), 139–58, at 148: "My third class of moral situation constitutes what I take to be the simplest variety of moral dilemma in the full sense. The characterization of this class is as follows: a man ought to do something and ought not to do that thing." See also Alan Donagan, "Moral Dilemmas, Genuine and Spurious: A Comparative Anatomy," *Ethics* 104 (1993), 7–21, at 9: "Given what morality is, what would a moral dilemma be, if there were such a thing? A common answer – indeed the one that immediately comes to mind – is that it would be a situation in which, according to the true principles of morality, a moral agent was obliged both to perform an action of a specified kind, and not to perform it."

a greater number of impending obligations that cannot be consistently fulfilled.[7]

The number of philosophers and theologians of the medieval period who discussed situations satisfying this general definition of moral dilemma is large, so some selection has been necessary for a volume of this sort. In one way it would be premature to attempt a comprehensive history of moral dilemma theory of the Middle Ages, since the writings of a great number of canonists, philosophers, and theologians are not yet available in critical editions. Even though the account given here is far from exhaustive, it seeks to be representative of the medieval period, as the principal figures covered in this book satisfy several criteria. They each: (1) are presently recognized as major figures in the history of medieval philosophy, theology, or canon law; (2) have theorized with a view to what their predecessors have said on the subject; (3) have expanded what they have received from their predecessors in a significant or noteworthy way; and finally, (4) represent a major school of the period (e.g., Dominican, Franciscan, Thomistic). What follows, therefore, can be viewed as a set of snapshots of select medieval thinkers who epitomize moral dilemma theorizing during the medieval period. While not a comprehensive history, the chapters that follow can be viewed collectively as an argument to establish the neglected medieval period in its rightful place in the history of moral dilemma theory.

Even though this work looks to an earlier time for theorizing on a subject of great interest to contemporary philosophers, it attempts to avoid the anachronistic pitfall of projecting present-day assumptions onto the medieval period. This concern is particularly important given that the very project of assembling a history of medieval philosophy has fallen under scrutiny in recent years, as some have alleged that current philosophical categories do not necessarily best explain how medieval thinkers viewed their

---

[7] Some theorists also have general definitions broad enough to include both kinds of moral dilemmas. See Earl Conee, "Against Moral Dilemmas," *The Philosophical Review* 91 (1982), 87–97, at 87: "Call an agent's predicament a 'moral dilemma' just when the agent cannot do everything that it is morally obligatory for him to do in the situation, though he can carry out each obligation"; Christopher W. Gowans, "The Debate on Moral Dilemmas," in *Moral Dilemmas*, ed. Gowans, 3–33, at 3: "A moral dilemma is a situation in which an agent *S* morally ought to do *A* and morally ought to do *B* but cannot do both, either because *B* is just not-doing-*A* or because some contingent feature of the world prevents doing both." Also notable is the definition offered by Daniel Statman, *Moral Dilemmas* (Amsterdam: Rodopi, 1995), 16: "We are speaking of a situation in which the agent must choose between two courses of action, A and B, and the following conditions obtain: 1. The agent ought to do A and also ought to do B. 2. A and B are incompatible in this situation. 3. Both A and B involve doing evil. 4. The evil is serious, 'dramatic.' 5. No moral consideration allows us to say that one of the options overrides the other. 6. The agent knows conditions 1–5." Statman does not preclude the possibility that A and B could be contradictories.

own projects.[8] Medieval theorists possessed their own set of assumptions, and their conceptions of the boundaries of particular intellectual disciplines (including philosophy) differ greatly from our own.

The greatest divide between medieval moral dilemma theory and its present-day counterpart concerns the basic moral category under which moral dilemmas are considered. For medieval thinkers it was sin, rather than simply moral failure or moral transgression. The theorists examined in this volume considered moral dilemmas primarily for what their existence might entail for the state of one's soul in the afterlife. For example, medieval proponents of moral dilemmas frequently had to counter the objection that claimed moral dilemmas cannot exist, for their existence would make sin necessary and salvation impossible. These otherworldly concerns of sin, salvation, heaven, and hell are almost never broached by twentieth-century philosophers engaged in moral dilemma theory. In one way, the search for moral dilemma theory in the Middle Ages is much like the search for moral philosophy in the Middle Ages. Admittedly, some have argued that there is no such moral philosophy in the Middle Ages – only moral theology. Nevertheless, the sophistication of medieval argumentation and the clear analogues to contemporary concerns cannot be avoided. Both medieval and present-day theorists are concerned with whether moral dilemmas exist, how their existence might be demonstrated, and what implications their existence might have for such issues as free will, the development of the virtues, and general moral theory.

The present book is sensitive to these historiographical concerns. While my interests are primarily philosophical, I draw from a range of sources that include documents in theology and canon law, in addition to those that are more easily recognized as philosophical. I have provided relevant biographical information for each of the principal medieval thinkers considered in this volume, and I have attempted to be sensitive to aims and presuppositions guiding the various medieval discussions and to note them when necessary.

TERMINOLOGY

Bringing medieval thinkers into a contemporary debate first presents a problem of terminology. Medieval thinkers who discuss moral dilemmas

---

[8] Works of particular note include John Inglis, *Spheres of Philosophical Inquiry and the Historiography of Medieval Philosophy* (Leiden: Brill, 1998); John Marenbon, *Later Medieval Philosophy (1150–1350): An Introduction* (London: Routledge, 1991), 83–90; John Marenbon, *Early Medieval Philosophy (480–1150): An Introduction*, rev. edn (London: Routledge, 1991), vii–xii; and Mark D. Jordan, "Medieval Philosophy of the Future," in *The Past and Future of Medieval Studies*, ed. John Van Engen (Notre Dame: University of Notre Dame Press, 1994), 148–65.

customarily speak of an agent as being perplexed (*perplexus*) or suffering from perplexity (*perplexitas, perplexio*). For instance, a thirteenth-century compendium of theological terms offers the following definition:

> Perplexity is an entrapment between opposites, so that one seems always to be bound to sin, in whatever side one might choose (*Perplexitas est involutio inter opposita, ita quod videtur semper vergere in peccatum, quamcumque partem eligat*).[9]

This definition is consistent with the one adopted for this volume, although the presence of the qualifier "seems" offers the possibility that situations of moral entrapment might be apparent rather than real. In contrast to the standard medieval nomenclature that speaks of an agent as *perplexed* when unable to avoid wrongdoing, contemporary philosophers tend to state simply that an agent is *in a moral dilemma*. These expressions are not inconsistent, but some clarification is required to forestall confusion. A difficulty is that *perplexitas* and its cognates admit of two meanings. First, the literal or etymological meaning of *perplexitas* is the condition of being entangled, ensnared, or intertwined, as when one is caught in a trap without the means of escape. This sense of the word is of particular relevance to the present volume. Second, the extended or metaphorical sense of *perplexitas* is the condition of being confused.[10] It could be said that the first sense is primarily ontological, and the second is epistemic. Of particular concern for this study are those situations where an agent is described as *perplexus* in the sense of being confused because the agent is *perplexus* in the sense of being trapped by conflicting moral obligations. Of course, an agent may be confused in the absence of genuine moral entanglement, since what an agent initially judges to be a moral dilemma may, upon reflection, be realized to be merely an apparent one with the discovery of some previously unrecognized and morally permissible option. In those cases, the perplexity would be subjective, but not objective.

This twofold sense of *perplexitas* to mean entanglement as well as confusion is quite ancient, as it is found in the Roman legal tradition of the

[9] The authorship of the *Statement of the Terms of Theology* (*Declaratio terminorum theologiae*) is contested. A modern edition of this work is printed in Bonaventure, *Opera omnia*, ed. A. C. Peltier, 15 vols. (Paris: Vivès, 1864–1871), VII: 232–9, with the cited text at 237.
[10] For the various senses of the terms *perplexus* and *perplexitas*, see *Thesaurus Linguae Latinae*, vol. X, I, fasc. XI *pernumero-persuadeo* (Stuttgart and Leipzig: B. G. Teubner, 1998), 1650–3. An instance of *perplexus* in its primary sense of "entangled" is present in Lucretius's *On the Nature of Things* (*De rerum natura*). The philosophical poem accounts for the origin of visible objects by stating that atoms falling through the void become *perplexi*. See Lucretius, *De rerum natura* 2, 102. See also the appearance of *perplexus* in Vergil, *Aeneid* 9, 391.

casus perplexus or "perplexing case."[11] The expression was used to designate instances where jurists were left to render a decision in confusing situations where laws conflicted or where litigants had equally pressing claims. One classic example is the case of a testator who leaves a will containing mutually inconsistent prescriptions, thereby leaving jurists to wrestle with a conflicting set of instructions. Juridical perplexity is, of course, a topic of interest well beyond the ancient Roman period. The best-known philosopher to approach the issue was Gottfried Leibniz, whose 1666 doctoral *On Perplexing Cases in Law* (*De casibus perplexis in jure*) set forth an ambitious method for resolving difficult or uncertain cases.[12] The present volume will touch upon legal perplexity only to the extent that it concerns agents obliged to select among morally impermissible options.

A PRÉCIS OF CHAPTERS

This book divides into six chapters. It begins with the thought of Gratian, the twelfth-century founder of the science of canon law. The influence of the canon law tradition on medieval philosophical and theological thought is at times unrecognized, but this chapter establishes its clout through several centuries of medieval moral dilemma theorizing. In the thirteenth distinction of his *Decretum*, Gratian argues that agents who find themselves in moral dilemmas should appeal to the principle of the lesser of two evils. In support of his view, Gratian marshals the authority of Gregory the Great, and in doing so inaugurates a controversy over the meaning of Gregory's texts that will persist for centuries. The multi-authored medieval commentary on Gratian's *Decretum*, known as the *Glossa ordinaria*, is surprisingly quite critical of Gratian, precisely because the glossators who authored it reject the possibility that agents are ever inescapably bound to commit moral transgressions. The adoption of Gratian's *Decretum* as the standard medieval textbook for the study of canon law, together with the widespread reading of it with the *Glossa ordinaria*, set forth two opposing

---

[11] For a discussion of *casus perplexus* in the Roman legal tradition, see Reinhard Zimmermann, *The Law of Obligations: Roman Foundations of the Civilian Tradition* (Oxford: Clarendon Press, 1990), 721–2; Ralph Backhaus, *Casus perplexus: Die Lösung in sich widersprüchlicher Rechtsfälle durch die klassische römische Jurisprudenz* (Munich: C. H. Beck'sche Verlagbuchhandlung, 1981); and Stéphan Geonget, *La notion de perplexité a la Renaissance* (Geneva: Librairie Droz, 2006), especially chap. 1: "*Casus perplexus* et antinomies des lois," 23–59.

[12] Gottfried Wilhelm Leibniz, *Disputatio de casibus perplexis in jure*, in *Sämtliche Schriften und Briefe* (Berlin: Darmstadt: Otto Reichl Verlag, 1930), VI.1: 231–56. For an evaluation of this work, see Hanina Ben-Menahem, "Leibniz on Hard Cases," *Archiv für Rechts- und Sozialphilosophie* 79 (1993), 198–215.

yet equally authoritative positions as the intellectual inheritance for later medieval theorists on the question of moral dilemmas. Gratian and his critics framed the issue of moral dilemmas for generations of medieval thinkers.

The second chapter examines a pair of major summaries of theology from the early thirteenth century, the *Summa aurea* of the Parisian secular master William of Auxerre (*c.* 1140–1231), and the later Franciscan compendium known as the *Summa Halesiana*, associated with Alexander of Hales (*c.* 1185–1245). Both works were quite influential in forming the philosophical and theological thought of the high scholasticism of the later thirteenth and fourteenth centuries, and both contain extended discussions of moral dilemmas. The authors of those works demonstrate a familiarity with Gregory's defense of moral dilemmas, perhaps through the work of Gratian, and they put Gregory's words to various uses. Particularly valuable in these *summae* are analyses of twenty alleged moral dilemmas. Most of these dilemmas ultimately are judged to be merely apparent, as the authors of both works propose that there exists a previously unconsidered and morally permissible option for the agents described in the majority of cases. A few of the dilemmas, however, are deemed true moral dilemmas by the authors of each work, as the agents in those remaining cases are judged to be unable to escape some degree of moral wrongdoing. Both works promote the principle of the lesser evil as a way for agents trapped in moral dilemmas to minimize their moral transgressions.

The quasi-autobiographical *Vita coaetanea* or *Contemporary Life* of Raymond Lull (*c.* 1232–1316) is the subject of the third chapter. This quite remarkable medieval work was dictated by Lull to monks near the end of his life, and in it the philosopher and Christian apologist recounts four moral dilemmas he experienced, adding in each case an explanation of how he was miraculously saved from committing wrongdoing. In describing his dilemmas, Lull uses the philosophical terminology of thirteenth-century discussions of perplexity of conscience, so his work manifests an acquaintance with moral psychology controversies of the period. Lull's *Vita* asserts the existence of moral dilemmas as part of the moral life and exhibits a highly unusual theological strategy for how agents should deal with them. The *Vita* suggests that agents who find themselves trapped in situations of inescapable moral wrongdoing should engage in petitionary prayer, for God is able to remove prayerful agents from the dilemmas they experience. In Lull's account, moral dilemmas admit of no intrinsic resolution, but only an extrinsic one where agents are supernaturally extracted by divine intervention. In the absence of providential interventions, individuals remain hopelessly trapped and unable to avoid wrongdoing.

Thomas Aquinas (1225–74) is the subject of the fourth chapter of the present volume. Shortly before Easter in 1272, Aquinas conducted a quodlibetal disputation on a variety of issues, one of which was *Whether Someone is Able to be Perplexed* (*Utrum aliquis posit esse perplexus*). Unfortunately, no authentic text survives for this portion of Aquinas's disputation beyond the title. Had the full text survived, it would be the only autonomous treatment of moral dilemmas in the corpus of Aquinas's writings. Nevertheless, Aquinas broaches the subject as a side issue in several works throughout his career, so it is possible to piece together what he might have said at this disputation, assuming that his remarks there were consistent with his other considerations of the subject. In the surviving texts, Aquinas analyzes eighteen moral dilemmas. Many such dilemmas ultimately are judged by him to be merely apparent, as he often discerns previously unconsidered options that individuals can perform to keep all obligations fulfilled. Central to Aquinas's analysis of the remaining cases is his denial that innocent agents will ever find themselves in moral dilemmas and that guilty ones often will. Some texts suggest that the lingering after-effects of prior faults can render the fulfillment of future obligations impossible. In all his examples of these prior-fault or self-imposed dilemmas, however, Aquinas identifies a way in which agents can somehow still undo the ill-effects of the past wrongdoing to allow all future obligations to be fulfilled. While Aquinas's examples are consistent in this regard, Aquinas never categorically states that all agents in prior-fault dilemmas can so escape an additional moral failure. Not surprisingly, twentieth-century commentators on Aquinas have disagreed over whether Aquinas allows for strictly irresolvable prior-fault dilemmas.

The penultimate chapter explains more fully Aquinas's account of a mistaken conscience. In particular, it investigates a potential problem of Aquinas's moral psychology: how is his doctrine of the infallibility of the habit of self-evident principles (synderesis) compatible with his admission that malformed-conscience dilemmas exist? This chapter highlights Aquinas's view that errors in minor premises are the common source for errors in practical reasoning, and it concludes with a consideration of similar views in later medieval moral dilemma theory.

The last chapter examines the principal issue left unresolved by Aquinas's explicit texts on moral dilemmas, namely, whether the Thomistic ethical framework allows for the existence of irresolvable prior-fault dilemmas. As Aquinas's texts provide no categorical answer to this question, a solution is sought in the work of Johannes Capreolus (*c.* 1380–1444), whose massive

Arguments Defending the Theology of St. Thomas Aquinas (*Defensiones theologiae Divi Thomae Aquinatis*) is the earliest complete presentation of the Thomistic philosophical and theological system. In light of the influence of that work, Capreolus bears the honorific title *Princeps Thomistarum* or "Prince of Thomists." Written during the first third of the fifteenth century, the *Defensiones* broaches the subject of moral dilemmas in three articles of the second book. Central to Capreolus's discussion is an analysis of a moral dilemma featuring an agent who is unwittingly deceived by a demon into believing that it is a lesser evil to blaspheme or hate God than not to do so. This section of the *Defensiones* is particularly valuable because it contains a systematic critique of the principle of the lesser evil defended by earlier theorists. While Capreolus states explicitly at the beginning of the *Defensiones* that he intends for the most part to defend Aquinas using texts from the Thomistic corpus, Capreolus's discussion of moral dilemmas appears to be one of the few areas where he goes well beyond Aquinas's works and provides supplementary argumentation. In doing so Capreolus borrows heavily from the arguments of the Augustinian Gregory of Rimini (1300–58) and the Englishman Thomas Bradwardine (1290–1349) to complete Aquinas's account. Capreolus thereby offers a negative answer to the question that Aquinas had left open, namely, whether Thomism allows the existence of irresolvable prior-fault dilemmas.

The conclusion of this book affirms that the medieval debate on the existence of moral dilemmas exhibits a tendency common to other key controversies of philosophy and theology in the Middle Ages: that of creative appropriation. The thinkers covered in this volume theorized with careful attention to their predecessors, but found new ways to be original within the framework defined by tradition. The systematic investigation of whether moral dilemmas exist is not primarily an achievement of modern or contemporary philosophy. Rather, in the medieval period the subject of moral dilemmas was first subjected to substantive analysis. One may ask why medieval theorizing on moral dilemmas appears to have been lost to later philosophy. The chapter proposes that the medieval contributions to moral dilemma theory were eclipsed by the rise of the casuistic tradition, which appropriated many of the examples of moral dilemmas from medieval theorists but transformed them into case studies of moral uncertainty. This transformation is particularly acute in the moral theory of late scholasticism known as probabilism.

This book demonstrates that a satisfactory history of moral dilemmas must acknowledge the medieval contributions to the subject. As I have sought to write a book that will interest the specialist in the history of philosophy as well as those whose training has been more systematic than historical, I have included translations of all Latin texts. While I have intended to make a contribution to the history of philosophy, I expect that it will be of interest to contemporary philosophers working on the problem of moral dilemmas who are open to considering the largely untold history of the subject. It seems reasonable that the analyses and insights propounded by medieval thinkers concerning moral dilemmas could contribute to contemporary theorizing about the subject. At a minimum, medieval texts can augment the standard set of examples of moral dilemmas considered by contemporary philosophers, a set which at present is quite small and is largely taken from cases that originate in literary works, such as Greek tragedy or contemporary novels. The forgotten medieval tradition, explored here, can restore to the discipline of philosophy its own set of examples to supplement these literary borrowings.

CHAPTER I

Gratian and his glossators on conflicts in the natural law

Gratian is considered the founder of the scientific or systematic study of canon law on the basis of his influential synthetic work, the *Decretum*.[1] An early section of that book deals with moral dilemmas, and this chapter will examine its argumentation and early reception. While the *Decretum* is well known, the same cannot be said of the details of its author's life. The amount of legend that surrounds the twelfth-century jurist is inversely proportional to the verified facts about him. If one listens to the former, one will hear that Gratian was a monk, either Benedictine or Camaldolese; that he resided at the monastery of Saints Felix and Nabor in Bologna and taught canon law there; that he was the brother of the Parisian theological master Peter Lombard; that his first name was Franciscus (or perhaps Johannes); and that during his ecclesiastical career he rose to the rank of abbot, bishop, or even cardinal. All of these claims have been found to be largely unconfirmed and traceable to questionable sources at times centuries removed from Gratian's day.[2] What is verified is quite minimal: Gratian finished the *Decretum* sometime after 1139 and before 1158, he resided for a time in Bologna, and in addition to legal interests he also held theological ones.[3] Whether he was a layman or a cleric, an academic professor of law or a practicing lawyer, or a young author at the completion of the *Decretum*

---

[1] The English translations of the *Decretum* and the *Ordinary Gloss* cited below are taken from Gratian, *The Treatise on Laws (Decretum DD. 1–20) with the Ordinary Gloss*, trans. Augustine Thompson, OP and James Gordley (Washington, DC: The Catholic University of America Press, 1993), with some minor alterations. In the absence of modern critical editions for both works, this chapter uses *Decretum Magistri Gratiani*, ed. Aemilius Friedberg, *Corpus iuris canonici*, vol. 1 (Leipzig: Tauchnitz, 1879), and *Decretum Gratiani emendatum et notationibus illustratum unà cum glossis* (Rome: 1582). A digitized version of the latter is available at http://digital.library.ucla.edu/canonlaw/toc.html.

[2] The historically unfounded status of nearly every traditional biographical tenet concerning Gratian was argued by John T. Noonan, Jr., "Gratian Slept Here: The Changing Identity of the Father of the Systematic Study of Canon Law," *Traditio* 35 (1979), 145–72.

[3] See Noonan, "Gratian Slept Here," 159, 172. Noonan's arguments have not been entirely persuasive to Stephan Kuttner, who, while conceding that in Gratian's biography "nearly everything remains as uncertain as it ever was," nevertheless is well disposed to the evidence suggesting that Gratian was a monk, a teacher of canon law, and perhaps even a bishop. See Kuttner, "Research on Gratian: Acta

or a mature one, will remain unknown absent the discovery of some new source material.

I.I GRATIAN'S *DECRETUM*: ITS INFLUENCE AND METHOD

Unquestionable is the influence of the *Decretum* in both ecclesiastical and civil law in the medieval period and beyond. Soon after its completion it was adopted as the standard textbook of canon law and held this privileged place for about 750 years in the Catholic church, while also contributing significantly to the development of the secular Western legal tradition.[4] Moreover, the *Decretum*'s legal content is replete with foundational analyses of philosophical and theological topics, and these discussions were crucial in framing approaches to many issues treated by theorists of the later Middle Ages. Perhaps it was in light of these contributions that Dante depicted Gratian in paradise in the company of such medieval luminaries as Albert the Great, Thomas Aquinas, Peter Lombard, and Boethius.[5]

The original title of the *Decretum* is instructive for explaining the work's approach. Gratian named it *Concordia discordantium canonum* or *Harmony of Discordant Canons*. That title employs a musical metaphor by suggesting a harmony or *concordia* will be produced from dissonant materials.[6] The work is not simply a compilation or *florilegium* of existing authoritative texts, but Gratian attempted a systematization of the variegated sources of canon law, including the sacred scriptures, papal pronouncements, writings of the Church Fathers, documents from Church councils, and other ecclesiastical texts. While Gratian did have predecessors who attempted to syncretize elements of church law, none approached the wide range of canonical sources incorporated into the *Decretum*. That the swath

---

and Agenda," in *Proceedings of the Seventh International Congress of Medieval Canon Law* (Vatican City: Biblioteca Apostolica Vaticana, 1988), 3–26, at 5, 6–8.

[4] For recent assessments of its influence, see Peter Landau, "Gratian and the *Decretum Gratiani*," in *The History of Medieval Canon Law in the Classical Period, 1140–1234: From Gratian to the Decretals of Pope Gregory IX*, ed. Wilfried Hartmann and Kenneth Pennington (Washington, DC: The Catholic University of America Press, 2008), 22–54; James A. Brundage, *The Medieval Origins of the Legal Profession: Canonists, Civilians, and Courts* (University of Chicago Press, 2008), esp. chap. 3: "The Legal Revival of the Twelfth Century," 75–125; as well as Peter Landau, "The Development of Law," in *The New Cambridge Medieval History*, vol. IV, pt 1, ed. David Luscombe and Jonathan Riley-Smith (Cambridge University Press, 2004), 113–47, at 128–9.

[5] Dante, *Paradiso*, x, 97–129.

[6] See Brundage, *The Medieval Origins of the Legal Profession*, 97. See also Stephan Kuttner, "Harmony from Dissonance: An Interpretation of Medieval Canon Law," *Wimmer Lecture* x (Latrobe, PA: Archabbey Press, 1960), 1–16, at 4–5.

of ecclesiastical material at the jurist's disposal was written over a period covering the greater part of a millennium adds to Gratian's impressive achievement. That at times canonical texts were found to be in conflict cannot be surprising; the sheer variety of his source materials were written in differing styles and represented divergent genres. Jurists could easily devise contradictory answers to legal questions depending on which authoritative sources they consulted. A formal synthesis of such heterogeneous materials was needed to assist in the practice of law as well as in the teaching of it. Naturally, therefore, the early part of the *Decretum* contains several sections that explain Gratian's method for adjudicating among conflicting authorities. He articulates a hierarchy of ecclesiastical ordinances (canons) and introduces distinctions in an attempt to produce the desired *concordia* among his materials. While certainly conflicts among laws can create difficulties for the practice of law, they can also generate dilemmas for agents who feel obliged to honor the prescriptions of opposing authorities. Gratian was interested not only in organizing a legal system, but also in how agents should respond to the imposition of a barrage of conflicting obligations generated by competing authorities. In other words, his concerns appear to be legal as well as moral, and in many texts it would be difficult to separate the two domains.

Gratian has often been credited with establishing canon law as a distinct discipline separate from theology and philosophy. Nevertheless, the domain of canon law as understood by Gratian was fairly broad in virtue of sources of obligation referenced by its canons. In addition to appeals to divine revelation and to the juridical authority of ecclesiastical pronouncements, it numbered among its sources a variety of natural law principles as expressed by Christian saints and scholars. To these sources of obligation were added the requirements of ecclesiastical offices, the duties of which were set forth by the long-standing practices of the church. Gratian's attempt to harmonize the various fonts of canon law can be seen as an attempt to adjudicate among sources of obligation for agents falling under these manifold juridical norms of the medieval church. How Gratian went about this task of conciliation offers a helpful analogue with some features of present-day discussions of moral dilemmas, if only because many present-day theorists have considered moral dilemmas to result from a conflict in the sources of obligation. For example, in an article that became influential among twentieth-century theorists, E. J. Lemmon proposed that moral dilemmas occur when "oughts" conflict and he offered a threefold genealogy of such oughts. These oughts are either:

(1) duties (those resulting from a special office or status position),
(2) obligations (those resulting from a contract or promise), or
(3) moral principles (those resulting from the adoption of a particular outlook).[7]

On this view, a moral dilemma is simply a situation where oughts conflict, and such situations should be expected as part of the moral life given the diversity of offices, contracts, and outlooks that can bind an agent in the course of a life. Similarly, Thomas Nagel provided a wider classification of the categories of obligation, arguing that there are "five fundamental types of value" that generate moral conflicts. These five categories are incommensurable, and are identified as "obligations, rights, utility, perfectionist ends, and private commitments."[8] It can be helpful to consider such present-day taxonomies alongside Gratian's views. As shall be seen below, even though Gratian attempts to reconcile conflicts among authorities, in the end he concedes that moral dilemmas are still possible, as not all sources of moral obligation will always be successfully integrated. In this crucial respect the twelfth-century jurist has surprisingly much in common with some twentieth-century defenders of moral dilemmas.

The original Decretum

Much of modern scholarship on the *Decretum* has concerned the issue of interpolations to Gratian's original document. It has long been recognized that additions to Gratian's text were made shortly after its completion. Quite recently, Anders Winroth has identified the original version of the text, and this discovery must now inform all subsequent approaches to the *Decretum*.[9] This "first recension" is only about half the length of the longer, supplemented version (or "second recension") that circulated through the ages, largely augmented by the inclusion of a significant amount of Roman law materials. Dating these earlier and later recensions, however, is difficult apart from two facts: the first recension references the Second Lateran Council of 1139, and hence the *Decretum*'s completion cannot predate that year; and the second recension was quoted by Peter Lombard in his *Sententiae* by 1158, so the first recension must have been completed before that time.[10] That this first recension circulated as a completed project

---

7 See E. J. Lemmon, "Moral Dilemmas," *The Philosophical Review* 70 (1962), 139–58.
8 Nagel, "The Fragmentation of Value," in *Mortal Questions* (Cambridge University Press, 1979), 128–41, at 129, 131.
9 Anders Winroth, *The Making of Gratian's* Decretum (Cambridge University Press, 2000).
10 Winroth, *The Making of Gratian's* Decretum, 140–2.

before being expanded into a second recension can be established because at present it survives in several manuscripts.[11] At some point between 1139 and 1158 the first recension was expanded substantially, and this twofold transmission of the *Decretum* prompts the question of whether Gratian was also the author of the second recension. Winroth calls the authors of the respective recensions "Gratian 1" and "Gratian 2," but notes that such labels should be considered neutral concerning whether they reference the same person. Nevertheless, he ultimately questions whether one person "could have undergone the intellectual development that is reflected in the differences between the two recensions."[12] If Gratian 1 and Gratian 2 are the same person, then after the completion of the first recension Gratian became thoroughly immersed in Roman law before giving life to the *Decretum's* second iteration.

The present chapter restricts itself to the texts by the so-called "Gratian 1," the author of the first recension of the *Decretum*.[13] This Gratian – the one who with confidence can be called Gratian – defends the existence of moral dilemmas as part of the moral life in distinction 13 of his famous work. In arguing for the reality of moral dilemmas, Gratian finds support in a short text from the Eighth Council of Toledo (commenced in 653) as well as in a lengthy extract from the *Moralia in Job* by Gregory the Great (*c.* 540–604). Both texts serve as authoritative supports for Gratian's defense of the existence of moral dilemmas. Although Gratian's own comments on the issue of moral dilemmas are brief, they are remarkable for the distinctive position they stake out, particularly in light of the scathing responses to them preserved in the *Glossa ordinaria* or *Ordinary Gloss*, an influential collection of multi-authored marginal notes – called glosses – that gradually accrued to the text of the *Decretum* and ultimately became its quasi-official commentary.[14] The glossators' collective opposition to Gratian's view on the subject of moral dilemmas in the *Decretum* is noteworthy and will be examined in the latter part of the present chapter. By way of preview, it can be said that distinction 13 of the *Decretum* defends the possibility of conflicts in the natural law, from which it follows that agents may find

---

[11] Ibid., 130.   [12] Ibid., 194.

[13] In restricting the account here to the first recension, this chapter follows the appendix "The Contents of The First Recension of Gratian's *Decretum*," in Winroth, *The Making of Gratian's* Decretum, 197–227.

[14] The *Glossa ordinaria* on Gratian's *Decretum* should not be confused with the twelfth-century commentary on the Latin vulgate with the same name. See *Biblia Latina cum Glossa ordinaria: Facsimile Reprint of the editio princeps*, ed. Karlfried Froehlich and Margaret T. Gibson, 4 vols. (Turnhout: Brepols, 1992), and Lesley Smith, *The* Glossa Ordinaria: *The Making of a Medieval Bible Commentary* (Leiden: Brill, 2009).

themselves entangled in situations of inescapable moral wrongdoing. The glossators, in turn, sharply criticize Gratian and the authorities he cites, deploying a variety of arguments in the course of rejecting the jurist's position.

1.2 CONFLICT AND *CONCORDIA*

Conflicts among laws can threaten the integrity of any legal system, ecclesiastical or otherwise. While Gratian's original title for the *Decretum, Concordia discordantium canonum*, appears to presuppose that at least some church canons stood in opposition to each other, not all early jurists on Gratian's text appear willing to concede this point. From a present-day perspective, Gratian's systematization of the sources of canon law parallels Peter Lombard's scholastic achievement in gathering philosophical and theological sources for his *Sententiae*, but not all contemporaries were willing to admit that the authoritative sources of a particular discipline could be in conflict. Several twelfth-century commentaries on the *Decretum* alleged that Gratian's purpose was to clear up confusions about law rather than treat of laws that required reconciliation. A work from the 1170s, the *Summa antiquitate et tempore*, put the issue this way: "[Gratian] speaks of discordant canons, not because they are really discordant, but because they seem to be (*Discordantium dicit non quia vere discordant, sed quia videntur discordare*)."[15] In similar fashion, the author of the *Summa Parisiensis* on Gratian's *Decretum*, completed in 1170, noted that "we explicate 'of discordant canons' not as those which are, but as those which seem to be (*exponimus 'discordantium canonum', non qui sint, sed qui videntur esse*)."[16] Present-day interpreters are not as restrained as their twelfth-century predecessors in assessing whether Gratian believed real oppositions or contradictions to obtain among laws.[17] A close examination of the beginning of the *Decretum* supports this interpretation: distinctions 8 through 12 largely constitute a catalogue of principles to be used when two authorities are discovered to

---

[15] *Prefaces to Canon Law Books in Latin Christianity: Selected Translations, 500–1245*, ed. Robert Somerville and Bruce C. Brasington (New Haven: Yale University Press, 1998), 211; *Die Geschichte der Quellen und Literatur des Canonischen Rechts*, ed. Johann Friedrich von Schulte, 3 vols. (Stuttgart: Ferdinand Enke, 1875–80 [repr. Union, NJ: The Lawbook Exchange, 2000]), I: 250.

[16] *Prefaces to Canon Law Books in Latin Christianity*, 202; *The Summa Parisiensis on the Decretum Gratiani*, ed. Terence P. McLaughlin (Toronto: The Pontifical Institute of Mediaeval Studies, 1952), 1.

[17] See Kuttner, "Harmony from Dissonance," 3–4; Constant Van de Wiel, *History of Canon Law* (Louvain: Peeters, 1991), 98; James A. Brundage, *Medieval Canon Law* (London: Longman, 1995), 47–8; and Peter Landau, "Gratian and the *Decretum Gratiani*," 22, 35, 42.

be in conflict. Gratian there introduces in piecemeal fashion a taxonomy of classes of authorities and recommends that texts from higher classes take precedence over those from lower ones when opposition is found. A canon from a more highly ranked authority is thereby held to restrict the force of a canon from a lower authority.

A taxonomy of authorities

In assimilating evidence for his taxonomy of authorities, Gratian cites a wide range of materials and intersperses these materials with interpretive comments, known as *paragraphi*, or more commonly, as *dicta*. In the words of one modern interpreter, Gratian "interweaves the collected texts with his own statements, or rather uses the collected texts only as *argumenta auctoritatis* for his reasoning."[18] Each *dictum* is a formulation of one of Gratian's views, and several early ones manifest not only his hierarchical approach to classes of authorities – ecclesiastical as well as secular – but also his principles for adjudicating among competing laws. Some *dicta* promote the authority of scripture over commentaries and treatises.[19] Another privileges the authority of explicit divine commandments over the statements of bishops.[20] Still others promote the authority of the natural law (*ius naturale*) over all customs as well as both secular and ecclesiastical enactments.[21] In each of these *dicta*, Gratian establishes a rule for privileging the statement of one authority over another, should they be found to be in conflict. As

---

[18] Stephan Kuttner, "The Father of the Science of Canon Law," *The Jurist* 1 (1941), 2–19, at 15. Kuttner contends earlier in the article that Gratian's methodology exhibits Abelardian influence and is indebted to earlier scholastic theological models that privileged dialectic (see 9–11). See also D. E. Luscombe, *The School of Peter Abelard: The Influence of Abelard's Thought in the Early Scholastic Period* (Cambridge University Press, 1970), esp. chap. 9, "Abelard and the 'Decretum' of Gratian," 214–23.

[19] See, for example, "Equal authority should not be ascribed to the canonical Scriptures and commentaries on them (*Non debetur par reuerentia canonicis scripturis et expositionibus earum*)," *Decretum*, dist. 9, c. 10, 18 (Thompson, 32); "Treatises are subject to the canonical Scriptures (*Scripturis canonicis tractatorum litterae deseruiunt*)," *Decretum*, dist. 9, c. 3, 17 (Thompson, 29).

[20] "Let not the words of any bishop be advanced as a subterfuge against divine commandments (*Contra diuina mandata calumpniae non colligantur ex quorumlibet dictis episcoporum*)," *Decretum*, dist. 9, c. 9, 18 (Thompson, 31).

[21] See, for example, "So whatever has been either received in usages or set down in writing is to be held null and void if it is contrary to the natural law (*Quecunque enim uel moribus recepta sunt, uel scriptis comprehensa, si naturali iuri fuerint aduersa, uana et irrita sunt habenda*)," *Decretum*, dist. 8, d. p. c. 1, 13 (Thompson, 25); "Thus is it obvious that custom is subordinate to natural law (*Liquido igitur apparet, quod consuetudo naturali iuri postponitur*)," *Decretum*, dist. 8, d. p. c. 9, 16 (Thompson, 28); "Therefore both ecclesiastical and secular enactments are to be rejected entirely if they are contrary to natural law (*Constitutiones ergo uel ecclesiasticae uel seculares, si naturali iuri contrariae probantur, penitus sunt excludendae*)," *Decretum*, dist. 9, d. p. c. 11, 18 (Thompson, 32).

a modern analogue, some twentieth-century theorists on moral dilemmas have suggested that agents can resolve their moral dilemmas by adopting a serial ordering of precepts whereby an ought from one source is held always to trump an ought from another source. Lemmon summarizes this view as, "we may hold to some very sweeping 'higher-order principle' such as 'Always prefer duty to obligation' or 'Always follow moral principles before duty or obligation.'"[22] For Gratian, it appears that natural law holds a supreme place in this hierarchy of authorities. Although the expression *ius naturale* is used in several senses in the *Decretum*, it appears to be Gratian's term to refer to the human discovery and conception of order, because Gratian notes it "began with the appearance of rational creatures and does not change over time, but remains immutable (*Cepit enim ab exordio rationalis creaturae, nec uariatur tempore, sed immutabile permanet*)."[23] Gratian contends that all laws must yield to it.

In sum, Gratian contends that conflicts among ecclesiastical laws, as well as conflicts between ecclesiastical and civil laws, are to be adjudicated according to a hierarchy of authorities that ultimately privileges the natural law. Thus, for Gratian, there is a provisional solution to conflicts found among laws: the higher authority in his taxonomy prevails over the lower authority, and the ultimate authority is the natural law.[24]

1.3 CONFLICTS WITHIN THE *IUS NATURALE*

Having touted the natural law as the ultimate authority for conflicts among secular and ecclesiastical authorities, Gratian asks in distinction 13 of the *Decretum* whether there can be conflicts within the natural law itself. The jurist's tentative yet affirmative answer is indicated with this *dictum*:

No dispensation is permitted from natural law except perhaps when one is compelled to choose between two evils (*Item aduersus naturale ius nulla dispensatio admittitur; nisi forte duo mala ita urgeant ut alterum eorum necese sit eligi*).[25]

Cases of irresolvable conflict were not envisioned among the ecclesiastical and secular laws discussed in distinctions 8–12, since conflict in those realms was to be adjudicated on the basis of the hierarchy of authorities where the natural law holds the highest place. Here, however, Gratian envisions scenarios where two evils so press upon someone that it is necessary to

---

[22] Lemmon, "Moral Dilemmas," 151.   [23] Gratian, *Decretum*, dist. 5, d. a. c. 1, 7 (Thompson, 16).

[24] It should be noted that Gratian's precise view concerning the relationship of the natural law to the will of God or divine law is much contested.

[25] Gratian, *Decretum*, dist. 13, d. a. c. 1, 31 (Thompson, 48).

choose one of them. Although the presence of the word "perhaps" (*forte*) in the text appears to leave open the question of whether such situations exist, Gratian's next *dictum* supports the view that they do, because he gives counsel for agents who find themselves in such situations: "The lesser of two evils is to be chosen (*Minus malum de duobus est eligendum*)."[26] This counsel takes the form of a strong recommendation: the use of the passive periphrastic implies necessity or obligation and exhibits a standard medieval formula for expressing moral imperatives. These two *dicta* of Gratian jointly assert the existence of situations of inescapable moral wrongdoing and prescribe a course of action for agents who might find themselves in such situations.

The issue here is whether moral dilemmas exist, that is, whether agents are ever unable to avoid moral wrongdoing because of irreconcilable obligations. Gratian proposes that a dispensation (*dispensatio*) is required from the natural law when an agent cannot follow all of its commands or precepts in a given situation. This concept of a dispensation is key to Gratian's account; it presupposes that there is no way to defuse a genuine conflict generated from inconsistency within the natural law. While the obligatory force of some secular or ecclesiastical law can be vacated with an appeal to higher authorities, there is no higher authority than the natural law. Surely one approach would be simply to maintain that there are no conflicts possible within the natural law. On such a view every agent always encounters the natural law as issuing perfectly consistent commands and there is no possibility of encountering contradictory obligations; the integrity of the natural law would be such that at all times and places agents could perform permissible actions and avoid moral wrongdoing. Gratian, however, does not follow this line of thinking. As shall be considered below, he credits the activities of the devil as the source of disorder for agents who experience an irresolvable tension between impending moral obligations.

The principle of the lesser evil

By advising that an agent in a moral dilemma choose the lesser of two evils, Gratian invokes an ethical maxim with a lengthy ancestry. The maxim existed in Plato's time, for it is referenced enthymematically in the *Gorgias* and is presupposed in Socrates's well-known defense of the view that it is a lesser evil to suffer injustice than to commit it.[27] Aristotle reports the maxim as, "one should take the least of evils (*ta elachista lēpteon tōn kakōn*),"

---

[26] Gratian, *Decretum*, dist. 13, c. 1, 31 (Thompson, 49). [27] Plato, *Gorgias*, 509c.

invoking it in the *Nicomachean Ethics* while defending the celebrated doctrine of virtue as a mean between two vices.[28] Aristotle explains that while two vices surround each virtue, both are not equally difficult to avoid, since people usually tend toward one extreme rather than the other. To increase one's chances of hitting the mean, Aristotle advises that one tend toward the vice that is less erroneous. Among Latin philosophers, Cicero famously appealed to the principle twice in *On Duties* (*De officiis*), rendering it as "*minima de malis*" and noted its high status among *philosophi*.[29] Its use, then, certainly predates Cicero in the Latin tradition of moral philosophizing. Cicero considered it to be proverbial, and he appealed to it in his defense of Marcus Atilius Regulus, a Roman consul who chose to fulfill a vow even though doing so involved extreme physical suffering. Regulus's choice, Cicero notes, is supported by the maxim because undergoing pain is a lesser evil than breaking a vow, and hence the consul acted correctly. Not all defenders of the principle of the lesser evil were philosophers, however. Perhaps the most influential medieval Latin exponent of the maxim was Thomas À Kempis (*c.* 1380–1471), who advised in his spiritual handbook *The Imitation of Christ* (*De imitatione Christi*) that, "Of two evils the lesser is always to be chosen (*De duobus malis minus est semper eligendum*)."[30] As shall be seen, the principle was also well known in the medieval canon law tradition prior to Gratian, as the Council of Toledo text defending it was excerpted in earlier collections prior to the *Decretum*, including the works of Ivo of Chartres (*c.* 1040–1116).[31]

Which evil is the lesser one?

Gratian offers no original examples of conflicts where an agent is left to resort to the principle of the lesser evil, but he transmits the examples of other theorists. To supplement his account, Gratian appeals to two authoritative texts that are generous with examples, and he incorporates extracts directly into the *Decretum* following the synthetic procedure that largely accounts for the bulk of the work. The first, from the second chapter of the Eighth Council of Toledo, begins with a warning that individuals should cautiously guard against such situations where they must select between a pair of evils. The Council then advises:

---

[28] Aristotle, *Nicomachean Ethics*, 2.9 1109a35–1109b1.   [29] Cicero, *De officiis*, 3.29.105, 3.29.105.

[30] Thomas À Kempis, *De imitatio Christi*, 3.12, in *De imitatio Christi libri quatuor*, ed. Eusebius Amort (Cologne, 1759), 60.

[31] For a list of Gratian's predecessors who excerpted the Council of Toledo's texts on the principle of the lesser evil, see *Decretum Magistri Gratiani*, ed. Friedberg, 31, n. 1.

If an inescapable danger compels one to perpetrate one of two evils, we must choose the one that makes us less guilty (*si periculi necessitas unum ex his temperare compulerit, id debemus resoluere, quod minori nexu noscitur obligari*).[32]

Here Gratian clarifies how he envisions conflicts within the natural law. When agents finds themselves in situations of inescapable moral wrong-doing, such conflicts do not render all moral obligations meaningless, for agents are still obliged to minimize, to the extent possible, the degree of evil done and thereby ought to select the lesser of two evils. Even though there is a dilemma, an agent is not permitted to choose either of the options indiscriminately, for the force of law obtains even in cases of conflict. When agents select the lesser evils, they are still committing evils, for the lesser evils do not simply cease to be evil just because there are worse evils that could be done.

To put it another way, when an agent is in a moral dilemma, unable to avoid choosing one of two evils, the agent is exempted from the prohibition that normally attaches to the lesser evil. In a dilemma of $\{x, y\}$, where x is the greater evil and y the lesser, even though the agent must choose one, x and y are not to be given equal consideration, since there remains the obligation always to privilege the lesser evil. The dispensation always attaches itself to y and never to x. Even though the agent is entangled in conflicting obligations, the agent is not released from participation in the moral life since the agent is still obliged to minimize the evil done. Apart from a dilemmatic situation of this kind, one could never advise the agent to pursue actions of the type y; the obligation to choose y only obtains when the lesser evil is the only alternative alongside some greater evil. Even as one of the two options of a moral dilemma, the lesser evil does not cease to be evil; it retains its status as the *lesser* evil and is simply preferable to the greater evil. In speaking of a dispensation, Gratian is not saying that in a dilemma an agent is dispensed from the guilt or effects of having performed an evil, but rather the agent is dispensed from the principle that actions of type y ought never to be done. In the dilemma, the agent should perform y, even though y is wrong.

The status of an evil as the lesser evil is only intelligible in relation to other possible evils that are greater. The designation *lesser* simply indicates a comparative relation, since the obligation to pursue the lesser evil in a

---

[32] Gratian, *Decretum*, dist. 13, c. 1, §1, 31 (Thompson, 49). A full text for the *Concilium Toletanum VIII* is given in *Concilios Visigóticos e Hispano-Romanos*, ed. José Vives, Tomás Marín Martínez, and Gonzalo Martínez Díez (Barcelona-Madrid: Consejo Superior de Investigaciones Científicas, Instituto Enrique Flórez, 1963), 260–93, with the cited text at 273.

moral dilemma is contingent upon two extrinsic factors: that the range of an agent's actions is limited, and that every remaining possibility of that range involves the commission of greater evils. Any designation of an evil as the lesser evil is impossible apart from its relation to at least one other action. Presumably an action that is designated as the lesser evil in one dilemma could be designated as a greater evil in another, given a different range of actions available to an agent. The existence of the dispensation does not eradicate the moral dilemma but rather indicates which of the two options of the dilemma ought to be chosen once an agent becomes entangled by evils. The agent does not escape morally unscathed from the dilemma, since the agent ends up committing *some* evil. The dispensation is not a dispensation from committing evil, but is a dispensation from the prohibition that outside the dilemma would proscribe the action that is the lesser evil.

Gratian's *dicta* and the Council of Toledo text also clarify the essential structure of moral dilemmas. Both note that an agent in such a dilemma is compelled to select from among two and only two options, both of which are evils that so impress themselves on an agent as to render a choice between them unavoidable. There is no appeal to a third option that can defuse the situation; the range of options is apparently exhausted by the two evils. Gratian and his authorities never discuss "trilemmas" or "tetralemmas," but only consider situations composed of two options. Perhaps Gratian has in mind an action and its omission as the two options for every case of inescapable moral wrongdoing. One might suspect further that Gratian's preference for dilemmas (over trilemmas, tetralemmas, etc.) is that any dilemma composed of an act and its omission is expressible as a pair of contradictories and constitutes the simplest situation of inescapable moral wrongdoing.

The Council of Toledo passage cited by Gratian offers one substantive comment about how agents should divide pairs of evils into the categories of lesser and greater. The Council enjoins agents to do so "by the sharpness of pure reason (*purae rationis acumene*)."[33] This obligation of careful discernment is particularly significant because it precedes the impending commission of some evil act; care is to be taken to ensure that one does not act worse than one could, even though some evil will be unavoidably performed. At the end of this process of discernment, the lesser evil ought to be chosen. Notably, another manuscript tradition of the Eighth Council of Toledo contains the words "by the sharpness of prayer (*orationis acumene*)"

---

[33] Gratian, *Decretum*, dist. 13, c. 1, §2, 31 (Thompson, 49).

in the place of "by the sharpness of pure reason (*purae rationis acumene*)."[34] On that reading, petitionary prayer is the recommended course for agents who find themselves trapped between the commission of two wrongs and are left to assess their respective gravity. These two manuscript readings advise agents to pursue divergent routes in assessing pairs of evils: the invitation to righteous prayer is a theological route, while the invitation to use the sharpness of reason is a philosophical one. The text of the Council of Toledo transmitted through the canon law tradition in Gratian's *Decretum* is the philosophical route, as it presents the Council's words as "by the sharpness of pure reason."[35]

An infelicitous oath dilemma

The extract from the Council of Toledo given by Gratian contains the first of several examples of moral dilemmas present in distinction 13 of the *Decretum*. The example is brief and illustrates the characteristics of moral dilemmas that previously were only approached abstractly or theoretically in Gratian's *dicta* and in the earlier part of the Council of Toledo passage. The facts of this case can be summarized as:

An agent swears to commit a crime, and afterwards is faced with the choice of either fulfilling the promise by committing the crime, or not committing the crime and failing to fulfill the promise.

This example features an agent who infelicitously promises to commit a crime (*noxia*) and is faced with the choice of either doing the deed or omitting it.[36] While neither Gratian nor the Toledo text specifies that the dilemma can be expressed as a pair of contradictories, it seems appropriate to approach the dilemma as one, and so the dilemma can be expressed as $\{a, \sim a\}$, where a represents the doing of the crime and $\sim a$ represents its omission. Either a or $\sim a$ is logically unavoidable for the agent in this case, since there is no middle way between them. In support of this view, it should be noted that a and $\sim a$ are presented in the text as exhausting the range of options available for the agent. The agent must choose between them, and both are presented as morally impermissible. If the agent performs a, the evil performed is the unspecified but presumably serious crime. If the agent

---

[34] *Concilios Visigóticos*, 273.

[35] The philosophical route is presented in the *editio Romana* (63–4) and in Friedberg's edition (31). It is also present, for instance, in Gratian, *Decretum cum apparatus* (Venice: Baptista de Tortis, 1500), 9v.

[36] Gratian, *Decretum*, dist. 13, c. 1, §2, 31 (Thompson, 49).

decides to omit *a*, opting for ∼*a*, then the evil performed is the violation of a promise. Even though both options are designated as evil, they can still be analyzed or evaluated with respect to their gravity, and ought to be so evaluated, given the injunction stated beforehand that the lesser evil should always be chosen in such cases.

The Toledo passage then concludes its presentation of this example by indicating that the violation of the oath is the lesser evil because it is not injurious to the community in the way that the performance of crime would be, and hence it is the lesser evil and should be chosen. The method used to determine the lesser evil in this dilemma is curious; presumably it exhibits an exercise of the "sharpness of pure reason" identified earlier. In short, the violation of the promise is identified as the lesser evil because it simply harms the agent and offends God, whereas the commission of the crime would not only likewise harm the agent and offend God, but additionally would harm the victim of the crime. Some sort of calculus establishing the lesser and greater evil in this dilemma is implied with the conclusion that "In the former case we perish by a two-fold lance of guilt, in the latter we are slain three ways (*Illic enim duplici culparum telo perimimur, hic tripliciter iugulamur*)."[37] In this case, the identification of an additional recipient of evil in one prong of the dilemma is key to establishing the greater evil. While the determination of the lesser evil in this case appears relatively straightforward, it shall be seen that the struggle of identifying the lesser evil will be a theme of later medieval theorists dealing with moral dilemmas.

1.4 GRATIAN'S GREGORIAN DEFENSE OF MORAL DILEMMAS

In Gratian's text the Council of Toledo passage is followed immediately by a second and much larger extract taken from the thirty-second chapter of Gregory the Great's *Moralia in Job*.[38] The *Moralia* was a revised set of talks that Gregory had given to fellow monks who had accompanied him when he was sent from Rome to Constantinople by Pelagius II as a papal ambassador. The monks had asked him to explicate the book of Job with a view to morality, and the text that exists today is the result of the revisions of the talks he undertook after being elevated to the papacy. That the selections from the *Moralia* excerpted by Gratian dovetail with the Council of Toledo passage is suggested by Gratian's extremely brief

---

[37] Gratian, *Decretum*, dist. 13, c. 1, §2, 31 (Thompson, 49).
[38] Gregory the Great, *Moralia in Iob*, ed. Marcus Adriaen, 3 vols. (Turnhout: Brepols, 1979–85), III: 1656–8; *Morals on the Book of Job*, 3 vols. (Oxford: John Henry Parker, 1844–50), III.2: 538–40.

introductory *dictum* to it, which says simply, "Concerning the same matter (*De eodem*)."³⁹

Inescapable moral wrongdoing

Both authorities – the Council of Toledo and Gregory – assert the existence of morally dilemmatic situations and both enjoin agents who find themselves in such situations to choose the lesser of the two evils. While the Council offers more detailed remarks concerning how an agent might identify the lesser evil, enjoining agents to evaluate options according to the "sharpness of pure reason," Gregory offers a fuller account of the structure of moral dilemmas. In a passage that would become the most frequently cited text in later medieval discussions of moral dilemmas, perhaps due in no small part to Gratian's promotion of it in the *Decretum*, Gregory contends:

> Thus, many commit sins when, because they want to avoid one sin, they cannot escape the snare of another, and thus they commit one fault to avoid another. They find no way to escape one sin without consenting to the other . . . When the mind is torn between greater and lesser sins, if absolutely no path of escape lies open without sin, lesser evils are always to be chosen (*ut plerosque ita peccare faciant, quatenus si fortasse fugere peccatum appetant, hoc sine alio peccati laqueo non euadant, et culpam faciant dum uitant, atque nequaquam se ab una ualeant soluere, nisi in alia se consentiant ligare . . . ut cum mens inter minora et maxima peccata constringitur, si omnino nullus sine peccato aditus patet, minora semper eligantur*).⁴⁰

This text succinctly asserts that there are situations where wrongdoing is inescapable, even for those who want to avoid sin, and it advises that the lesser evil should be chosen in such cases. Gregory does not indicate how frequently such situations might arise in the course of an individual's life, but he simply suggests that many people are subject to them. The text appears consistent with the statements by Gratian and the Council of Toledo, but its suggestion of the pervasiveness of such situations in the moral life may give one pause. For instance, one might be tempted to hold that the existence of situations of inescapable moral wrongdoing vitiates the prospect of progress or success in the moral life. The Christian theological goal of moral perfection would seem to be even farther removed from realization when the moral landscape is dotted with such situations. In commenting on Gregory's text, the twentieth-century

---

³⁹ Gratian, *Decretum*, dist. 13, c. 2, 31 (Thompson, 50). In a section not extracted by Gratian, the Council does reference the discussion of moral dilemmas from the *Moralia* of "Beatus Papa Gregorius." See *Concilios Visigóticos*, 276.
⁴⁰ Gratian, *Decretum*, dist. 13, c. 2, §1, 31–2 (Thompson, 50–1).

ethicist Alan Donagan appears to follow this line of thinking, concluding that "It was a respectable theological opinion that the devil could bring about situations in which common morality prescribes that a certain kind of action both be done and not done . . . That such entrapment should be possible was terrible to the early faithful."[41] Gregory, however, does not appear to consider the belief in moral dilemmas to be as threatening to the moral life as Donagan does, since, at the very end of the extract cited by Gratian, he contends that agents in dilemmatic situations of inescapable moral wrongdoing can still make progress in the moral life by choosing the lesser evil over the greater one. In doing so, Gregory maintains, such agents thereby acquire greater virtues.[42]

Gregory defends the permissibility of the principle of choosing the lesser evil in moral dilemmas by introducing a vivid analogy. The lesser evil, he contends, should always be chosen when one is caught in a dilemma, much like a fugitive who becomes trapped on a building or on a tower while fleeing an enemy should always jump off where the wall is lowest.[43] Presumably, for agents to choose the greater evils in moral dilemmas would be equivalent to fugitives who choose to jump where the wall is higher, thereby unnecessarily rendering themselves susceptible to greater injury than is required. This analogy highlights the key to Gregory's analysis: moral improvement is possible simply with the avoidance of graver evils, even though an agent cannot expect to have a moral life free from the commission of some lesser evils. Of course one may ask why there need be any such situations where an agent is forced to choose from a slate of evil options differing by degrees. Gregory's answer, it seems, concerns the activity of the devil, who is said to trick humans with suggestions (*suggestiones*).[44] Gratian appears to follow Gregory in identifying the devil as the primary cause for why agents experience a disorder in the natural law and thereby find themselves in moral dilemmas.[45]

---

[41] Alan Donagan, *The Theory of Morality* (University of Chicago Press, 1977), 144.

[42] See Gratian, *Decretum*, dist. 13, c. 2, §3, 33 (Thompson, 52). Isidore of Seville notes in *Etymologiae*, 10, B that "We call a person good if evil does not have the upper hand in him, and we call that person best who sins least (*Eum autem dicimus bonum cui non praevalet malum: eumque optimum qui peccat minimum*)." See *The Etymologies of Isidore of Seville*, trans. Stephen A. Barney, W. J. Lewis, J. A. Beach, Oliver Berghof, and Muriel Hall (Cambridge University Press, 2006), 214; *Etymologiae sive origines*, ed. W. M. Lindsay, 2 vols. (Oxford: Clarendon Press), I: 393.

[43] Gratian, *Decretum*, dist. 13, c. 2, §3, 32 (Thompson, 51).

[44] See Gratian, *Decretum*, dist. 13, c. 2, §1, 31 (Thompson, 50).

[45] For a characterization of the Gregorian tradition as "La perplexité demoniaque," see Stéphan Geonget, *La notion de perplexité a la Renaissance* (Geneva: Librairie Droz, 2006), 186–206. Geonget argues that Gregory's discussion of perplexity in the *Moralia* should be viewed as the background for understanding the perplexity experienced by literary figures such as Faust.

Three cases of perplexity: The Murderous Adulterer Dilemma,
The Worldly Superior Dilemma, *and* The Simony Dilemma

The larger part of Gregory's text extracted by Gratian is particularly important because of its discussion of three detailed examples of moral dilemmas
that are deployed to illustrate the view that inescapable moral wrongdoing
is part of the moral life. It is reasonable to infer that Gratian finds these
examples to support his *dicta* concerning moral dilemmas, since in his
citation he has condensed a larger text of Gregory while preserving the
three examples. Admittedly, the examples are unusual and are unlikely to
recur frequently in the world, but the simple possibility that they could
occur is sufficient to make claims about the moral life. The three dilemmas
set forth by Gregory there can be summarized as:

1. *The Murderous Adulterer Dilemma*
   A man binds himself to a friend with an oath prescribing that he will
   keep his friend's confidence, only afterwards to discover that the friend
   to whom he swore the oath is committing adultery and planning to kill
   the husband of the adulteress.[46]

2. *The Worldly Superior Dilemma*
   A subordinate binds himself in obedience with an oath to a spiritual
   advisor for the sake of abandoning the things of this world and making
   progress in the spiritual life. Soon afterward, the advisor commands the
   subordinate to pursue the things of the world and to avoid the things of
   God.[47]

3. *The Simony Dilemma*
   A cleric rises to an ecclesiastical office by bribery and thereby acquires
   the pastoral care of others, only to repent later of his crime of simony. He
   fears for the well-being of the members of his flock should he abandon
   them by leaving the illicitly obtained office.[48]

In these three examples, the agent in each case is presented as entangled or
bound (*ligatus*) in a situation and unable to avoid committing a morally
wrong action. In the first case, the *Murderous Adulterer Dilemma*, the agent
is ensnared between the options of revealing the friend's intention of homicide and not revealing it. This action and its omission both appear to be
impermissible, since, as Gregory explains, the agent must select between
being guilty of a perjurious violation of an oath or being an accomplice

---

[46] See Gratian, *Decretum*, dist. 13, c. 2, §2, 32 (Thompson, 50).
[47] See Gratian, *Decretum*, dist. 13, c. 2, §2, 32 (Thompson, 50).
[48] See Gratian, *Decretum*, dist. 13, c. 2, §2, 32 (Thompson, 50–1).

to adultery and homicide. Neither option from this contradictory set is favorable and neither option is presented as preserving the moral integrity of the agent. In the second example, the *Worldly Superior Dilemma*, a subordinate finds himself bound by obedience to a spiritual advisor who issues commands incompatible with the spiritual life. The dilemma here involves the prongs of obedience or disobedience to a superior. If the subordinate follows the commands of his superior, he will live a worldly existence, and if disobeys, he will be in violation of his vow. With either contradictory, it appears that a wrong will be committed by the subordinate. The strict view of promises and oaths exhibited in the *Murderous Adulterer Dilemma* and the *Worldly Superior Dilemma* may be puzzling to the contemporary reader, so it should be noted that the binding character of such pledges was a debated issue in medieval thought. A strict view of promises and oaths was often bolstered by a reading of Judges 11:29–40, where Jephthah appears to fulfill an infelicitous vow and sacrifice his only daughter. Strict defenders of pledges were not difficult to find among medieval biblical commentators.[49] Finally, in the *Simony Dilemma*, a cleric is faced with the dilemma of either remaining in an illicitly obtained office or abandoning it. With the former prong, the cleric stains the office he procured by bribery and he exercises its authority unworthily, while with the latter, he scandalizes the flock entrusted to him and leaves them shepherdless. Again, it appears that there is no morally permissible course of action for the agent in this case, since either contradictory seems to involve moral wrongdoing. This dilemma presupposes the Patristic and medieval notion of scandal that considered the leading of another into sin to be itself gravely sinful. Jerome had authoritatively defined a scandalizer as "one who by word or deed gives to anyone an occasion for falling (*qui dicto factoue occasionem ruinae cuiquam dederit*)."[50] As shall be seen in later chapters, the avoidance of scandal is identified as one prong of several moral dilemmas discussed by many medieval theorists after Gregory. In the three cases here, the man, the subordinate, and the cleric each face a dilemma composed of an act and its omission, and both the act and the omission are held to be impermissible. Since the act and the omission in each case are presented as contradictories that exhaust the range of options available to each agent, moral wrongdoing is judged to be imminent and unavoidable for each of them.

---

[49] For a survey of medieval understandings of vows in light of Jephthah's case, see John L. Thompson, *Writing the Wrongs: Women of the Old Testament among Biblical Commentators from Philo through the Reformation* (New York: Oxford University Press, 2001), esp. chap. 2: "Jephthah's Daughter and Sacrifice," 100–78.

[50] Jerome, *Commentariorum in Mathaeum libri IV*, ed. D. Hurst and M. Adriaen, *Corpus Christianorum series Latina*, vol. LVII (Turnhout: Brepols, 1969), 129; *Commentary on Matthew*, trans. Thomas P. Scheck (Washington, DC: The Catholic University of America Press, 2008), 179.

These three examples given by Gregory and extracted by Gratian for inclusion in the *Decretum* are meant to illustrate the view that agents can experience the natural law as imposing conflicting claims, and the sole recourse for them is to analyze each set of contradictories into the categories of greater and lesser evils. Gratian and Gregory believe that for each of the pairs of contradictories composing these moral dilemmas, one of the contradictories under examination by "sharpness of pure reason" will be discovered to be the lesser evil. There is no suggestion, at least, that the agent's evaluative calculus will conclude that the set of contradictories expresses two evils of equal moral gravity. In cases 1–3, the identified lesser evils are to be preferred, but nonetheless they do not lose their status as evils. Surprisingly, neither Gregory nor Gratian explicitly identifies the lesser evil for any of the three moral dilemmas. The only detail in this regard is that the agent in the *Simony Dilemma* is presented as judging the abandonment of his flock as the "graver fault (*gravius delictum*)" but the retaining of the office as the "worse sin (*deterior culpa*)."[51] Gratian's Gregorian view, then, is that there are situations where the best an agent can hope for is the avoidance of a more serious moral failure, and the agent must at times be content with the commission of less grave offences. The identification of greater and lesser evils, however, is no mean task. This distinctive position on moral dilemmas was not favorably received by certain early commentators on the *Decretum*.

1.5 A DENIAL OF MORAL DILEMMAS IN THE *GLOSSA ORDINARIA*

It is possible to evaluate the early reception of Gratian's view of moral dilemmas by examining the collective remarks preserved in the *Glossa ordinaria*, a compendium of footnote-like comments or glosses that accrued to Gratian's text in the late twelfth and early thirteenth centuries (with some additions later) and thereafter came to have the status of a quasi-official guide to interpreting the *Decretum*.[52] The influence of this work should not be understated; it was studied by nearly every student of canon law because of its inclusion in most of the later medieval manuscripts of the *Decretum* as well as in the printed versions of Gratian's work that appeared from the late fifteenth through the seventeenth centuries.[53] The

---

[51] Gratian, *Decretum*, dist. 13, c. 2, §2, 32 (Thompson 51).

[52] For an account of the earliest reception of Gratian's view of moral dilemmas among those who wrote other commentaries on the *Decretum*, see Stephan Kuttner, *Kanonistische Schuldlehre von Gratian bis auf die Dekretalen Gregors IX: Systematisch auf Grund der handschriftlichen Quellen dargestellt* (Vatican City: Biblioteca Apostolica Vaticana, 1935), 257–91.

[53] See Rudolf Weigand, "The Development of the *Glossa ordinaria* to Gratian's Decretum," in *The History of Medieval Canon Law in the Classical Period, 1140–1234: From Gratian to the Decretals*

inclusion of the *Glossa ordinaria* with the 1582 edition of the *Decretum* authorized by Gregory XIII affirmed its standing as an authoritative guide to Gratian's work.[54] The two principal figures who organized the *Glossa ordinaria* are known: Johannes Teutonicus (*c.* 1170–1245) completed his editing project of the *Glossa ordinaria* around 1215, and Bartholomaeus Brixiensis (fl. 1234–58) added to Johannes Teutonicus's version around 1245.[55] Many of the glossators are known by name, but it is difficult to assign individual glosses to a particular glossator. When a jurist's abbreviated name follows a particular comment it is at times ambiguous and could refer to more than one author, and even when an unambiguous abbreviated name appears it is possible that the name was added at a much later time. So, even though names appear for many glosses, such identifications are unreliable.[56] The commentary tradition on the *Decretum* that is preserved in the various iterations of the *Glossa ordinaria* is remarkable for the present study because it suggests that Gratian's heirs in canon law were unequivocally unwilling to take seriously the jurist's view that the moral life lays impossibilities upon individuals. In short, the glossators jointly reject Gratian's view that moral dilemmas exist, and they subject Gratian's texts to a firestorm of criticism.

The glossators against Gratian

The early part of the *Glossa ordinaria* on distinction 13 of the *Decretum* asserts that while dispensations are permitted in the case of other laws, there are none from the provisions of the natural law that is expressed in precepts and prohibitions. It continues, "Nevertheless, the Master makes one exception in the case of perplexity, but he does so badly (*magister tamen excipit unum casum de perplexitate, et male*)."[57] Here the glossator, who, in the words of one modern commentator, has been "shocked into

---

of *Pope Gregory IX*, ed. Wilfried Hartmann and Kenneth Pennington (Washington, DC: The Catholic University of America Press, 2008), 55–97, at 82–91, and Kenneth Pennington, "Johannes Teutonicus," in *Dictionary of the Middle Ages*, vol. VII, ed. Joseph R. Strayer (New York: Charles Scribner's Sons, 1986), 121–2, at 122.

54 The publication of the *editio Romana* was a culmination of an immense editing project formalized by Gregory XIII in 1578 and brought to completion by a group of jurists collectively known as the *Correctores Romani*.

55 See Kenneth Pennington, "Medieval canonists: a bio-bibliographical listing," pre-published at http://faculty.cua.edu/pennington/biobibl.htm in preparation for inclusion in *History of Medieval Canon Law*, ed. Wilfried Hartmann and Kenneth Pennington, 11 vols. (Washington, DC: The Catholic University of America Press 1999–).

56 For a list of glossators of the *Glossa ordinaria* and a discussion of the difficulties of trusting the names appended to some glosses, see the appendix "Jurists in the Gloss," in Gratian, *The Treatise on Laws*, 122–3.

57 *Glossa ordinaria*, XIII, f, 63 (Gordley, 48). Here and below the references to the *Glossa ordinaria* follow the ordering of glosses by letter given by Gordley rather than the ordering in the *editio Romana*.

open disapproval" by Gratian's *dicta*, issues this surprising comment.[58] Referring to Gratian by the traditional title of "Master," the glossator expresses the judgment that Gratian has erred badly (*male*) by claiming that there can be dispensations from the natural law. A bit later in the text, another condemnation of Gratian's position surfaces, this time in a gloss to which is appended the name of Archidiaconus, Guido de Baysio (d. 1313). This gloss begins with a brief grammatical clarification on a portion of the text, and then is followed by a substantive judgment that straightforwardly states, "In truth, however, there is no perplexity (*in veritate tamen perplexio nihil est*)."[59] Such categorical rejections of moral dilemmas in the *Glossa ordinaria* are remarkable. These two glosses on the text of the *Decretum* summarily reject the notion that moral dilemmas exist. No pious qualms about deferring to the Master of canon law arise, and instead Gratian's text is subjected to a critical commentary. At issue is whether agents ever find themselves in a state of moral perplexity (*perplexitas*) or are ever perplexed (*perplexi*) such that they are genuinely unable to avoid moral wrongdoing. Gratian's *dicta* and the authorities he marshals in support of his position jointly argue that such dilemmatic situations exist as part of the moral life, but the glossators categorically deny this. The glossators attempt to defend their denial of moral dilemmas with a variety of arguments, and they pointedly take issue with the alleged examples of moral dilemmas set forth in Gratian's extracts from the Council of Toledo and Gregory's *Moralia*.

The chief tactic favored by the jurists of the *Glossa ordinaria* to combat Gratian's position on moral dilemmas is to argue that every instance of *perplexitas* is simply a subjective epistemic condition rather than real moral entanglement. That is, in the view of the glossators, to be *perplexus* stems simply from an agent's limited grasp of real alternatives that if pursued would allow an agent in every situation to avoid the commission of an evil. In light of this view, the appeal to the principle of the lesser evil becomes superfluous. In formulating their position, the glossators exploit that the term *perplexus*, much like its English cognate, can refer to an epistemic state as well as to an ontological condition, and they use the former sense to argue against the existence of true moral dilemmas. The twofold sense of the term *perplexus* can be shown by its English cognate: solvable as well as unsolvable puzzles can perplex someone, but to be perplexed by ignorance is a far different thing from being perplexed because a puzzle is intrinsically

---

[58] Jean Porter, *Natural and Divine Law: Reclaiming the Tradition for Christian Ethics* (Grand Rapids, MI: Eerdmans, 1999), 149.
[59] *Glossa ordinaria*, XIII, d, 65 (Gordley, 50).

unsolvable. This dual sense of the term *perplexus* in Latin is reflected in its ability to mean *entangled* or *intertwined* as well as *baffled* or *confused*. Etymologically the term derives from the verb *plectere*, meaning *twine* or *interweave*, and the Latin *plectere* comes from the Greek word *plekein*, which carries the same meaning.[60] In both Latin and Greek, the literal or foundational sense of being *entangled* is extended to a metaphorical sense of being *confused*. Gratian's *dicta* and the cited texts from Gregory and the Council of Toledo jointly favor the literal or foundational sense of *perplexus*, in contrast to the glossators who emphasize the metaphorical and epistemic sense of the term, and this conflict inaugurates a controversy over moral dilemmas that will extend well into the later Middle Ages.

The glossators on foolish agents

Several texts from the *Glossa ordinaria* on distinction 13 jointly explain the view that dilemmas must be simply epistemic. One of the longest glosses contains a concise argument against the reality of moral dilemmas. It wastes no time in rejecting Gratian's position:

> But it must be stated that no one can really be perplexed between two evils in this way. For it would then follow that necessity can make one do something evil . . . Therefore, the person's perplexity cannot really arise from the matter itself, but it must arise in the mind and from foolish opinion (*Sed dicendum est, quod nullus potest esse perplexus inter duo mala: quia secundum hoc sequeretur, quod aliquis ex necessitate teneretur facere malum . . . perplexio ergo quantum ad rem nihil est: sed quantum ad animum, et ad stultam opinionem*).[61]

This text is important because it denies that moral dilemmas can be anything more than cognitive. Perplexity cannot be caused by the order of things (*res*), but simply occurs in a mind (*animus*) that holds an opinion that is foolish (*stulta*). On this view, minds that are presumably not foolish will never be stultified into thinking there is a dilemma forcing wrongdoing in any given case, because such privileged minds will always be able to discern a course of action that is morally permissible in any given set of circumstances. According to the glossator, the moral order is always consistent and the natural law can always be viewed as issuing

---

[60] *Oxford Latin Dictionary*, ed. P. G. W. Glare (Oxford: Clarendon Press, 1982), 1351, 1389; *A Latin Dictionary*, ed. Charlton T. Lewis and Charles Short (Oxford: Clarendon Press, 1962), 1352, 1386; *A Greek–English Lexicon*, ed. Henry George Liddell, *et al.* (Oxford: Clarendon Press, 1996), 1415. See also *Mediae Latinitatis lexicon minus*, ed. J. F. Niermeyer and C. Van de Kieft (Leiden: E. J. Brill, 1993), 789.

[61] *Glossa ordinaria*, XIII, f, 63 (Gordley, 49).

observable precepts. To put the matter in more contemporary language, the glossator here defends the traditional view that "ought implies can." If a moral obligation obtains, it is possible to be fulfilled. Perhaps the glossators also have in mind the principle of Roman law that states "There is no obligation to the impossible (*impossibilium nulla obligatio est*)."[62] This line of interpretation continues when the glossators turn from Gratian's *dicta* to comment on the authorities the jurist deployed in his defense. The glossators first criticize the extract from the Council of Toledo, particularly where it enjoined those who find themselves in moral dilemmas to choose the lesser of two evils. Regarding that prescription, the gloss notes:

This should be understood as the idea of one who stupidly believes himself to be perplexed, and you should so understand everything said here. Indeed, it is not really true that both courses of action are evil, although he thinks that both are evil (*intellige quantum ad fatuam illius opinionem qui se credit perplexum; et sic intelligas omnia verba hic posita: non enim utrumque illorum malum est: licet ille opinetur utrumque esse malum*).[63]

Again, this text attempts to locate the condition of *perplexitas* on the side of the subject rather than in a state of affairs; those individuals in moral dilemmas are said to be perplexed because of stupidity rather than as a result of a true extra-mental condition. This text explicitly denies that a situation composed of two and only two courses of action can have both actions as genuine evils. In case any readers remain unclear about their position, the glossators continue to assert that the necessity to choose between two evils is not real: it simply seems so given the postulation of some foolish opinion (*opinio stulta*) on the part of the agent.[64] In sum, they contend, regarding two evils "one or the other of two does not obligate him (*alterum illorum non obligat ipsum*)."[65]

Concerning the agent described in the Council of Toledo text as believing himself to be caught between committing a crime and violating a promise, the glossators contend that the agent's error is considering the promise to be obligatory. Hence, as one of the contradictories has no obligatory force, there is no dilemma. The *Glossa ordinaria* simply states, "one is permitted not to fulfill such an oath (*licet non servet tale iuramentum*)."[66] According to the glossators, therefore, the church council errantly draws the conclusion that a choice must be made between evils.

---

[62] *Codex Justinianus*, 50.17.185. See *The Digest of Justinian*, ed. Theodor Mommsen and Alan Watson, 4 vols. (Philadelphia: University of Pennsylvania Press, 1985), IV: 968.

[63] *Glossa ordinaria*, XIII, a, 64 (Gordley, 49).

[64] *Glossa ordinaria*, XIII, f, a, g, 63, 64, 65 (Gordley, 49, 50).

[65] *Glossa ordinaria*, XIII, d, 64 (Gordley, 49).   [66] *Glossa ordinaria*, XIII, e, 64 (Gordley, 49).

Unsurprisingly, Gregory fares no better than the Council of Toledo at the hands of the glossators. The three moral dilemmas set forth by Gregory are dismissed as illusory, and the reader is again urged to understand them simply as cases where agents are deluded by foolish opinion (*opinio stulta*).[67] In the first example that concerned a man who swore an oath of confidentiality only thereupon to learn of his friend's adultery and murderous plans, the glossators identify a variety of permissible courses of action, suggesting either that the oath is not binding, or that the man could warn the husband of the impending murder attempt without revealing the name of the would-be murderer, or that the man could convince the would-be murderer not to carry through with the plan. The dilemmatic structure, according to the glossators, is not real, since there is no obligation to keep quiet about the murderous plans, and even if there were, there are the aforementioned alternative actions available. The contradictories of revealing the friend's intention of homicide or not revealing it do not constitute a moral dilemma, because revealing the intention is not proscribed by a binding oath, and even if it were, not revealing the intention can be permissibly performed provided that other actions are taken to prevent the murder, such as persuading the confider to pursue an alternative course of action or warning the adulterer in a very general way. Hence, the glossators find here no dilemma of inescapable moral wrongdoing. Similarly, the glossators find little merit in the second dilemma concerning the subordinate whose spiritual director advises the avoidance of the things of God and the pursuit of the things of the world. If the man is certain about the character of the advice, it should not be followed; but if the man is in doubt (*dubitet*) about whether the advice is bad, he should nevertheless submit.[68] In short, the glossators reject the obligatory character of any vow that does not concern what is "lawful, just, and honest (*de licitis et iustis et honestis*)."[69] The contradictory set of obedience and disobedience fails to generate a moral dilemma because obedience is not necessarily obligatory. Finally, regarding the third dilemma involving a simoniacal cleric who is faced with a choice of remaining in an illicitly obtained office or abandoning it, the glossators find no obligation to retain the office. They simply judge that the agent must leave the illicitly procured office, but there is some disagreement over whether the cleric should obtain permission prior to leaving. The glossators simply discern no dilemma here, advising that the cleric should leave and enter perpetual penance.

---

[67] *Glossa ordinaria*, XIII, g, 65 (Gordley, 50): "*secundum opinionem eorum stultam semper intelligas.*"
[68] *Glossa ordinaria*, XIII, i, 66 (Gordley, 51).   [69] *Glossa ordinaria*, XIII, i, 66 (Gordley, 51).

This position of the glossators that holds every instance of *perplexitas* to be simply a subjective epistemic condition rather than genuine moral entanglement has much later adherents as well. In addition to Kant's well-known denial of conflicts of duty, one should consider the statement of Thomas Hill Green:

> There is no such thing really as a conflict of duties. A man's duty under any particular set of circumstances is always one, though the conditions of the case may be so complicated and obscure as to make it difficult to decide what that duty really is. That which we are apt to call a conflict of duties is really a competition of reverences for imagined imponents of duty, whose injunctions, actual or supposed, do not agree.[70]

Both the medieval and more recent defenders of this position identify the resolution to purported moral dilemmas to be simply the acquisition of knowledge or the removal of mistaken views of obligation.

Four additional cases of perplexity: The Marital Intercourse Dilemma, The Killers of Christ Dilemma, The Hiding Fugitive Dilemma, *and* The Alcohol Abuser Dilemma

A lengthy comment of the *Glossa ordinaria* on distinction 13 discusses several more cases of alleged moral perplexity, inspired in part from diverse sections of the *Decretum*, and then it argues that the situations are really only superficially or epistemically dilemmatic. The four cases can be summarized as:

1. *The Marital Intercourse Dilemma*
   A wife, boiling with passion (*effervere*), seeks sex from her husband. If the husband refuses his marital obligation, he sins mortally, and if he accedes, he sins venially. He is thereby *perplexus*, unable to avoid sin either way.[71]

2. *The Killers of Christ Dilemma*
   The men who crucified Christ appeared *perplexi* between two mortal sins. They sinned mortally if they killed the Son of God, and they sinned

---

[70] Thomas Hill Green, *Prolegomena to Ethics*, ed. A. C. Bradley (Clarendon Press, 1883 [repr. Bristol: Thoemmes Press, 1997]), 355. For a similar statement, see R. M. Hare, *Moral Thinking: Its Levels, Method, and Point* (Oxford University Press, 1981), 26: "Those who say, roundly, that there can just be irresoluble conflicts of duties are always those who have confined their thinking about morality to the intuitive level. At this level the conflicts are indeed irresoluble; but at the critical level there is a requirement that we resolve the conflict, unless we are to confess that our thinking has been incomplete."

[71] See *Glossa ordinaria*, XIII, f, 63 (Gordley, 49).

mortally likewise by not killing, since on the latter option they each
would be acting against conscience (*praeter conscientiam*) that informed
by religious tradition dictates that those who call themselves the Son of
God must be put to death.[72]

3. *The Hiding Fugitive Dilemma*

A man demands from a third party to know the location of an enemy
who happens to be hiding with the third party. If the third party reveals
the enemy, he commits an act of betrayal and sins mortally. If he denies
the enemy is there, he lies and sins venially. Along either route, the
third party is *perplexus* between sins, since he is not able to avoid the
commission of at least one sin.[73]

4. *The Alcohol Abuser Dilemma*

A man promises to drink more than he is able. In this case, he is *perplexus*
between two venial sins: if he attempts to drink in such an excessive
way, he sins, and if he does not drink and violates his promise, he also
sins. Either way, he cannot avoid sin.[74]

From the glossators' earlier attempts to dismantle the one Toledan and the
three Gregorian examples of moral dilemmas discussed above, it should
not be difficult to anticipate their responses to these additional four. Again
the glossators collectively consider moral dilemmas to be only epistemic
rather than real; dilemmas result from ignorance or foolishness of the mind
rather than from inconsistent obligations issuing from the natural law.
Regarding the first of the four examples, the *Marital Intercourse Dilemma*,
where there is a man whose wife is boiling with passion for a sexual act,
the recommendation is simply to accede to the wishes of the wife. The
glossator notes, "I do not believe that this enjoyment is a sin (*non credo
quod talis delectatio sit aliquid peccatum*)."[75] The dilemma is no dilemma
at all, since the belief that the satisfaction of the wife's wish is sinful is
identified as outrightly mistaken.[76] Similarly, with the second example, the

---

[72] See *Glossa ordinaria*, xiii, f, 63 (Gordley, 48–9). This dilemma is privileged in other canonical
literature and in theological works. For a discussion, see Artur Michael Landgraf, "Der ʿCasus
perplexusʾ in der Frühscholastik," *Collectanea Franciscana* 29 (1959), 74–86, and John O'Neill, "ʿThe
Same Thing Therefore Ought to Be and Ought not to Beʾ: Anselm on Conflicting Oughts,"
The Heythrop Journal 35 (1994), 312–14. Peter Abelard provides an extended consideration of this
dilemma; see *Peter Abelard's Ethics*, ed. and trans. D. E. Luscombe (Oxford: Clarendon Press, 1971),
24–9.

[73] See *Glossa ordinaria*, xiii, f, 63 (Gordley, 49).

[74] See *Glossa ordinaria*, xiii, f, 63 (Gordley, 49).   [75] *Glossa ordinaria*, xiii, f, 63 (Gordley, 49).

[76] This alleged example of *perplexitas* becomes a repeated one in the canon law tradition and is
examined in detail by some of Gratian's most notable heirs, including Rufinus (fl. 1150–91) and
Huguccio of Ferrara (fl. 1180–1210). For a summary of the discussion, see John W. Baldwin, *The
Language of Sex: Five Voices from Northern France around 1200* (University of Chicago Press, 1994),
192–4, 283.

Killers of Christ Dilemma, the men who crucified Christ under the dictate of conscience were negligent, according to the glossator, in not consulting the Apostles and the sacred scriptures, which presumably would have removed the force of conscience's dictate. Laboring under such a culpable mistake, they "were not perplexed except in their minds (*non erant perplexi nisi quantum ad animum*)."[77] Regarding the third example, the *Hiding Fugitive Dilemma*, involving one who houses the enemy of another, the glossators advise that there is another unseen option apart from betrayal and lying: the third party should remain silent and will not be responsible even if the enemy presumes something from silence, for silence does not always mean consent. This example is an ancient one, surfacing in Augustine of Hippo, examined famously in the eighteenth century by Immanuel Kant, and still debated today as a popular question in contemporary discussions of moral dilemmas, often supplemented with details to make the example about Nazis looking for hiding Jews.[78] The inclusion by the glossators of this case is a particularly pointed critique of Gratian's view because the stipulated facts include a designation of gravity for each of the prongs of the dilemma, as betrayal is designated as a mortal or serious sin, and lying is designated as a venial or lesser sin. Even in cases like these, the glossators imply, the principle of the lesser evil is superfluous, as no choice even between sins of manifestly unequal gravity is ever necessary. Regarding the fourth example, the *Alcohol Abuser Dilemma*, the glossators are silent. Perhaps they judged that their comments on Gregory's examples were sufficient to demonstrate there is no obligation to follow vows contrary to justice.

In sum, the glossators provide a complete rejection of Gratian's contention that there need to be dispensations from the natural law to assist agents caught in moral dilemmas. This judgment of the glossators found favor with later jurists. While summarizing Gratian's influence on the canon law tradition, Stephan Kuttner observed, "Many of Gratian's opinions have completely reshaped canonical institutes, while others proved to be untenable," and then he offers as an example of the latter that Gratian "admits a dispensation from natural law" in the early part of the *Decretum*.[79] The view of the glossators on this point of moral dilemmas, it appears, outlasted that of Gratian within the medieval canon law tradition.

---

[77] *Glossa ordinaria*, XIII, f, 63 (Gordley, 49).

[78] Augustine, *De mendacio*, cap. 5–6, and *Contra medacium*, cap. 17; Immanuel Kant, *On the Supposed Right to Lie from Philanthropy*, in *Practical Philosophy*, ed. Mary J. Gregor (Cambridge University Press, 1996), 611–16.

[79] Stephan Kuttner, "The Father of the Science of Canon Law," 16.

1.6 GRATIAN'S LEGACY ON MORAL DILEMMAS

The *Decretum* and the *Glossa ordinaria* each represent distinct and opposed medieval viewpoints on the existence of moral dilemmas. Gratian argues in defense of the reality of moral dilemmas by contending that agents will need a dispensation from the natural law when certain situations oblige a choice between evils. The glossators, however, collectively find Gratian's view to be a serious threat to the integrity of the moral life and they vehemently oppose the Master. Their solution was to recast all purported cases of perplexity as simply situations where there is deficient knowledge on the part of the agent: foolish opinions, ignorance, or error cause such agents to believe themselves to be in dilemmas when there are always morally permissible alternative courses of action available. In the view of the glossators, an agent is never truly entangled by the world but is only confused because of a deficient cognitive state. The moral order is not disordered, but moral agents can be. The glossators hold that it is possible at all times for an agent to fulfill all moral obligations; the world will never present a situation where an agent cannot avoid doing evil.

Of course one might wish to ask the glossators what recourse there is for an unenlightened agent whose mind is filled with the aforementioned foolish opinions. Such agents will believe themselves to be perplexed on occasion, and that situation will result in moral wrongdoing save some infusion of knowledge. The only solution the glossators hint at in this case is the view that culpable negligence on the part of the agent is a necessary condition for entering into a perplexed state. On this line of thinking, then, the glossators might say concerning their proposed dilemmas that men should not marry prior to discerning what is permissible in marital relations; individuals should not acquire superiors until they are fully cognizant of the integrity of potential religious authorities, and promisors should not promise until they have discerned the integrity of promisees. In short, the glossators suggest that agents who believe themselves to be in moral dilemmas are always at fault. The theoretical articulation of this latent view of the glossators would not be formalized until later in the thirteenth century by Thomas Aquinas. In contrast to the glossators, Gratian's defense of moral dilemmas, inspired to a significant degree by Gregory, is a clear opponent to this position. The Master of canon law deserves to be recognized for this early distinctive view among medieval conceptions of moral dilemmas.

CHAPTER 2

Twenty moral dilemmas from two early thirteenth-century summaries of theology: William of Auxerre's Summa aurea and the Franciscan Summa Halesiana

The detailed remarks concerning moral *perplexitas* offered by the twelfth- and thirteenth-century commentators of the *Glossa ordinaria* on Gratian's *Decretum* should not suggest that the field of canon law was the primary locus for theoretical consideration of moral dilemmas in the Middle Ages. While canon law was the earliest discipline to regularize discussion of moral dilemmas among its practitioners, largely because of the subject's inclusion in Gratian's influential textbook, a parallel situation occurred among practitioners of theology in the thirteenth century for two reasons. First, the appearance of formal treatments of *perplexitas* within some early influential *summae theologiae* or "summaries of theology" insured that students of the period would consider the subject. Secondly, the gradual adoption of the university practice of commenting on Peter Lombard's *Sententiae* also helped, as Lombard's discussion of conscience in the second book of that work became the standard occasion for considering cases of *perplexitas* involving erroneously formed consciences.[1] While Lombard himself didn't use the term *perplexitas* in that discussion, many of his commentators did, including such major figures as Thomas Aquinas, Bonaventure of Bagnoregio (1217–74), and John Duns Scotus (1266–1308). This increase of interest in *perplexitas*, particularly among Parisian theologians of the thirteenth and early fourteenth centuries, was not of course without precedent. The previous chapter examined Gregory the Great's attention to the subject several centuries earlier in his *Moralia in Job*, a text that was quite influential for Gratian. The subject's solidification into a standard topic among professional theologians took some time to occur, despite some sporadic

---

[1] Peter Lombard, *Sententiae in IV libris distinctae*, II, d. 39. For a Latin text, see Peter Lombard, *Sententiae in IV libris distinctae*, 3rd edn, 2 vols. (Grottaferrata: Editiones Collegii S. Bonaventurae ad Claras Aquas, 1971–81), I.2: 553–6, and for an English translation, see Peter Lombard, *The Sentences*, trans. Giulio Silano, 4 vols. (Toronto: Pontifical Institute of Mediaeval Studies, 2007–10), II: 195–8.

discussions arising among some minor twelfth-century theologians.[2] By the first half of the thirteenth century, however, the subject of moral *perplexitas* was sufficiently recognized among professional theologians to warrant substantive treatment in the earliest of the comprehensive *summae theologiae* at the University of Paris.

From this intense period of theological activity are two towering works that attempted to present the whole scope of theological knowledge: the *Summa aurea* authored by William of Auxerre (*c.* 1140–1231) and the *Summa Halesiana* associated with Alexander of Hales (*c.* 1185–1245).[3] Each of these massive works devotes a distinct section to the problem of moral *perplexitas*, and those discussions testify to the importance of moral dilemmas among professional theologians of the period. Their respective treatments are remarkable for the large quantity of examples of dilemmas, the categorization of dilemmas by type, the articulation of some metaphysical claims about the possibility of dilemmas arising in the moral life, as well as the inclusion of advice for agents who might find themselves in such situations.

2.1 TWO *SUMMAE* AND THEIR AUTHORS

The present chapter sets forth the doctrine on moral dilemmas present in the *Summa aurea* and the *Summa Halesiana* and divides into five sections. First, it considers the historical context of each work, and in the case of the *Summa Halesiana*, reviews the contested issue of the identity of its author. Secondly, it examines some of the theoretical claims about the possibility of moral dilemmas that both works set forth at the beginning of their respective treatments of *perplexitas*. The next two sections analyze twenty moral dilemmas presented by these works, divided according to a distinction between spiritual perplexity and corporeal perplexity. Finally, the endorsement of the principle of the lesser evil in both works as a practical solution to moral dilemmas is examined. In sum, this chapter demonstrates that, despite early denials in both *summae* that situations of inescapable moral wrongdoing exist, both works offer the surprising conclusion that there are some situations where moral wrongdoing is unavoidable, despite the best efforts of moral agents who come to find themselves trapped in such situations. This chapter interprets the *Summa aurea* and the *Summa*

---

[2] See the overviews in Artur Michael Landgraf, "Der '*Casus perplexus*' in der Frühscholastik," *Collectanea Franciscana* 29 (1959), 74–86, and in Richard Schenk, OP, "*Perplexus supposito quodam*: Notizen zu einem vergessenen Schlüsselbegriff thomanischer Gewissenslehre," *Recherches de Théologie et Philosophie médiévales* 57 (1990), 62–95, at 68–79.

[3] The authorship of the *Summa Halesiana* will be discussed shortly below.

Halesiana on moral dilemmas in contrast to the received view of both *summae*, since it argues that both works defend the existence of moral dilemmas.

William of Auxerre's Summa aurea

William of Auxerre (Guillelmus Altissiodorensis) was arguably the most prominent Parisian master of theology of the early thirteenth century.[4] He is credited with shaping the development of theology during his time, largely through the organization and treatment of topics in his master-work, the *Summa aurea* or "golden summary" of theology. The adjective appearing in the title *Summa aurea* may be unoriginal and only later given in recognition of its achievement; the work appears in some manuscripts as *Summa in IV Sententiarum, Summa theologica, Summa theologiae*, or even just *Summa*.[5] Written between 1215 and 1229, his theological synthesis has been rightly characterized as "one of the most widely circulated and influential theological summas of the first half of the thirteenth century," and it represents the transition between the scholastic thought of the twelfth century and the full scholasticism to come later.[6] Its influence in the medieval period was further extended in its tendency to be reproduced in summary form, and several thirteenth-century abridgments are extant.[7] The work's significance can be seen by its content as well as its style, since, as arguably the first complete *summa* of the period, it "inaugurates a new genre of theological literature."[8] The doctrinal positions of the *Summa aurea* were widely influential in its day and in the later part of the thirteenth century, cited by such thinkers as Alexander of Hales and Thomas Aquinas. Notably, William's *Summa aurea* was one of the first major theological works to synthesize newly rediscovered Aristotelian texts with Christian theology. Despite all of this, there has been a tendency among some historians to view William simply as a transitional figure. A recent commentator reports that the "prevalent scholarly estimation of William can be stated

---

[4] Important studies include Jean Ribaillier, "Guillaume D'Auxerre. La vie et l'oeuvre," in *Summa Aurea*, ed. Jean Ribaillier, 7 vols. (Paris: Editions du Centre National de la Recherche Scientifique, 1980–7), I: 1–24; Walter Henry Principe, CSB, *William of Auxerre's Theology of the Hypostatic Union* (Toronto: Pontifical Institute of Mediaeval Studies, 1963); Boyd Taylor Coolman, *Knowing God by Experience: The Spiritual Senses in the Theology of William of Auxerre* (Washington, DC: The Catholic University of America Press, 2004); Jules A. St. Pierre, "The Theological Thought of William of Auxerre. An Introductory Bibliography," *Recherches de théologie ancienne et médiévale* 33 (1966), 147–55.
[5] Principe, *William of Auxerre's Theology*, 159, n. 29; Ribaillier, "Guillaume D'Auxerre," 16.
[6] St. Pierre, "The Theological Thought of William of Auxerre," 147.
[7] See Ribaillier, "Guillaume D'Auxerre," 16–24.   [8] Coolman, *Knowing God by Experience*, 12.

briefly: he is a pioneer who falteringly, hesitantly, initiates and anticipates the flowering of the scholastic genius among his successors."[9] Neverthe-less, there is an ongoing assessment of the distinctiveness and novelty of his philosophical and theological contributions, with renewed interest in his views concerning sacramental theology, moral theory, psychology, and theological method.[10] While the *Summa aurea* comprises four books and largely follows the subject order of Peter Lombard's *Sententiae*, it is not sim-ply a commentary. In the words of one interpreter, it is "an independent work with its own organization and method."[11]

In addition to writing the *Summa aurea*, William also authored the *Sum-mary of Ecclesiastical Duties* (*Summa de officiis ecclesiasticis*), a wide-ranging treatise whose prologue indicates its threefold subject matter. William there states that he will discuss the offices of the church, the persons to whom the celebration of the divine office belongs, and lastly the reading of rele-vant books of theology.[12] William's theoretical interest in church matters appears to span several of his works, for as shall be seen below, he devotes a considerable portion of his analysis of moral dilemmas to those that arise for ecclesiastics who are engaged in the exercise of their church offices.

William's life was not one of a quiet Parisian secular master. In addi-tion to fulfilling his academic obligations, he was Archdeacon of Beauvais and served as a representative for both King Louis IX and Gregory IX in diplomatic and administrative capacities, and at times he traveled to Rome for these affairs, including a lengthy stay in that city in 1230–31.[13] During William's last visit to Rome, Gregory IX appointed him to a commission to examine the physical treatises of Aristotle, as they had been subject to censure in Paris in 1210 by the provincial synod of Sens. That synod, which included the bishop of Paris as a member, had commanded that "neither the books of Aristotle on natural philosophy nor their commentaries are to be read at Paris in public or in secret, and this we forbid under penalty of excommunication (*nec libri Aristotelis de naturali philosophia nec commenta*

---

[9] Coolman, *Knowing God by Experience*, 9. Coolman argues, however, that William's contributions to the question of human knowledge of God are particularly original, even if they were not followed by later scholastics.

[10] See Principe, *William of Auxerre's Theology*, 16.   [11] Principe, *William of Auxerre's Theology*, 15.

[12] While the *Summa de officiis ecclesiasticis* does not exist at present in a printed modern critical edition, an online critical edition has been completed recently by Franz Fischer. See www.thomasinst.uni-koeln.de/sdoe/start.html. For a discussion of this work, see Fischer's *Einführung* (www.thomasinst.uni-koeln.de/sdoe/aux/intro.html), as well as Ribaillier, "Guillaume D'Auxerre," 6–15. There has been a tradition of attributing to William some *quaestiones disputatae*, a gloss on Porphyry's *Isagoge*, as well as a commentary on Alan of Lille's *Anticlaudianus*, but William's authorship of these works has generally been doubted.

[13] See Ribaillier, "Guillaume D'Auxerre," 4–5.

legantur Parisius publice vel secreto, et hoc sub pena excommunicationis inhibemus)."[14] Despite that proscription, it appears that Aristotle's physical treaties were not entirely abandoned and they continued to be read. On 23 April 1231, Gregory IX instituted the commission and commanded William, along with Symon of Alteis and Stephen of Provins, to examine Aristotle's books on nature and to exclude anything that was "erroneous or likely to give scandal or offense to readers (*erronea seu scandali vel offendiculi legentibus*)."[15] It appears, however, that William's death in Rome in the fall of that year occurred before this project of expurgation could be completed.

Alexander of Hales *and the* Summa Halesiana

Among those influenced by William of Auxerre was his younger contemporary at the University of Paris, Alexander of Hales.[16] Known to later ages as *Doctor Irrefragabilis* or the "Invincible Doctor," Alexander was a prominent theologian whose fame and reputation extended well beyond his lifetime. Jean Gerson (1363–1429) reports the possibly apocryphal story that upon being asked about the best way to study theology, Thomas Aquinas replied "to train oneself especially with one teacher," and, when asked further who he had in mind, Aquinas had responded, "Alexander of Hales."[17] The title "*Doctor Irrefragabilis*" likely originates in the praise posthumously bestowed upon Alexander by Alexander IV, who in the papal bull *De fontibus paradisi* of 1256 extolled Alexander's scholarly achievements and noted especially that Alexander had composed "a *Summa* about theological questions . . . in which ranks of irrefragable sentences are arranged to crush the obstinacy of contentious falsehood with the weight of truth (*super quaestionibus theologicis . . . Summam . . . in qua sententiarum irrefragabilium ordinatae sunt*

---

[14] The text of the condemnation of 1210 is present in *Chartularium Universitatis Parisiensis*, ed. Henricus Denifle, OP, 4 vols. (Paris: Delalain, 1891–9 [repr. Brussels: Culture et Civilisation, 1964]), I: 70. The English translation is taken from *A Source Book in Medieval Science*, ed. Edward Grant (Cambridge, MA: Harvard University Press, 1974), 42.

[15] For the text of Gregory IX's commission, see *Chartularium Universitatis Parisiensis*, I: 143–4. The English translation is from *A Source Book in Medieval Science*, 43.

[16] For the biographical facts of Alexander's life, the best account is the introductory material titled "Vita Alexandri," in Alexander de Hales, *Glossa in quatuor libros Sententiarum Petri Lombardi*, 4 vols. (Quaracchi, Florence: Collegium S. Bonaventurae, 1951–7), I: 7*–75*. See also Raphael M. Huber, OFM Conv., "Alexander of Hales, O.F.M. (ca. 1170–1245)," *Franciscan Studies* 5 (1945), 353–65, and more recently, Kenan B. Osborne, OFM, "Alexander of Hales: Precursor and Promoter of Franciscan Theology," in *The History of Franciscan Theology*, ed. Kenan B. Osborne, OFM (St. Bonaventure, NY: The Franciscan Institute, 1994 [repr. 2007]), 1–38.

[17] Jean Gerson, *Epistola ad quemdam fratrem Minorem* (1426), excerpted in "Vita Alexandri," 39*.

acies ad obterendam veritatis pondere contentiosae pervicaciam falsitatis)."[18]
An Englishman by nationality, and born to a wealthy but not noble rural
family, Alexander went to the University of Paris as a young man to study
arts, becoming *magister in artibus* and teaching at least by the year 1210.
He pursued further studies in theology, ultimately attaining the rank of
magister regens to hold a chair in theology at the university in 1220 or 1221.
Like William of Auxerre, Alexander is often viewed as a transitional figure
whose contributions to the discipline of theology preserved earlier discussions, anticipated the interest in certain areas of later scholastic thought,
and shaped considerably the formulation of problems for later generations
of thinkers. His use of the writings of Anselm of Canterbury (1033–1109),
for instance, is often noted as crucial to popularizing the Benedictine archbishop for later thinkers, as Alexander was one of the first to incorporate
Anselm's so-called "ontological" argument into thirteenth-century discussions of natural theology. Also, like William, Alexander belongs to the
group of early theologians who appropriated the writings of Aristotle for
use in Christian theological thinking. Alexander is credited with initiat-
ing in 1223 the practice of reading Peter Lombard's *Sententiae*, rather than
scripture, as an exercise of the theological faculty.[19] As commenting on the
Sententiae would become a regularized activity for medieval theologians
until well into the fifteenth century, Alexander played a decisive role in
promoting Lombard's work as a basis for doing theology.[20] In this capac-
ity Alexander is generally recognized as the first to divide Lombard's text
into smaller sections or *distinctiones*.[21] He also is credited with helping to
formalize the scholastic *disputatio*, and among his writings survive many
disputed and quodlibetal questions.[22] Apart from his distinct theoretical

[18] An English translation of the bull *De fontibus paradisi* is given in Robert Prentice, OFM, "The 'De
     fontibus paradisi' of Alexander IV on the 'Summa theologica' of Alexander of Hales," *Franciscan
     Studies* 5 (1945), 350–1. A Latin text for this work is printed in Alexander of Hales, *Summa theologica*,
     4 vols. (Clarae Aquae [Quaracchi]: Typographia Collegii S. Bonaventurae, 1924–48), I: VII–VIII.

[19] Roger Bacon observes the novelty of Alexander's use of Lombard's work as a textbook, noting that
     "Alexander was the first who read [the *Sentences*] (*Alexander fuit primus qui legit*)." Roger Bacon,
     Opera, in *Opera quaedam hactenus inedita*, ed. J. S. Brewer, vol. 1 (London: Longman, 1859 [repr.
     New York: Kraus, 1965]), 329.

[20] For an account of Alexander's *Gloss on the Four Books of the Sentences* (*Glossa in IV libros Sententiarum*),
     see Victorin Doucet, OFM, "A New Source of the 'Summa Fratris Alexandri': The Commentary
     on the Sentences of Alexander of Hales," *Franciscan Studies* 6 (1946), 403–17; and more recently,
     Hubert Philipp Weber, "The *Glossa in IV libros Sententiarum*," in *Mediaeval Commentaries on the
     Sentences of Peter Lombard*, ed. Philipp W. Rosemann (Leiden: Brill, 2010), 79–109.

[21] A review of the evidence is given by Ignatius Brady, OFM, "The Distinctions of Lombard's Book
     of Sentences and Alexander of Hales," *Franciscan Studies* 25 (1965), 90–116.

[22] Alexander of Hales, *Quaestiones disputatae 'antequam esset frater,'* 3 vols. (Quaracchi, Florence:
     Collegium S. Bonaventurae, 1960). His *Quodlibeta* have not been edited in a critical edition. For the

contributions to the discipline of theology, therefore, it is unquestionable that his method of doing theology was extraordinarily influential.

Like William of Auxerre, Alexander also lived a busy life in service to the church and the university. He served as a canon of St. Paul's in London and was Archdeacon at the cathedral of Coventry. From 1229 to 1231 he was in Rome representing the interests of the University of Paris to the pope, joining William of Auxerre and others in defending the institution during a tumultuous period. He also served as a diplomat assisting Henry III of England in seeking peace with the French in 1235. Shortly before his death he worked with his fellow Englishman, the theologian Robert Grosseteste (*c.* 1168–1253), on the canonization commission for Edmund Rich of Abingdon.

Alexander is most frequently regarded as the founder of the "Franciscan school" of theology.[23] This attribution has received careful consideration, since the bulk of his theological career took place before his decision, at age fifty, to join the Franciscan order in 1236. When he entered, William possessed a chair in theology at the University of Paris, so with his admission into the order he became the first Franciscan to possess a university chair. One commentator notes that Alexander's change in ecclesiastical status "caused some stir within the university community, but which, in various accounts of Alexander's life, has been mythically imbued with undeserved significance."[24] The Franciscan Roger Bacon (1214/20–*c.* 1292) provides some detail about Alexander's admission to the mendicant order, reporting that, "when Alexander entered the Franciscan order, there was about him a great commotion (*quum intravit ordinem fratrum Minorum, fuit de eo maximus rumor*),"[25] and "the friars and others shouted praises to heaven (*fratres et alii exaltaverunt in coelum*)."[26] It does not appear that Alexander had to modify any of his theological opinions as a condition for entering the order, and there is no record of any opposition by the order to his completed works; commentators have long discussed the compatibility between the theological orientation of Alexander and the spirituality of the Franciscans.[27] Despite his late entrance into the order, his influence on

---

few parts of the *Quaestiones disputatae 'postquam fuit frater'* that have been edited, see the references in Weber, "The *Glossa*," 82, n. 15.

[23] J. Guy Bougerol, OFM, *Introduction to the Works of Bonaventure*, trans. José de Vinck (Paterson, NJ: St. Anthony Guild Press, 1964): "The fame of Alexander extends beyond the University of Paris: he may truly be seen as the founder of the Franciscan school, for he gave that school both its body of teachings and its characteristic spirit," 15.

[24] Osborne, "Alexander of Hales," 4.

[25] Quoted from Huber, "Alexander of Hales," 357. See Bacon, *Opera*, 325–6.

[26] Bacon, *Opera*, 326.   [27] For a discussion, see Osborne, "Alexander of Hales," 20–3, 37.

the other great Franciscan thinkers of the period is significant. Bonaventure, John of Rupella (*c.* 1190/1200–45), and Richard Rufus of Cornwall (fl. 1231–56) are counted among his students. Bonaventure at times even refers to Alexander as his "father and master (*pater et magister*)."[28]

The authorship of the Summa Halesiana

The authorship of the *Summa Halesiana* has been contested since the late nineteenth century even though for earlier centuries it was generally unquestioned that Alexander of Hales had composed it. The titles under which this massive work circulated, first in manuscript and then in printed form, were the *Summa theologica*, the *Summa fratris Alexandri* (*Summary [of Theology] of Brother Alexander*), or simply the *Summa*, among others, and both the manuscript and printed traditions almost invariably promote Alexander as its author.[29] It is true that Roger Bacon had written wryly that others had produced "that great *Summa*, which weighs more than a horse (*magnam summam illam, quae est plusquam pondus unius equî*)," alleging that it was ascribed to Alexander simply "out of reverence (*propter reverentiam*)," but this assertion appears to have been largely forgotten and only rediscovered in the mid-nineteenth century with the editing of Bacon's works.[30] On the other hand, Alexander IV considered the *Summa* to be authored by Alexander of Hales when he described it in *De fontibus paradisi*, noting that Alexander had left it unfinished at his death while enjoining the Franciscans to bring it to completion. In the late nineteenth and early twentieth centuries, some commentators began to notice that the *Summa* contained interpolations from the works of Bonaventure among others and that the style of writing differed in sections of the *Summa*. When the Franciscan fathers at Quaracchi began to edit the critical edition of the work in the early part of the twentieth century, they nevertheless worked under the assumption that Alexander was the sole author, publishing the first three volumes under that view, and they downplayed the scholarly doubts about the work's authorship. Such a practice elicited much criticism by scholars, including Étienne Gilson.[31] A change in editorship of the project

---

[28] For an account of the relationship of the two men, and a list of texts where this epithet occurs in Bonaventure's corpus, see Bougerol, *Introduction to the Works of Bonaventure*, 4, 203, and "Vita Alexandri," 20*.

[29] See the "Prolegomena" in Alexander of Hales, *Summa theologica*, 4a: L–LIV.

[30] Bacon, *Opera*, 326.

[31] For an account of the production and early reception of that edition of the *Summa Halesiana*, see Ignatius Brady, OFM, "The 'Summa Theologica' of Alexander of Hales (1924–1948)," *Archivum Franciscanum Historicum* 70 (1977), 437–47, at 444.

for the final volume of the *Summa* at Quaracchi yielded a new approach to examining the question of origins of the *Summa*. In the judgment of one commentator, this new change in direction would "restore the honor of the College" of the editors at Quaracchi.[32] In the early part of 1948 a prologue to the fourth and final volume of the critical edition of the *Summa* was published that considered the contested question of its authorship.[33] After examining a wide range of evidence, it concluded:

Alexander himself in some way produced the *Summa* (external criteria), but with other collaborators (internal criteria); also, chiefly from his writings, but also from others. Therefore, it is possible to call the *Summa* in some way authentic and Halesian, but not, however, unqualifiedly (*Ipse Alexander quodammodo Summam fecit (critica externa), sed collaborantibus aliis (critica interna); item, ex propriis maxime scriptis, sed etiam ex alienis. Quare et authentica et halesiana quodammodo Summa dici potest, non autem simpliciter*).[34]

Since then, it has become customary to consider Alexander of Hales to be an initiator, compiler, or co-compiler, rather than single author, of the *Summa Halesiana*. Books I, II, and III appear to have been mostly completed between 1241 and 1245,[35] prior to the death of Alexander, and much of the content is taken from Alexander's earlier authentic works, especially the *Glossa in IV libros Sententiarum*.[36] It is generally accepted that Alexander had some editorial or supervisory role in the organization and compilation of the first three books, but beyond this there is room for debate and interpretation.[37] All present-day interpretations appear to be somewhere between Alexander IV's claim that Alexander of Hales wrote

---

[32] Brady, "The 'Summa Theologica,'" 447.

[33] The "*Prolegomena in librum III necnon in libros I et II 'Summae Fratris Alexandri'*" by Victorinus Doucet, OFM is the first part of vol. IV of the Quaracchi edition of the *Summa theologica*. In recognition of the question of contested authorship of the *Summa*, this volume and the final one completing the critical edition of the *Summa Halesiana* were published with the expanded title of *Summa theologica seu sic ab origine dicta "Summa Fratris Alexandri."* A major part of the *Prolegomena* (pages LIX–LXXXI) was published in English two years previously as Victorin Doucet, OFM, "The History of the Problem of the Authenticity of the Summa," *Franciscan Studies* 7 (1947), 26–41, 274–312, and both works are the best assessments of the state of the question of the authorship of the *Summa Halesiana*. Important more recent assessments include Osborne, "Alexander of Hales," 1–38.

[34] Doucet, "*Prolegomena*," CCCLXIX.   [35] Doucet, "*Prolegomena*," CCCVI, CCCLIV–CCCLV.

[36] See Doucet, "A New Source," 403–17. Book IV is considered to be the work by William of Militona (d. 1257/60).

[37] One commentator writes, "[Alexander's] role in its composition, in a word, must have involved something more than merely supplying much of the material it contains. Was it because he was the one who first conceived of composing the work and outlined its general plan? Or did he perhaps go further, functioning as a director or general supervisor of the work? These are questions we cannot answer with any measure of certainty today," in Meldon C. Wass, OFM, *The Infinite God and the Summa Fratris Alexandri* (Chicago: Franciscan Herald Press, 1964), 8. See Bougerol, *Introduction*

the entire first three books of the *Summa* and Roger Bacon's claim that he wrote none of it.

Given the reappraisal of Alexander's role in the composition of the *Summa*, it has now become customary to privilege other works from the Halesian corpus in the determination of Alexander's view on any particular position.[38] The interpolation of texts from other Franciscans in the *Summa Halesiana* renders it more an expression of early Franciscan theology rather than a distinctive work expressing the outlook of the historical Alexander of Hales, who appears to many now to be a different figure from the literary Alexander of Hales who had been believed for centuries to have authored the *Summa Halesiana* and whose fame has rested nearly entirely on this association. Nevertheless, the work has exercised a considerable influence in the history of philosophy, as it was an official textbook for Franciscan education in the fourteenth century.[39] This chapter will refer to Alexander of Hales as the author of the *Summa Halesiana*, with the recognition that his role may simply be that of inspiration for the work.[40] The views on moral dilemmas expressed in the *Summa Halesiana* may reflect the outlook of another Franciscan (such as John of Rupella), rather than Alexander of Hales, but this question cannot be resolved unless more evidence about the particular composition of the various chapters of the *Summa Halesiana* is discovered.

2.2 TWO DISCUSSIONS OF *PERPLEXITAS*

William of Auxerre devotes the fifty-fourth section of the third book of the *Summa aurea* to a consideration of moral dilemmas.[41] This portion of the work, titled *De perplexitate*, comprises three chapters and is arguably the earliest substantive treatment of moral dilemmas by a major theologian in the thirteenth century. A similarly detailed discussion of moral dilemmas appears in the *Summa Halesiana* as chapter IV of question III of the second part of the second book, titled *De perplexitate conscientiae*, and it

---

to the Works of Bonaventure, 15: "The 'Summa of Alexander of Hales' is the product of a team of theologians, disciples of the master to whom the entire work is ascribed in its title."

[38] This procedure is defended by Walter Principe, CSB, *Alexander of Hales' Theology of the Hypostatic Union* (Toronto: Pontifical Institute of Mediaeval Studies, 1967), 15.

[39] For an estimation of its value as a compendium of early Franciscan thought, see Étienne Gilson, *History of Christian Philosophy in the Middle Ages* (New York: Random House, 1955), 327.

[40] While perhaps imprecise, this choice is perhaps better than other options, such as referring to the authors of the *Summa Halesiana* as "'the Summists.'" See Wass, *The Infinite God*, 30.

[41] Texts cited below from the *Summa aurea* are from Guillelmus Altissiodorensis, *Summa aurea*, ed. Jean Ribaillier, 7 vols. (Paris: Editions du Centre National de la Recherche Scientifique, 1980–1987), III.2: 1044–54. The translations are my own.

comprises two articles.[42] Alexander explicitly notes his dependence on his predecessors, saying that he will be using "examples from the Masters (*casus a Magistris*)," and chief among them is William of Auxerre.[43] Alexander's dependence, however, goes beyond the simple borrowing of examples from the *Summa aurea*, as he also incorporates several of William's significant theoretical claims about moral dilemmas. Alexander should be viewed as an appropriator and exponent of William of Auxerre's views on moral perplexity, but not as an uncritical one, for Alexander does not hesitate to omit some of William's examples while adding his own.

Perplexitas *as an equivocal term*

Both William and Alexander begin their respective treatments of moral dilemmas by disambiguating three senses of the term *perplexitas*.[44] First perplexity (*prima perplexitas*) is the perplexity of the understanding of sacred scripture (*perplexitas intelligencie Sacre Scripture*). Second perplexity (*secunda perplexitas*) is the perplexity of understanding what should be done (*perplexitas intelligencie faciendorum*), and third perplexity (*tertia perplexitas*) is the perplexity of the inevitability of sinning (*perplexitas inevitabilitas peccandi*). According to both thinkers, first and second perplexity result from deficient epistemic states that can be rectified with additional knowledge. For instance, they argue that first perplexity can be remedied by the use of the traditional tools available to exegetes of sacred scripture, such as making distinctions among ambiguous terms, or making temporal distinctions when interpreting texts. These suggestions are not novel, but simply repeat standard Christian hermeneutical approaches that were articulated by Augustine of Hippo in the third book of *De doctrina Christiana*. Second

---

[42] Texts cited below from the *Summa Halesiana* are from Alexander of Hales, *Summa theologica*, III: 391–7. The translations are my own.

[43] *Summa Halesiana*, 393. Alexander also takes three examples from the *Summa de vitiis* of John of Rupella, of which two are found in Gregory the Great. See Doucet, *Prolegomena*, CCLXXXVIII, and Alexander of Hales, *Summa theologica*, III: 393, n. 12. These examples will be discussed in detail below. The *Summa de vitiis* was completed around 1235. On that work, see Doucet, *Prolegomena*, CCXIV, and more recently, Silvana Vecchio, "The Seven Deadly Sins between Pastoral Care and Scholastic Theology: The *Summa de vitiis* by John of Rupella," in *In the Garden of Evil: The Vices and Culture in the Middle Ages*, ed. Richard Newhauser (Toronto: The Pontifical Institute of Mediaeval Studies, 2005), 104–27. Extracts of the *Summa de vitiis* are given in Odon Lottin, *Psychologie et morale aux XIIᵉ et XIIIᵉ siècles*, 6 vols. (Louvain: Abbaye du Mont César, 1942–60), II: 361–3. For an assessment of the general dependence of the *Summa Halesiana* on the *Summa aurea*, see "Prolegomena," in Alexander of Hales, *Summa theologica*, 4a: CXXXII.

[44] *Summa aurea*, 1044–5; *Summa Halesiana*, 391–2. This threefold division is adopted by later medieval writers. See, for example, Pseudo-Bonaventure, *Centiloquium*, par. 1, sec. 2, in Bonaventure, *Opera omnia*, ed. A. C. Peltier, 15 vols. (Paris: Vivès, 1864–71), VII: 356.

perplexity, a general perplexity about how one should live one's life, can be solved by prayer, as the Holy Spirit can instruct all those who request assistance. William adds that first and second perplexity have even been experienced by saints, and even though the darkness of ignorance can constrain such individuals, it cannot completely overcome them. The authors of both *summae* consider first and second perplexity to be generated by vincible ignorance that can be easily remedied, and neither type is broached again by the authors. Third perplexity – the inevitability of sinning – is the true subject for both investigations into perplexity.

William of Auxerre on the necessity of sinning

William's prefatory remarks on perplexity occur in a section titled *What Perplexity Is* (*Quid sit perplexitas*).[45] After noting the aforementioned threefold senses of perplexity and highlighting third perplexity as the subject to be treated for the remainder of the discussion, William of Auxerre argues that one who investigates whether "someone is perplexed through the perplexity of sinning (*aliquis sit perplexus perplexitate peccandi*)" should recall that Gregory the Great had argued for the existence of such situations.[46] Here William references the discussions from Gregory's *Moralia* that were privileged by Gratian in the jurist's defense of cases of inescapable moral wrongdoing. William observes that "Gregory would not have said this, unless someone were perplexed between sins (*Gregorius non dixisset hoc, nisi aliquis esset perplexus inter peccata*)."[47] Nevertheless, it becomes clear that William seeks to mollify the force of Gregory's contention that individuals can be forced to sin. As evidence against Gregory's position, William observes that the Lord invites all sinners to repent, and therefore it should be concluded that in whatever state a sinner resides, a return to the Lord is possible. He then provides what seems to be a fairly decisive judgment about moral dilemmas: "therefore we are not perplexed; and thus no one is unqualifiedly perplexed (*ergo non sumus perplexi; et ita nullus est perplexus simpliciter*)."[48] Since the existence of moral dilemmas, conceived in the manner of Gregory, casts serious doubt on ultimate salvation, William concludes that to be unqualifiedly perplexed or in a state of *perplexus simpliciter* is not possible. The claim that "*nullus est perplexus simpliciter*"

---

[45] *Summa aurea*, 1044–5.
[46] *Summa aurea*, 1045. See Gregory the Great, *Moralia in Iob*, ed. Marcus Adriaen, 3 vols. (Turnhout: Brepols, 1979–85), III: 1656–8; *Morals on the Book of Job*, 3 vols. (Oxford: John Henry Parker, 1844–50), III.2: 538–40.
[47] *Summa aurea*, 1045.   [48] *Summa aurea*, 1045.

appears to be an unequivocal rejection of moral dilemmas at the start of his discussion. He states this position more strongly a bit further in the text, saying:

Accordingly we say that perplexity is nothing, for it exists only in a qualified way, according to an erroneous conscience (*Unde dicimus quod perplexitas nichil est, est enim secundum quid, secundum erroneam conscientiam*).[49]

Here William locates the genesis of moral perplexity in an erroneous conscience, seemingly restricting cases of inevitable sinning to the prior adoption of some errant moral view. Perplexity is nothing (*nichil*) in itself, but only exists qualifiedly (*secundum quid*). There is no necessity or inevitability of sinning in an unrestricted sense, he maintains, since any such situations presuppose some prior disorder at the level of conscience. William then attempts to reconcile his position with that of Gregory by generously stating that Gregory's discussion of perplexity should only be "understood hypothetically and not unqualifiedly (*secundum ypotesim intelligitur non simpliciter*)."[50] In other words, William invites the reader to consider Gregory's account to be a thought experiment rather than a real description of the moral life. Such a characterization is consistent with the qualification that the glossators made on Gregory's and Gratian's account of moral dilemmas, when they said "in truth, however, there is no perplexity (*in veritate tamen perplexio nihil est*)."[51]

To illustrate that perplexity presupposes some prior disorder in an agent's conscience, William deploys the first of the twenty moral dilemmas presented in the two *summae*. It appears to be a traditional one, for it was analyzed by the authors of the *Glossa ordinaria*. William's understanding of the basic facts of the dilemma can be summarized as:

1. *The Killers of Christ Dilemma*
   The men who killed Christ were *perplexi*, obliged to kill Christ and not kill Christ. They were obliged to kill him because their consciences dictated that they should do so, and they were obliged not to kill him because some of them believed him to be the Messiah on account of signs and miracles.[52]

William's analysis is largely consonant with the analysis of the glossators: the men who killed Christ possessed erroneous consciences and such errors were within their power to be avoided. Christ's miracles, such as the resuscitation of Lazarus, should have been evidence of divine authority, sufficient

---

[49] *Summa aurea*, 1046.   [50] *Summa aurea*, 1046.
[51] *Glossa ordinaria*, XIII, d, 65 (Gordley, 50).   [52] See *Summa aurea*, 1046–7.

to manifest to them that Christ was a superior to those who commanded Christ's killing. The agents remain perplexed only as long as they maintain culpably malformed consciences. William's contention that they "were not perplexed (*non erant perplexi*)" means that they were not entangled by true conflicting moral obligations.[53] Of course, they may still have been perplexed in the sense of being confused, but William here is more concerned with an investigation into the reality of moral dilemmas than with a particular individual's state of ignorance. While William's analysis of this dilemma up to this point is standard medieval fare, at least when viewed in light of the canon law tradition, he does introduce some novelty worthy of mention. William presents two provisional arguments in defense of the killers of Christ, only to show afterward that the force of those arguments does not hold. First, he proposes that the conscience of a killer of Christ is similar to the conscience of another man who, upon seeing someone else, falsely believes the other to be the king. That man, believing the other to be king, appears obliged to honor the other as king, and if no honor is given, an insult occurs to the king. Secondly, William hypothesizes that a person who mistakenly believes a certain creature is God seems obliged to confer honor on the creature as if it were God. In these two cases, it is alleged, the agents should not be considered to be guilty of sin when they honor the apparent king or worship a creature as divine, because they are bound to offer honors or worship according to their mistaken consciences. In responding to these two arguments, however, William decisively rejects their conclusions, saying:

> The worship owed to God is attributed to a creature; therefore it is idolatrous; therefore [the agent] sins mortally (*Cultum Deo debitum attribuit creature; ergo est ydolatra; ergo mortaliter peccat*).[54]

In William's view, errors in conscience do not shield agents from responsibility for disordered actions, even if such actions are performed with good intentions. He contends that perplexity "is solved through the putting away of the erroneous conscience (*solvitur per depositionem erronee conscientie*)."[55] To act according to an erroneous conscience, according to William, exhibits a "presumption of the intellect (*presumptio intellectus*)" for which the agent is to be held responsible.[56] With this declaration, William concludes his prefatory discussion of moral dilemmas and begins to consider additional cases of perplexity.

---

[53] *Summa aurea*, 1046.   [54] *Summa aurea*, 1047.
[55] *Summa aurea*, 1045.   [56] *Summa aurea*, 1047.

The Summa Halesiana *on the necessity of sinning*

Alexander of Hales's prefatory remarks on moral perplexity occur in a section of the *Summa Halesiana* titled *Whether There Is Perplexity of Conscience* (*Utrum sit perplexitas conscientiae*).[57] His account appears generally consonant with that of William, as Alexander likewise advises that perplexity is solved "through the setting aside of the erroneous conscience (*per depositionem erroneae conscientiae*)."[58] Like William, Alexander begins by referencing Gregory the Great's discussion of perplexity, indicating that Gregory's arguments suggest that there is perplexity in the sense of an inevitability of sinning.[59] In the "on the contrary" section of his reply, however, Alexander questions that assumption with the following argument:

No one sins in that which one is not able to avoid; therefore there is no inevitability of sinning; therefore there is no perplexity (*Nullus peccat in eo quod vitare non potest; ergo non est inevitabilitas peccandi; ergo non est perplexitas*).[60]

This argument against perplexity appears to reject categorically that one is ever in such a situation of inescapable moral wrongdoing. Further, it appears to commit Alexander to a medieval version of the principle "ought implies can." While this argument might seem to settle the issue for Alexander, three additional arguments are added to this *contra* portion of the discussion, and surprisingly these three collectively support the view that there are dilemmas, but God saves certain individuals from them. Since these three arguments appear to presuppose the existence of perplexity – which is precisely what is denied in the first argument of the *contra* – it will be in the *solutio* portion of the analysis that Alexander's considered view will be found. These other three *contra* arguments are worth noting. First, Alexander there states that as long as one is an earthly wayfarer (*viator*), sanctifying grace is available to remove perplexity. Secondly, the Psalms suggest that "God saves from perplexity (*Deus salvat a perplexitate*)." Finally, Alexander adds that Augustine's works imply that if a man should pray incessantly, God "will extract him from perplexity (*eruet eum a perplexitate*)."[61] These

---

[57] *Summa Halesiana*, 392.   [58] *Summa Halesiana*, 392.

[59] The invocation of Gregory the Great as an authority on *perplexitas* first by Gratian, and later by William and Alexander, establishes Gregory's text as an unavoidable authority for many later medieval discussants of moral dilemmas. In the pseudo-Bonaventurian theological compendium *Pharetra*, extracts from Gregory form the beginning of an entry on *perplexitas*. See pseudo-Bonaventure, *Pharetra*, lib. 2, cap. 14, in Bonaventure, *Opera omnia*, ed. Peltier, VII: 78. See also the entry for *perplexitas* by Albericus de Rosate (1290–1354/60) in his alphabetic dictionary *Lexicon sive dictionarium utriusque iuris* (Pavia: Michael et Bernardinus de Garaldis, 1498).

[60] *Summa Halesiana*, 392.   [61] *Summa Halesiana*, 392.

three arguments suggest that prayers, and the resulting divine help that is attendant upon such prayers, will protect agents from any situations that would involve the necessity of sinning. Alexander's contention that God will extract agents from such situations seems to presuppose that situations of perplexity exist, and that moral dilemmas will be experienced by those who do not petition for divine help. This theme will surface in the thirteenth century in greater detail with the thought of Raymond Lull, who shall be examined in the next chapter.

Perplexitas iuris *and* perplexitas facti

In the *solutio*, Alexander begins by offering a classification of types of perplexity not given in the *Summa aurea*. He contends that perplexity is twofold: there is perplexity of law (*perplexitas iuris*) and perplexity of fact (*perplexitas facti*).[62] Both kinds of perplexity can generate situations where there is an inevitability of sin (*inevitabilitas peccati*). The first type occurs when an agent is confused about the obligations imposed by law. No one needs to be perplexed in this sense, however, "for no one is in such a state so that the uncertainty of the law is not able to be removed by him (*nullus enim est in tali statu quin possit ab eo amoveri dubietas iuris*)."[63] Here Alexander appears to broach, albeit briefly, the subject of vincible epistemic perplexity. This distinction between two kinds of perplexity was also defended by Alexander's contemporary, the canonist and theologian Raymond of Peñafort (*c.* 1180–1275), whose brief comments on the topic can be helpful in understanding this distinction.[64] Raymond explains that perplexity of fact "is to be solved through the reconciliation of contraries: for in law there is no real contrariety, but superficial contrariety alone (*per contrariorum concordiam est solvenda: nam in iure nulla est contrarietas realis, sed superficialis tantum*)."[65] Therefore, according to Alexander and Raymond, perplexity of law never truly requires sinning, since the acquisition of knowledge defuses such dilemmatic situations. Turning to the second sense of perplexity, Alexander states that perplexity of fact occurs when "someone is able to be perplexed by one's own fault (*potest aliquis ex proprio vitio esse perplexus*)."[66] Alexander considers this perplexity to result

---

[62] *Summa Halesiana*, 392.   [63] *Summa Halesiana*, 392.

[64] See Raymond of Peñafort, *Summa*, lib. 3, *De scandalo, et perplexitate, et notorio*, §6, in *Summa de poenitentia et matrimonio cum glossis Ioannis de Friburgo* (Rome: Ioannes Tallinus Bibliopolus, 1603), 356. Raymond's account of this distinction was preserved by Albericus de Rosate in the entry for *perplexitas* in the *Lexicon sive dictionarium utriusque iuris*.

[65] Raymond of Peñafort, *Summa*, 356.   [66] *Summa Halesiana*, 392.

from an agent's prior misdeed that impedes the fulfillment of a future obligation. Again, Raymond can help, as he adds that this perplexity of fact occurs when the devil successfully suggests evils to an agent.[67]

To illustrate perplexity of fact, Alexander sets forth his first example of a moral dilemma, and it features a priest who finds himself celebrating a mass at the point of words of consecration, but because of some unspecified prior wrongdoing is in a state of mortal sin.[68] The priest in such a situation is perplexed, because to consecrate the Eucharist in a state of serious sin is to celebrate the sacrament unworthily, and yet if he does not proceed with the consecration he creates a grave scandal among those assisting him by not fulfilling his office as priest. Such a priest at that time appears unable to avoid sin, since by acting or not acting a moral failure is committed. Alexander's solution to this priest's state of *perplexitas* is simply repentance; if the priest repents of the prior fault then the impediment to consecration is removed. Alexander then draws a general conclusion about such cases of perplexity:

Accordingly, perplexity should not follow if the first fault be removed, but remaining in such a state one is able to be perplexed (*Unde si primo ablatum esset vitium, non sequeretur perplexitas, sed manente tali statu potest esse perplexitas*).[69]

Alexander here claims that the removal of first faults removes perplexity, but untreated first faults can generate this particular kind of dilemma. Alexander leaves unstated here whether it is *always* the case that prior wrongs can be sufficiently rectified, that is, whether in all cases of perplexity generated by prior moral failures agents can save themselves from additional wrongdoing through some rectifying act. Nevertheless, Alexander's theorizing here concerning this kind of moral dilemma – what might fittingly be called a *prior-fault dilemma* – is significant, and will be subject to greater analysis by later medieval thinkers.

Alexander adds that the entirety of Gregory's discussion of perplexity should be understood as an explication of situations of perplexity generated by prior wrongs that can be removed by subsequent rectifying acts. On this interpretation, the force of Gregory's defense of moral dilemmas is significantly evaded or at least downplayed. It should be noted that

---

[67] Raymond of Peñafort, *Summa*, 356. In his discussion, Raymond also extracts the standard discussion of perplexity found in Gregory the Great's *Moralia*.

[68] This example is likely a traditional one, as it is given by Stephen Langton (1150–1228) in his *Quaestiones*. There the priest is described as "perplexed between two mortal sins (*perplexus est inter duo mortalia*)" and is urged to determine the magnitude (*quantitas*) of each one so that the lesser can be chosen. For the text, see Landgraf, "Der '*Casus perplexus*' in der Frühscholastik," 82.

[69] *Summa Halesiana*, 392.

Alexander devotes some further remarks that assert a providential role to situations of perplexity. He states that the expression "necessity of sinning (*necessitas peccandi*)" can refer simply to a propensity to sinning, and God can liberate individuals from that propensity. Also, "necessity of sinning" can refer to the aforementioned prior-fault dilemmas, and Alexander contends that such situations assist in bringing sinners to salvation. He explains that the "Lord permits man to fall to the necessity of such perplexity so that thus man is dismayed over his sin (*Permittit tamen Dominus hominem cadere in huiusmodi necessitatem perplexitatis, ut sic confundatur homo super peccato suo*)."[70] According to this argument, providence allows agents to experience prior-fault dilemmas so that the experience will cause the agent to turn to God and seek repentance. This contention of Alexander that prior-fault dilemmas provide moral instruction to sinners is absent from William's account.

At this point, two questions can be raised about Alexander's discussion. The first is whether Alexander is defending the view that all moral dilemmas are prior-fault dilemmas. The second is whether all prior-fault dilemmas can be escaped with some rectifying act – such as repentance – that removes the after-effects of the original misdeed and allows the agent to escape further wrongdoing. As will be seen shortly, Alexander ultimately answers both questions in the negative.

2.3 MORAL DILEMMAS OF THE SPIRITUAL PERPLEXITY VARIETY

Both William and Alexander separate all moral dilemmas into the classes of: (1) perplexity in spiritual works (*perplexitas in operationibus spiritualibus*), and (2) perplexity in corporeal works (*perplexitas in operationibus corporalibus*). This twofold division receives no justification from either thinker, but the examples falling under each class provide evidence for the meaning of the distinction. All cases of spiritual perplexity involve agents who believe themselves unable to avoid wrongdoing in the exercise of a religious vocation. Hence, the agents featured in such dilemmas are priests, monks, deacons, or hermits. Corporeal perplexity, in contrast, is less restricted and covers situations unrelated to religious vocations. Examples of corporeal perplexity feature both lay people and religious who experience moral dilemmas when dealing with worldly situations, and such situations frequently involve money, food, or possessions. The examples of both spiritual and corporeal perplexity feature individuals who judge themselves compelled to perform an action and omit the same action at the same time

---

[70] *Summa Halesiana*, 392.

and are thereby considered perplexed. Collectively, William and Alexander discuss nine moral dilemmas of the spiritual perplexity variety, with five of the nine common to both thinkers.

The Fornicating Priest Dilemma *and* The Simoniacal Priest at Mass Dilemma

The first two of the five examples of spiritual perplexity common to William and Alexander feature priests who become perplexed while celebrating mass. The two moral dilemmas are:

2. *The Fornicating Priest Dilemma*
   A priest publicly known to keep a mistress is celebrating mass and arrives at the point where he is to say the words of consecration. He is *perplexus* because he is obliged to discontinue and not discontinue the mass. If he discontinues the mass, he causes a great scandal. If he continues the mass, he accepts the Eucharist unworthily and brings divine judgment upon himself.[71]

3. *The Simoniacal Priest at Mass Dilemma*
   A man is ordained a priest through simony and afterwards finds himself celebrating mass. He is *perplexus* because he is obliged to discontinue and not discontinue the mass. If he discontinues the mass, he causes a scandal. If he continues the mass, he celebrates unworthily and sins mortally.[72]

Both of these examples appear to be straightforward dilemmas of the prior-fault type discussed above. The priest who maintains a mistress (*fornicaria*) renders himself incapable of performing the sacrifice of the mass worthily, and he risks sacrilege by continuing or scandal by abandoning the mass.[73] Similarly, the priest whose past includes simony appears obliged to perform and not perform the mass. Both dilemmas have one prong that concerns scandal, that is, the leading of others into sin. The respective priests in these cases are guilty of prior wrongs that appear to preclude the fulfillment of their present obligations. The impediment to the fulfillment of present obligations is simply the result of a previous impermissible act, such as the generation of a relationship with a mistress or the purchase of

---

[71] See *Summa aurea*, 1050. Alexander uses the example prior to deploying the spiritual/corporeal distinction, as it occurs in his prefatory remarks on perplexity discussed above (*Summa Halesiana*, 392).

[72] See *Summa aurea*, 1050–1; *Summa Halesiana*, 393.

[73] Alexander does not identify this dilemma with Gregory's simoniacal priest dilemma, presumably because this dilemma pertains to the performance of a particular ecclesiastical duty rather than the possession of an ecclesiastical office as such. Alexander's does have an explicit treatment of Gregory's dilemma elsewhere, and it will be discussed shortly below.

a church office. In commenting on these examples, William introduces an important terminological qualification concerning prior-fault dilemmas, stating that a priest with a mistress is not unqualifiedly perplexed (*perplexus simpliciter*), but the priest is only perplexed as long as he persists in the intention (*propositum*) of maintaining the mistress. If the priest were to dismiss that intention, resolving to correct his life and to send the mistress away, he no longer would remain in the state of sin and could perform the sacrament without impediment.[74] William's analysis of this dilemma is followed without any significant change by Alexander. More heavily burdened than a fornicating priest, William contends, is a simoniacal priest. William particularly emphasizes the dilemmatic structure of that situation:

> It seems that he is perplexed from one side, because it is not permissible for such a one to celebrate; on the other side, if he refrains, he causes a great scandal, and thus he appears to be perplexed (*Videtur quod sit perplexus ex una parte, quia non licet tali celebrere, ex altera parte, si desistit, scandalum magnum facit, et sic videtur esse perplexus*).[75]

Such a priest appears hemmed in on both sides by the contradictories of acting or not acting. Alexander adds that the agent has committed two prior wrongs that are generating the dilemma: the first wrong was seeking ordination to the priesthood by simony, and the second was choosing to say mass upon being ordained. William and Alexander defend the same solution to this dilemma as they did in the *Fornicating Priest Dilemma*: the priest must repent of his sin of simony and then continue the mass. The justification for this solution, however, differs between the two authors. William contends that if the priest were to repent of his simoniacal act and resolve never to begin mass again absent a proper ecclesiastical dispensation, he would be free to continue the mass because the "power of the sacrament (*virtus sacramenti*)" would overcome his personal deficiencies in this case.[76]

It is not difficult to speculate that Alexander finds William's account of the situation to be wanting, for he provides much more detail in his analysis and his justification for the continuance of the mass diverges significantly from that of his predecessor. Rather than appealing to the notion of the power of a sacrament, Alexander invokes the principle of the lesser of two evils, and in doing so resurrects a line of thinking that was seen in Gratian's account of moral dilemmas. Of the choice between continuing or not continuing the mass, Alexander promotes the former, declaring that the priest "should perform the mass with sorrowful penitence, for in such

---

[74] *Summa aurea*, 1050.   [75] *Summa aurea*, 1050.   [76] *Summa aurea*, 1050.

a way he avoids the greater evil (*cum dolore poenitentiali Missam perficiat: sic enim vitat maius malum*)."[77] Alexander judges scandal to be a graver sin than sacrilege, perhaps because scandal corrupts others and sacrilege only corrupts the agent. Here Alexander disagrees with the view that the bad effects of prior-fault dilemmas can always be undone to allow for the completion of present obligations. The very appeal to the principle of choosing the lesser of two evils presupposes that all present obligations cannot be fulfilled. With his analysis here, Alexander joins Gregory and Gratian in positing a certain kind of moral dilemma, which might fittingly be called *irresolvable prior-fault dilemmas*.

While William believes that prior-fault dilemmas of the *Simoniacal Priest* variety can be resolved by repenting of the previous fault, and that such an act of repentance allows an agent to keep all moral obligations intact, Alexander takes a different route, insofar as he appeals to the principle of choosing the lesser of two evils. According to William's account, no evil is performed, while for Alexander a particular evil is performed, namely, the lesser one. This divergence will surface again in their analyses of additional dilemmas.

The Poor Parents Dilemma *and* The Hermit Dilemma

The next two of the five moral dilemmas of the spiritual perplexity variety common to both William and Alexander feature individuals who have taken religious vows, yet come to believe that they have obligations preventing them from fulfilling what they have vowed. They are:

4. *The Poor Parents Dilemma*

   A man whose parents are of little means takes a vow to leave the world and enter a monastery. After taking the vow, he is *perplexus*, because he seems obliged to fulfill the vow and not fulfill the vow. If he fulfills the vow, he leaves behind his indigent parents, thereby transgressing the Mosaic commandment that prescribes the honoring of one's parents. If he omits to fulfill his vow, he sins mortally by perjuring himself.[78]

5. *The Hermit Dilemma*

   A man fulfilling his vow to live as a hermit finds himself called back to the city by many people so that he might, by his counsel and example, persuade sinners to return to God. The hermit is *perplexus*, obliged to leave the city to save souls, and simultaneously obliged to stay away from the city to fulfill his vow.[79]

---

[77] *Summa Halesiana*, 393.   [78] See *Summa aurea*, 1051; *Summa Halesiana*, 394–5.
[79] See *Summa aurea*, 1048–9; *Summa Halesiana*, 393–4.

In the first of these two examples, an individual has vowed to enter a monastery but appears to have made no provision for the care of his parents, who are poor and unable to provide for themselves. In his depiction of this dilemma, William provides a bit more detail than Alexander, stipulating that the individual in question is "a certain just man who abides in charity (*aliquis iustus manens in caritate*)."[80] This assumption becomes key to William's analysis, because in his solution he surprisingly contests these very facts, arguing that if a just man abiding in charity were truly to make such a vow in those conditions, he would not be in doubt about how to proceed, because the anointing of the Holy Spirit would teach him in such a case. By attributing these virtues to the agent, William precludes himself from analyzing this situation as a prior-fault dilemma, as presumably the presence of the virtues of charity and justice would inoculate an agent from failing to overlook the care of parents. It takes no great imagination to infer that Alexander is unsatisfied with that account offered by William. Alexander sets forth the example but omits any reference to the agent's virtues. He argues that the man "is obliged to provide to parents concerning the good things which he has, as he is able, but he ought not to put away that vow he should satisfy (*tenetur providere parentibus de bonis quae habet, prout potest, sed non debet dimittere quin votum impleat*)."[81] Alexander notes that if there is some way the Mosaic commandment concerning one's parents and the vow can be fulfilled simultaneously, then both are to be carried out. If this is impossible, however, he simply ought to fulfill the vow. The justification for choosing to fulfill the vow over the obligation to one's parents is given as "what obliges more greatly is to be adhered to (*quod plus obligat adhaerendum est*)."[82] This principle, which appears to be a version of the principle of the lesser of two evils, suggests that the obligation to one's parents does not cease, but the failure to fulfill the vow would be a more grave wrongdoing. Alexander does not deny that there is a dilemma, nor does he treat this simply as prior-fault dilemma where a previous wrong can be undone; rather, he articulates the principle that the agent should choose to perform the act that fulfills the greater obligation. It is likely that Alexander's principle, which can be rephrased perhaps as "choose what obliges more greatly," does not differ in meaning from the principle he defended earlier in his analysis of the *Simoniacal Priest at Mass Dilemma* discussed above, namely, that of choosing the lesser of two evils. Alexander of Hales's account, therefore, in at least these two examples, seems to be close to Gratian's Gregorian view of moral dilemmas, insofar

---

[80] *Summa aurea*, 1051.   [81] *Summa Halesiana*, 394.   [82] *Summa Halesiana*, 394.

as he posits the existence of dilemmas of inescapable moral wrongdoing. To press this point further, it can be said that with the *Poor Parents Dilemma*, Alexander presents a prior-fault dilemma that does not admit of sinless or faultless resolution.

William and Alexander are in concert in their analyses of the *Hermit Dilemma*. The *prima facie* evidence identified by William and Alexander that seems to support the view that the hermit should abandon his vow and return to the city is varied, and includes the following considerations: there is no greater sacrifice than to offer God the soul of sinners; scriptural texts enjoin evangelization and apologetics; Blessed Hillary left his place to cure a matron's daughter; and finally, Augustine held that to feed the soul is greater than to feed the stomach. William and Alexander ultimately do not find this conglomeration of evidence to be convincing, however, and they both in due course contend that the hermit should remain where he is. In this way they appear to privilege the contemplative life over the active life. Their position is defended with the twofold observation that the good that the hermit may accomplish in the city is uncertain, and there would be no justification for the hermit ever to return to his vow if he left for a time, since there are always other souls that in principle could be assisted by him. The latter consideration appears to be a defense of the permissibility of the vowed life as such; the needs of others are always potentially pressing, and if such needs were always to be taken into consideration it would never be permissible for anyone to become a hermit. William and Alexander are in agreement in analyzing this case of perplexity, as they both judge that the apparent perplexity is resolvable because there exists no true obligation for the hermit to abandon his solitude for the sake of the city. In other words, there is no necessity to set the good he might accomplish in the city up against the good he will accomplish as a hermit. William and Alexander appear to resist any kind of utilitarian-style calculation where one must predict future goods to determine the best course of action. Both authors are willing to entertain arguments that assert the priority of spiritual goods over temporal goods, but here they resist comparing spiritual goods against any sort of utility standard. Rather, the integrity of the vow is considered inviolable and independent of any possible goods that might be brought about in the city.

A moral residue argument for The Hermit Dilemma?

Particularly noteworthy is an additional substantive discussion that William appends to his analysis of the *Hermit Dilemma* because it appears to anticipate a type of argument advanced by some twentieth-century defenders of moral dilemmas. Commonly called *moral residue* arguments, arguments of this type hold that the moral emotions or moral sentiments experienced by agents count as evidence for the reality of moral dilemmas. According to proponents of moral residue arguments, agents in moral dilemmas appropriately feel guilty or remorseful for choosing one course of action, and those feelings would accompany the agent had the agent chosen any other available option.[83] As one theorist summarizes, defenders of moral residue arguments simultaneously assert four points:

(1) when the agent acts, she experiences remorse or guilt;
(2) that she experiences these emotions is appropriate;
(3) had the agent acted on the other of the conflicting obligations, she would have experienced remorse or guilt; and
(4) in the latter case these emotions would have been equally appropriate.[84]

On the other hand, opponents of moral residue arguments have countered by stating that the moral emotions described as guilt or remorse can always be better characterized as other emotions that do not imply wrongdoing. For instance, simple regret has been put forward as the true emotion for such cases.[85] The strength of moral residue arguments, therefore, is contingent upon the true assessment of the particular moral sentiments or emotions of agents, as some sentiments and emotions clearly imply wrongdoing (e.g., guilt or remorse) while others do not (e.g., regret). This twentieth-century debate appears to be anticipated in an unusual supplemental discussion that William of Auxerre adds to his account of the *Hermit Dilemma*. After having completed the argumentation of the *Hermit Dilemma* described above, William surprisingly begins anew with an entirely different analysis, stating:

Let it be supposed, however, that [the hermit] is in doubt whether it is a sin to leave or not leave; if he leaves, he sins mortally, if he does not leave, similarly he sins (*Sed ponatur quod dubitat an peccatum sit exire vel non exire; si exit, peccat mortaliter; si non exit, peccat similiter*).[86]

Here the hermit believes himself to be in possession of morally compelling reasons in support of both staying and leaving. William focuses on the

---

[83] Prominent defenders of moral residue arguments include Bernard Williams, "Ethical Consistency," in *Problems of the Self: Philosophical Papers 1956–1972* (Cambridge University Press, 1973), 166–86; Ruth Barcan Marcus, "Moral Dilemmas and Consistency," *The Journal of Philosophy* 77 (1980), 121–36; and P. S. Greenspan, *Practical Guilt: Moral Dilemmas, Emotions, and Social Norms* (New York: Oxford University Press, 1995).

[84] Terrance C. McConnell, "Moral Residue and Dilemmas," in *Moral Dilemmas and Moral Theory*, ed. H. E. Mason (New York: Oxford University Press, 1996), 36–47, at 37–8.

[85] See McConnell, "Moral Residue and Dilemmas," 38.   [86] *Summa aurea*, 1049.

agent's state of mind, underscoring the doubt that the agent experiences upon considering the two incompatible options. The agent in this case would continue to be tormented over the souls that could have been saved should the vow have been preserved, and the agent would continue to be tormented about the broken vow should he have left to serve the city. With this new presentation, William envisions the two prongs of the dilemma to be equally compelling and the moral sentiments held by the hermit for each view equally appropriate.

William then augments this discussion by proposing a highly unusual analogy: the hermit's situation is comparable to a scenario where a wife seeks to have marital relations with her husband, but the husband is unclear about whether his wife is really his wife:

And similarly it is inquired concerning one who is in doubt regarding whether a woman is his, and she asks for the marital debt; either he is obliged to render or not; if he renders he sins mortally, because he doubts her to be his; if he does not render, similarly [he sins mortally] (*Et similiter queritur de illo, qui dubitat de aliqua utrum sit sua et illa petit debitum, aut tenetur reddere aut non; si reddit peccat mortaliter, quia dubitat ipsam esse suam; si non reddit, similiter*).[87]

Such a husband remains in doubt about his marital obligations, in the sense of wishing to do the correct action but is unsure about whether to act in a particular circumstance. The analogy here appears to be grounded on a parallel between the hermit's vow to remain as a hermit, and a husband's vow to remain faithful to his wife. Such a man may be in doubt about whether he should or should not have marital relations with the woman, because on the one hand, husbands are obliged to return the marital obligation to their spouses, yet on the other hand, from the husband's perspective, this petitioning woman may not be his wife.

Having introduced this analogy, William renders a new judgment about the hermit. He desists from reaffirming his previous line of reasoning that held that the hermit should privilege the vow over the needs of the people. Rather, the hermit should have recourse "to the Holy Spirit, who is the true master and will show him how he is obliged to act (*ad Spiritum Sanctum, qui est verus magister et docebit ipsum qualiter facere debeat*)."[88] This interpretation is difficult to reconcile with his earlier account, as the newer one appears to leave open the possibility that both leaving and staying are equal options. Neither option is identified as permissible; rather, this new analysis presumes that both are impermissible. William concludes his discussion of his analogy by noting that the husband should also have

[87] *Summa aurea*, 1049.   [88] *Summa aurea*, 1049.

recourse to prayer, but as long as there is doubt, he is not obliged to return the marital debt.

William's mandate that the agent turn to prayer in his supplemental account of the *Hermit Dilemma* is not a claim that the hermit needs a divine infusion of knowledge. That is, William is not positing a foolish agent of the type discussed by the glossators on Gratian's *Decretum*, who collectively had argued that all moral dilemmas are simply generated by culpable ignorance. In this analysis, praying is the invocation of a third party to assist an agent in selecting from equally impermissible options. Since the hermit's alternatives do not admit of greater or lesser gravity, a divine judgment between them is deemed necessary. This new presentation of the *Hermit Dilemma* is remarkable for its compatibility with moral residue arguments, and its contention that a divine judgment is required in cases where an agent is presented with a set of equal options is fairly distinctive. Perhaps it should be noted that Alexander does not see fit to represent this unusual analysis in his discussion.

The Latrine of the Devil Dilemma

The last dilemma of the spiritual perplexity variety common to both *summae* is notable, if simply for its vivid presentation. William and Alexander describe the following situation:

6. *The Latrine of the Devil Dilemma*
   A person reveals to a priest during confession that he persists in a state of unrepented mortal sin, and later that person petitions the priest for the Eucharist in public. Such a priest is thereby rendered *perplexus*, as he is obliged to give and not to give the Eucharist to the petitioner. If the priest refuses, he betrays the secrecy of the confession, manifesting the hidden sin of the person and causing scandal. If the priest gives the Eucharist to the unrepentant sinner, he "throws the body of Christ into the latrine of the devil (*proicit corpus Christi in latrinam diaboli*)."[89]

In this case the priest appears caught between violating the secrecy of confession by exposing a sinner and desecrating the Eucharist by throwing it into "the latrine of the devil," i.e., giving it to the unworthy and defiant sinner. The priest appears to have the simultaneous obligations of protecting the secrecy of confession and avoiding the desecration of the Eucharist. Given that the sinner seeks the Eucharist in public, it seems that the priest is unable to escape committing one of the two impermissible

---

[89] See *Summa aurea*, 1047–8; *Summa Halesiana*, 393.

actions. The details of this dilemma, as well as the analysis of it, are largely the same for William and Alexander, even though Alexander adds that the priest and the sinner are in a relation of superior and subordinate, so the priest in virtue of this relationship must therefore especially "desire the salvation of the subordinate as well as his own (*debeat diligere salutem subditi et propriam*)."[90] If such a sinner were to petition for the Eucharist in private, a refusal would be obligatory for the priest. But in this public request, William and Alexander argue, the solution is that the priest must give the Eucharist to the sinner, so that the scandal of exposing a sinner and violating the secrecy of confession is avoided. In support of their view, they note that Christ gave the Eucharist to Judas at the last supper, and Christ gave himself to the Jews at Cana while knowing they were in a state of mortal sin. In their solution, William and Alexander contend that the option of giving the Eucharist to the sinner is only apparently proscribed and can be performed without sin.

Alexander adds two more notable details in his analysis. First, he observes that if the sinner's failings were publicly known, there would be no difficulty in recommending that the priest should refuse to give the Eucharist to the sinner, as no new scandal would result. Secondly, and more significantly, Alexander observes that "nor then is it properly said that the priest gives the Eucharist, but rather the sinner is said to seize it (*nec ipse dicitur tunc proprie dare, sed alius dicitur rapere*)."[91] In other words, the state of affairs where the Eucharist is in the "latrine of the devil" is more rightly considered to be a state brought about by the sinner than by the priest, so the responsibility for any desecration of the Eucharist belongs entirely to the sinful petitioner. The situation should therefore be analyzed as an impermissible action on the part of the sinner rather than a decision to be made on the part of the priest. In sum, for William and Alexander, the *Latrine of the Devil Dilemma* is not a true case of moral perplexity, because there is a morally permissible route of action for the priest, namely to give the Eucharist to the sinner who is asking for it.

The Pretend Priest Dilemma *and* The Chanting Deacon Dilemma

In addition to the preceding five cases of spiritual perplexity common to William and Alexander, there are other examples particular to each work. Present in William's *Summa aurea* but absent from the *Summa Halesiana* are two additional cases of spiritual perplexity:

---

[90] *Summa Halesiana*, 393.   [91] *Summa Halesiana*, 393.

7. *The Pretend Priest Dilemma*

A pretend priest is celebrating mass and approaches the point of con-secration. He is *perplexus* because he is obliged to say the words of consecration and not to say the words of consecration. If he does not proceed, he causes a scandal to those present, and if he does proceed, he sins mortally by attempting to say mass.[92]

8. *The Chanting Deacon Dilemma*

A deacon clothes himself with the vestments of the diaconate to assist a particular priest at mass who is notoriously known to have a fornicatress. When the deacon arrives at the point of the mass where he is obliged to chant the gospel, he is *perplexus* between continuing and serving the sinful priest, and not continuing and scandalizing those present, including the dean and the religious chapter.[93]

William's presentation and discussion of the first of these two examples is brief. From his remarks, it appears that he envisions a situation where an individual is attempting to concelebrate with priests rather than celebrating mass alone, for his recommendation ultimately hinges on whether there are many standing with the priest or there are few. William argues that if there are few with him, he is obliged to step away and substitute someone else for the words of consecration, whereas if there are many present, he is to repent having begun but to avoid scandal he need not stop, presumably because the mass will be valid by the actions of the concelebrating priests. While he should not have begun, the avoidance of the great scandal of interrupting mass in the presence of many justifies his continuance of the mass, even though he is not the one who actually brings about the consecration at the mass. William's analysis, to be sure, is lacking, for it doesn't account for a situation where there is a single celebrant.

For the *Chanting Deacon Dilemma*, William contends that if the deacon knows about the priest's fornicatress prior to vesting for the chanting of the gospel and he vests anyway, the deacon at that time sins mortally. Nevertheless, when he arrives at the gospel he should chant, because it is not fitting for the deacon to correct the priest at that point. Those present in the church already likely know of the priest's fornicatress, as the relationship with her is notorious. At issue is the timing of fraternal correction; members of a community have an obligation to admonish those who persist in sin. The deacon has sinned by delaying fraternal correction

---

[92] See *Summa aurea*, 1050–1. For a text variant, see Guillermus Altissiodorensis, *Summa aurea in quattuor libros Sententiarum* (Paris: Philippus Pigouchet, 1500 [repr. Frankfurt/Main: Minerva, 1964]), fol. CCXLI, *verso*.

[93] See *Summa aurea*, 1051.

to a point where it is not fitting to do it, so he must chant to avoid a second sin, namely, that of producing scandal. On this account, William locates the moral failure to occur at the moment that the deacon is vesting, and there is no additional failure when the deacon fulfills his obligation to chant. This example differs from the standard prior-fault dilemmas such as the *Fornicating Priest Dilemma* and the *Simoniacal Priest at Mass Dilemma* discussed above, where the prior sin seemingly makes a present obligation unfulfillable. Rather, the issue here is the omission of fraternal correction. The deacon only mistakenly believes that continuing to chant is impermissible. William, therefore, does not ultimately consider the *Pretend Priest Dilemma* or the *Chanting Deacon Dilemma* to be actual dilemmas, but rather instances where each agent commits a single moral failure that does not necessitate a second one.

The Simoniacal Office Dilemma *and* The Worldly Superior Dilemma

Alexander includes examples of spiritual perplexity that are not present in William's *Summa aurea*. Two are borrowed from Gregory the Great's *Moralia*:

9. *The Simoniacal Office Dilemma*
   A man is promoted to an ecclesiastical office by means of simony. He is *perplexus* because he is obliged to maintain the position and abandon it. If he maintains it, he does so illicitly, and if he abandons it, he scandalizes the faithful.[94]

10. *The Worldly Superior Dilemma*
    A man renounces the world and vows to be obedient to a superior in all things that are not against the law of God. The superior, however, then commands him to act with those who are of the world. The man is *perplexus*, obliged to follow his superior and obliged to avoid the contagion of the secular life.[95]

These two examples from Gregory were also included by Gratian in distinction 13 of the *Decretum* and analyzed in some detail by the glossators of the *Glossa ordinaria*. While Alexander's analysis does not stray far from the lines of argument given by the glossators, he does not explicitly indicate any indebtedness to the canon law tradition. Regarding the first

---

[94] See *Summa Halesiana*, 393. See Gregory the Great, *Moralia in Iob*, III: 1656–8; *Morals on the Book of Job*, III.2: 538–40.
[95] See *Summa Halesiana*, 394.

example, Alexander decisively states that such a man must desert the office immediately, as this course is mandated by certain church documents. This dilemma presumably differs from the *Simoniacal Priest at Mass Dilemma* in that it concerns a particular ecclesiastical office rather than the status of priest as such; the agent in this case could likely abandon the ecclesiastical office and continue to serve as a priest. In his account, Alexander does not view it to be a true moral dilemma, since the concern for avoiding scandal among the faithful does not compete with the unquestionable impermissibility of maintaining a church office illicitly. As for the *Worldly Superior Dilemma*, perhaps it is fair to say that Alexander's version is more inspired by Gregory than borrowed from him. Gregory had envisioned that the superior was commanding the inferior to avoid the things of God, but here Alexander simply depicts the superior as commanding greater interaction with those who are worldly. As Alexander's version of the dilemma is more moderate than Gregory's, so too is his recommendation. In short, the inferior should obey the commands of the superior as long as they do not mandate doing what is against God or what is against the rule of the inferior's religious profession. Again, the perplexity here is only apparent.

2.4 MORAL DILEMMAS OF THE CORPOREAL PERPLEXITY VARIETY

The remaining moral dilemmas of the *Summa aurea* and the *Summa Halesiana* are presented as cases of corporeal perplexity. They often concern the use of temporal goods such as food or money. In all, William and Alexander jointly set forth and analyze ten situations of corporeal perplexity. Three are discussed in common, three are found only in the *Summa aurea*, and the remaining four occur only in the *Summa Halesiana*.

The Madman's Sword Dilemma

The first case treated by both thinkers is arguably the most famous and most ancient example of a moral dilemma from the western philosophical tradition, as a variant occurs in the first book of Plato's *Republic*.[96] This celebrated case gathered the attention of many medieval thinkers, but often it was broached to illustrate certain features of the virtues, rather than moral dilemmas as such.[97] William and Alexander present the dilemma as follows:

---

[96] Plato, *Republic* I, 331e–332a. See also Xenophon, *Memorabilia* 4.2, and Cicero, *De officiis* 3.25.

[97] See, for example, Ana Marta González, "*Depositum gladius non debet restitui furioso*: Precepts, *Synderesis*, and Virtues in Saint Thomas Aquinas," *The Thomist* 63 (1999), 217–40.

II. *The Madman's Sword Dilemma*

A man deposits his sword with another, and the receiver swears to return the sword whenever the owner requests it. Afterward, the owner of the sword becomes insane and asks for its return. The one who received the sword is *perplexus*, obliged to return and not return the sword. If he does not return the sword, he becomes a perjurer by violating his oath. If he returns the sword, he becomes an accomplice to homicide should the insane person use the sword for murder.[98]

William attributes this case to Augustine, who had described such a situation in a discussion of lying and truth-telling in his exposition of the fifth Psalm.[99] In concert with Augustine, William and Alexander argue that the sword is not to be returned to its owner as long as the condition of madness endures. William postulates that "in every oath a righteous condition is understood (*in omni enim iuramento intelligenda est pia conditio*)."[100] Alexander also makes reference to righteousness (*pietas*) as a condition for all oaths, and such a view appears consonant with present-day theorists who contend that implicit in every promise is an understanding that some future condition may make the fulfillment of the promise impermissible.[101] In the presentation by Alexander, however, the absence of a condition of righteousness does not wholly insulate the possessor of the sword from some degree of wrongdoing. In his analysis, Alexander again appeals to Gregory the Great, and the greater part of his answer is simply a quotation from Gregory that was previously put to use by Gratian in the *Decretum*:

When the mind is bound between greater and lesser evils, if there is not a way without evading sin, the lesser evils are to be chosen, because one who on all sides is encircled with walls, is blocked off, and cannot flee, there he casts himself in flight where the wall is found to be lower (*cum mens inter maiora et minora constringitur, si non sit sine peccato evadendi aditus, minora eligantur, quia qui murorum undique ambitu, ne fugiat, clauditur, ibi se in fugam praecipitat, ubi brevior murus invenitur*).[102]

The appeal to the Gregorian principle that there are situations where one is bound between evils and that the lesser is to be chosen exhibits that Alexander believes in some moral dilemmas. According to Alexander, the agent possessing the sword is unable to avoid some degree of wrongdoing,

---

[98] See *Summa aurea*, 1052–3; *Summa Halesiana*, 395.

[99] Augustine, *Enarrationes in Psalmos*, 5.2.　　[100] *Summa aurea*, 1052.

[101] See Alan Donagan, "Consistency in Rationalist Moral Systems," *The Journal of Philosophy* 81 (1984), 291–309, at 302–5.

[102] *Summa Halesiana*, 395; Gregory the Great, *Moralia in Iob*, III: 1658; *Morals on the Book of Job*, III.2: 540.

and at best can avoid committing a greater sin by preferring a lesser one. The defense of inescapable moral wrongdoing that began with Gregory and was continued by Gratian finds another exponent in the thirteenth century with Alexander. While William (together with Augustine, and arguably with Plato as well) contends that the one who keeps the sword from the madman commits no evil, Alexander marks out a very different position, even though they all agree that the sword is not to be returned as long as the owner is afflicted by madness.

The Usurer's Money Dilemma

The next case of corporeal perplexity common to William and Alexander possesses a structural similarity to the preceding dilemma, but some significant factual differences generate surprisingly subtle analyses. Instead of featuring the owner of a sword who suffers from madness, this example exhibits an owner of money who practices the vice of usury. William's promotion of this example is noteworthy because of his role in formulating the scholastic opposition to usury. He was largely responsible for framing the scholastic view that usury is intrinsically evil and contrary to the natural law, an outlook continued by Alexander and others.[103] The facts of this dilemma are:

12. *The Usurer's Money Dilemma*

    A usurer deposits money with another, and the receiver swears to return the money when the usurer requests it. When later the usurer requests his money, the receiver is *perplexus*, obliged to return it and not return it. If the receiver returns it, he sins more grievously than one who returns a sword to a mad person, since to allow someone to suffer spiritual death is more grave than to allow someone to suffer bodily death. If he does not return the money, he violates his oath and impermissibly handles what is not his.[104]

    In this scenario, the argument defending the prong of the dilemma that holds the money is not to be returned to the usurer is an *a fortiori* argument: since the goods that are likely to bring about bodily death (e.g., a sword) are not be returned, then more strongly are the goods that bring about spiritual death likewise not to be returned. As usury is considered a grave sin, the return of the usurer's money would allow the usurer to sin gravely

---

[103] John T. Noonan, Jr., *The Scholastic Analysis of Usury* (Cambridge, MA: Harvard University Press, 1957), 42–5.
[104] See *Summa aurea*, 1052–3; *Summa Halesiana*, 395.

and thus suffer a spiritual death. The other prong of the dilemma that argues for return of the money is, of course, grounded on the presumed obligatory nature of oaths, as the receiver of the money had promised to return it upon being asked. Surprisingly, in analyzing this dilemma both William and Alexander deny the analogy between it and the *Madman's Sword Dilemma*, and they contend that the money should be returned to the usurer. The key element of the disanalogy is that the usurer is in possession of his mental faculties, whereas the madman, by definition, is not. William notes that "we do not know whether that usurer has the will of devoting that money for usury (*nescimus enim si ille usurarius voluntatem habeat dandi pecuniam illam ad usuram*)."[105] To this point Alexander adds that since the usurer is in the possession of his mind (*mens*), one must presume that the Lord could bring the usurer to use the money well, so the agent need not assume that the money will be used usuriously. Neither William nor Alexander suggests that this dilemma should be conceived as a prior-fault dilemma, as they do not consider that the agent in this case erred in the initial act of receiving money from the usurer. Perhaps they assume the example could be reformulated easily so that the lender becomes a usurer only after the money has been deposited.

While it seems that for William the justification for returning the usurer's money is simply the obligatory character of the vow along with the possibility that the usurer might not use the money for usury, it becomes clear in his account that he still considers the return of the money to involve some level of wrongdoing. William argues that the agent must seek to minimize his wrongdoing, contending that the return of the money is less sinful than not returning it. The background for this analysis seems largely inspired by Gregory the Great, for in his solution William offers the following key principle or rule (*regula*):

The rule is: whenever someone appears perplexed between two vices, always the less difficult is to be done, or that which obliges more greatly (*Regula est: quandocumque aliquis videtur perplexus inter duo vicia, semper minus difficile faciendum est, vel illud quod magis obligat*).[106]

Here for the first time in his account of moral perplexity, William endorses a variation of the principle of the lesser evil. Alexander had made such

---

[105] *Summa aurea*, 1053.

[106] *Summa aurea*, 1052. Another manuscript tradition provides a modified version of this principle: "the general rule is to be applied: whenever such cases arise, that which is less dangerous is to be chosen (*generalis regula est adhibenda: quincunquae emergunt isti casus eligendum est illud quod minus periculosus est*)." See Guillermus Altissiodorensis, *Summa aurea in quattuor libros Sententiarum*, fol. CCXLI, *recto*.

a commitment to that principle in his analysis of the *Simoniacal Priest*, the *Poor Parents*, and the *Madman's Sword* dilemmas, as was seen above. By appealing to this principle that enjoins the selection of what is less difficult or what obliges more greatly among vicious options, William concedes that both options do oblige, and they do not cease to oblige, but a choice must be made between them on the basis of degrees of obligation. The agent cannot escape some wrongdoing and should avoid performing a greater wrong than necessary. William's analysis of the *Usurer's Money Dilemma* appears at odds with his denial of unqualified perplexity at the beginning of his discussion of perplexity, where he contended that *perplexitas* is nothing (*nichil*) and exists only qualifiedly (*secundum quid*).

The Usurer's Wife Dilemma

The theme of usury is continued in the last example of a case of corporeal perplexity common to both the *Summa aurea* and the *Summa Halesiana*. This time the focus is on one whose livelihood is involuntarily sustained by its practice. William and Alexander give the facts of the dilemma as:

13. *The Usurer's Wife Dilemma*

    The wife of a usurer possesses nothing other than what her husband obtains through usury. She is *perplexus*, obliged to abandon her husband and not abandon her husband. If she abandons him, she violates her vow to him. If she stays, she participates in usury insofar as she takes her sustenance from it.[107]

In his discussion of this dilemma, William is quick to assert that this example also falls under the *regula* noted above, for he states that "according to the previously stated rule that which obliges more greatly is to be done (*Secundum regulam predictam faciendum est quod magis obligat*)."[108] By invoking this principle again, William commits himself to the view that at times an agent cannot altogether escape moral wrongdoing, and the best such an agent can do is to minimize it. William and Alexander are largely in agreement in their analyses of the situation, arguing that the woman is not justified in abandoning her husband completely, as spouses are obliged to provide the marital right to each other. The wife of the usurer can seek a kind of separation from her usurious husband that would still allow for a minimized fulfillment of the vowed marital obligation. William specifies that the wife should give up cohabitation as long as the husband persists in usury, but she cannot go away completely. Alexander notes that

---

[107] See *Summa aurea*, 1053–4; *Summa Halesiana*, 395.   [108] *Summa aurea*, 1054.

she can send him from her bed for a time. William and Alexander both contend, however, that the wife is obliged to seek her sustenance elsewhere, such as from parents or strangers, even if she is reduced to begging. They underscore that because the moral failures of the usurious husband do not rise to the gravity of fornication, the marital vow is still binding, so complete abandonment of the marriage is unjustified. Nevertheless, the usury of the husband is a form of "spiritual fornication (*fornicatio spiritualis*)," and for this reason a temporary separation from living in the same house or sharing a bed is justified.[109] Unlike William, Alexander does not appeal to any version of choosing the lesser of two evils in his analysis of the *Usurer's Wife Dilemma*, and thereby he never suggests that the wife in this case is truly perplexed. On the other hand, William's appeal to the *regula* suggests that the wife is committing some wrongdoing in minimizing contact with her husband, but at least in doing so she does not commit the greater wrongdoing of obtaining her sustenance usuriously.

The Heretic's Money Dilemma

Having examined cases of spiritual perplexity common to the *Summa aurea* and the *Summa Halesiana*, it is fitting to consider those unique to each work. William introduces three further cases not discussed by Alexander, and the first is:

14. *The Heretic's Money Dilemma*
    A man deposits money with another, and the receiver swears to return it whenever the owner requests it. Afterwards, the depositor becomes a manifest heretic and intends to use the money for the subversion of the church. The receiver of the money is *perplexus*, obliged to return and not return the money. If he returns the money, he allows the heretic to kill himself and many others spiritually. If he does not return the money, he becomes robber or a thief, and sins mortally.[110]

This example obviously possesses structural similarities with the *Madman's Sword Dilemma* and the *Usurer's Money Dilemma*. The moral or mental condition of the owners in all these dilemmas causes the respective possessors of the sword and the money to question the permissibility of returning the items to their owners. In this example, the owner becomes a heretic, and William ultimately judges that the money is not to be returned to the owner as long as he persists in heresy. There are other permissible options available to the possessor of the heretic's money, such as giving the

---

[109] *Summa aurea*, 1053–4; *Summa Halesiana*, 395.   [110] See *Summa aurea*, 1052–3.

money to the heretic's heirs (provided that they endure in the faith), or disposing of the money as the church may direct, or retaining the money until the heretic returns to the faith. William argues that the unwilling possessor of the heretic's money does not possess the *ratio* or essence of a thief or robber, largely because there are permissible ways of disposing of the money rather than keeping it. It does not seem that William regards this situation as a true instance of inescapable moral wrongdoing. He does not invoke the principle of choosing the lesser of two evils, but instead outlines permissible courses of action available to the possessor of the heretic's money. This case is merely a purported moral dilemma that upon examination turns out to be only an apparent one.

The Monastery Dilemma *and* The Food Dilemma

The last two cases of corporeal perplexity particular to the *Summa aurea* both involve monks, but they are not spiritual cases insofar as they concern the use of temporal goods:

15. *The Monastery Dilemma*

    A monk knows that everything in his monastery comes from usury. He is *perplexus*, obliged to eat and not eat at the monastery. If he eats, he benefits from usury. If he does not eat, he acts against the precept of the abbot and scandalizes his brother monks, thereby sinning mortally.[111]

16. *The Food Dilemma*

    A monk is commanded by his abbot to carry some food to the monastery, and along the way he meets a certain person placed in extreme necessity. The monk is *perplexus*, because he is obliged to give and not to give the food to such a person. If he gives the food away, he violates the precept of the abbot. If he ignores the person in extreme necessity and takes the food to the monastery, he acts against the divine precept that commands the feeding of the hungry.[112]

The first of these cases, the *Monastery Dilemma*, bears some similarity with the *Usurer's Wife Dilemma*, as both of the agents in these dilemmas find their basic needs being fulfilled through the sin of usury. The usurer's wife and the monk are each bound by a vow to a particular way of life, and the issue of their respective dilemmas concerns their acceptance of the necessities of life that have been obtained illicitly. William quickly resolves the monastery dilemma by contending that the monk should simply leave his cloister and join himself to another community. There does not appear

---

[111] See *Summa aurea*, 1053–4.   [112] See *Summa aurea*, 1053–4.

to be a true dilemma here, as the monk can fulfill his vow to live as a monk if he simply attaches himself to a different monastery, after finding one that is not dependent upon usury. The precept of the abbot who commands the eating of the usuriously acquired food is not binding as it is said to transgress a divine precept.

The second dilemma here, the *Food Dilemma*, also features a monk and food, but in this case the monk is perplexed between continuing to fulfill the command of an abbot to carry food to the monastery and giving the food to a person who is *in extrema necessitate*. The context of this example is the juridical principle of extreme necessity, which developed in twelfth-century canon law and was examined by many theorists in the thirteenth and fourteenth centuries. The principle held that an individual in a dire situation could lawfully make use of what was normally considered the private property of others.[113] William's analysis of this second dilemma, and his proposed resolution to it, are quite unusual. He does not appeal to the notion that the abbot's command to the monk carries an implied exception regarding those who are in need, nor does he appeal to the view that the monk should assume that the abbot would qualify his command were he to know about the chance encounter with the person in extreme necessity. William judges that the person in extreme hunger should ultimately be in possession of the food and consume it, but he argues that the food can be transferred to the hungry person without having the monk violate his obligation to carry the food. In short, William contends that the transfer of the food must happen primarily as the act of the hungry person rather than as an act of the monk. William explains that it is possible for the hungry person to *take* the food, if he wishes. In this case, it is properly said of the monk that he does not *give* the food, but rather that he *abandons* it. On this account, the act of the transfer of the food belongs more properly to the hungry person than the monk, and thus the monk is held not to have violated his obligation of obedience to the abbot's command. This style of arguing, where the situation is re-analyzed with the identification of a new primary agent, was seen above with Alexander's discussion of the *Latrine of the Devil Dilemma*, where a sinner is said to *seize* the Eucharist rather than the priest *give* it. William's account here is unsatisfying, for it does not seem plausible that a monk who abandons food to have it seized by another has fulfilled the command of the abbot to take the

---

[113] On the development of this principle from Gratian through the later medieval period, see Virpi Mäkinen, "Rights and Duties in Late Scholastic Discussion on Extreme Necessity," in *Transformations in Medieval and Early-Modern Rights Discourse*, ed. Virpi Mäkinen and Petter Korkman (Dordrecht: Springer, 2006), 37–62.

food to the monastery. Perhaps William himself realizes the weakness of this account, for he qualifies his analysis by then suggesting a situation where the hungry person is in such a state that he cannot seize the food without some help from the monk. Should the monk extend the food to him in this case? William argues in the affirmative, and in this case the act of transferring the food seems to belong to the monk insofar as he extends it to the hungry person. William then re-analyzes the situation, arguing that the monk is obliged to extend the food to him, because "for in extreme necessity all things are in common (*in extrema enim necessitate omnia sunt communia*)."[114] With the introduction of this biblical and monastic principle, William seems to forgo the earlier account that held the monk should abandon the food to allow it to be seized by the hungry person. William again may not be satisfied with this newer account, for he appends to his discussion an entirely different justification, noting simply that both the precept of the Lord to feed the hungry and the natural law absolve (*absolvit*) the monk from the precept of the abbot. In sum, then, for a variety of reasons, each arguably possessing varying degrees of plausibility, William contends that the monk is not irresolvably perplexed, as he can dispatch his obligation to the hungry person without sinfully acting against the precept of the abbot.

The Homicidal Adulterer Dilemma, The Hiding Fugitive Dilemma, *and* The Eater's Dilemma

In the *Summa Halesiana*, there are four remaining dilemmas set forth by Alexander that are not derived from the discussions of *perplexitas* in William's *Summa aurea*. The first three are familiar and are found in earlier thinkers:

17. *The Homicidal Adulterer Dilemma*
    A man swears an oath to another that he will protect secrets in silence, and afterwards the one to whom he swore discloses adultery and plans the homicide of the spouse of the adulteress. The man is *perplexus*, obliged to keep silent and not keep silent. If he keeps silent, he is an accomplice to adultery and a participant in homicide, and if he does not keep silent he breaks his oath and is guilty of perjury.[115]

18. *The Hiding Fugitive Dilemma*
    A man is being pursued by a killer and is hiding in another's house. The pursuer asks the house owner, who knows the whereabouts of the hiding man, whether the man is in the house. The owner is *perplexus*,

---

[114] *Summa aurea*, 1054. Cf. Acts 4:32.   [115] See *Summa Halesiana*, 396.

obliged to lie about the whereabouts of the man and not lie. If the owner lies, he sins mortally; and if he does not lie, he betrays the man either by silence or by saying where he is.[116]

19. *The Eater's Dilemma*

A man promises to eat more than is fitting, and is thereby *perplexus* between two venial sins. He is obliged to eat more than is fitting and not eat more than is fitting. If he eats more than is fitting, he sins venially. If he does not, he also sins venially by going against his word.[117]

Alexander notes that the first dilemma is taken from Gregory the Great. The second and third were offered by the glossators on Gratian's *Decretum*, but Alexander gives no explicit reference to the canon law tradition. Alexander's treatment of all three is consonant with the analyses of the glossators. Alexander argues that the agent of the *Homicidal Adulterer Dilemma* can keep the vow to the murderously intentioned adulterer by pursuing fraternal correction, or warning the husband without revealing anyone's name, or telling a priest in a general way about the danger to the husband so that the priest might safeguard him. On these lines, Alexander maintains, the vow is not violated and the agent both protects the husband and avoids becoming an accomplice to any crimes. The main difference between Alexander's analysis and that of the glossators is that the glossators considered the possibility that such a vow may not be binding, but Alexander does not broach this possibility. As a resolution to the *Hiding Fugitive Dilemma*, Alexander follows the Augustinian line of thinking (also defended by the glossators) that claims that there is no dilemma between lying and betraying a fugitive, as the agent can simply be silent without sinning or proclaim to the murderous pursuer an unwillingness to reveal the whereabouts of the fugitive. There is no real perplexity here, as one of the prongs of the dilemma is only apparently proscribed. Finally, Alexander's resolution to the *Eater's Dilemma* is brief: one who has made such an indiscreet promise should do penance rather than attempt to eat more than one is able. It appears that Alexander considers the original promise itself to be the moral failure, and there is no additional moral failure when the individual does not proceed to eat.

The Venial Sin Dilemma

The last moral dilemma presented by Alexander of Hales in his *Summa aurea* is discussed only briefly, and his analysis of it concludes his account of moral perplexity:

---

[116] See *Summa Halesiana*, 396.   [117] See *Summa Halesiana*, 396.

20. *The Venial Sin Dilemma*

A man is *perplexus* about whether to commit a venial sin that will prevent another person from committing a mortal sin.[118]

In this case, an individual seems caught between the obligations of personally avoiding a minor sin and impeding another person from committing a major sin. Alexander is quite hesitant in his analysis, citing authorities who have argued in various ways, and ultimately concedes the minimal claim that there can be some pressure (*tentio*) to commit a minor sin to protect another from mortal sin. In his account there, however, he does not consider this case to be a true moral dilemma. The background for this discussion is likely distinction 14 of Gratian's *Decretum*. There, Gratian (followed by the glossators of the *Glossa ordinaria*) contended that there is no obligation to commit minor crimes for the sake of preventing others from committing greater ones. The glossators asserted that the use of the principle of the lesser evil "is not true (*non est verum*)" when used to justify sinning – however minor – in these situations.[119]

2.5 APPEALS TO THE LESSER EVIL PRINCIPLE

Having mined the discussions on perplexity from the *Summa aurea* and the *Summa Halesiana* to find twenty distinct moral dilemmas, we are now in a position to draw some general conclusions about the respective positions of William of Auxerre and Alexander of Hales on the question of whether there is inescapable moral wrongdoing. To begin, it should be stated that most of the examples of spiritual and corporeal perplexity were judged by them, either individually or jointly, to be only apparent moral dilemmas. Upon analysis they often revealed a permissible course of action that allowed each agent in such instances to act without committing a moral wrong. The thirteen cases judged in both works to be only apparent moral dilemmas were: *The Hermit Dilemma, The Latrine of the Devil Dilemma, The Pretend Priest at Mass Dilemma, The Chanting Deacon Dilemma, The Simonia-cal Office Dilemma, The Worldly Superior Dilemma, The Heretic's Money Dilemma, The Monastery Dilemma, The Food Dilemma, The Homicidal Adulterer Dilemma, The Hiding Fugitive Dilemma, The Eater's Dilemma,* and *The Venial Sin Dilemma.* These dilemmas account for the greater part

---

[118] See *Summa Halesiana*, 396.

[119] *Glossa ordinaria*, XIIII, c; *Decretum Gratiani emendatum et notationibus illustratum una cum glossis* (Rome: 1582), 67; Gratian, *The Treatise on Laws (Decretum DD. 1–20) with the Ordinary Gloss*, trans. Augustine Thompson, OP and James Gordley (Washington, DC: The Catholic University of America Press, 1993), 52.

of those examined in the two *summae*. In each of these thirteen cases, the agents only erroneously judged that both prongs of the dilemma were impermissible.

More significant, of course, are those cases that William and Alexander considered – either individually or jointly – to be resolvable prior-fault moral dilemmas. These were genuine moral conflicts where sin is capable of being evaded by some further action on the part of an agent. Such dilemmas had as a condition that there be some previous impermissible act that generated the moral dilemma. These cases are resolvable insofar as the constraining after-effects of the initial wrongdoing were able to be defused by a further act by the agent. The *Killers of Christ Dilemma* and the *Fornicating Priest Dilemma* were of this variety; those agents whose consciences dictated they should kill Christ remained unable to avoid further wrongdoing as long as they did not reform their culpably malformed consciences, much like the fornicating priest would sin at mass unless he repented immediately of his mistress. To those resolvable prior-fault dilemmas should be added William's account of the *Simoniacal Priest at Mass Dilemma*, as he advised repentance as a solution that would allow the priest to avoid a further wrongdoing. In all these situations, the moral law is not laying impossibilities upon unsuspecting and innocent agents, but rather prior misdeeds make the performance of present obligations impossible until the after-effects of the prior misdeeds are somehow removed. William and Alexander outlined simple routes for each agent in these cases to fulfill their present obligations: by repentance the after-effects of the prior sins that impede the performance of present obligations are removed. There is no necessity of sinning, since the newly reformed agents can thereby blamelessly dispatch all obligations.

The designation of certain cases as either apparent dilemmas or resolvable prior-fault dilemmas is easily reconcilable with the categorical statements about perplexity that William and Alexander set forth at the beginning of their respective treatments of moral dilemmas. In no uncertain terms they initially promoted the view that agents never experience an *inevitabilitas peccandi* or inevitability of sinning. William had said that "no one is unqualifiedly perplexed (*nullus est perplexus simpliciter*),"[120] and "perplexity is nothing, for it exists only in a qualified way (*perplexitas nichil est, est enim secundum quid*)."[121] Similarly, Alexander prefaced his presentation of cases of moral dilemmas with the statement that "there is no perplexity (*non est perplexitas*)."[122] If one were to use these categorical denials as the

---

[120] *Summa aurea*, 1045.   [121] *Summa aurea*, 1046.   [122] *Summa Halesiana*, 392.

basis to draw judgments about the respective ethical views of William and
Alexander, one would likely conclude that both thinkers deny that agents
are ever unable to avoid moral wrongdoing.[123] Admittedly, most of the
cases of moral dilemmas examined in the *Summa aurea* and the *Summa
Halesiana* are consistent with this prescription. Nevertheless, these categorical statements must be judged in light of the analyses of the remaining few
cases of moral dilemmas set forth by William and Alexander. Their subsequent analyses qualify, to a significant degree, the force of the categorical
statements that began both discussions, as each thinker increasingly allows
for the possibility of inescapable moral wrongdoing. This evolution occurs
slowly and incrementally, so it is worth summarizing how the development
takes place.

In analyzing the *Usurer's Money Dilemma* and the *Usurer's Wife Dilemma*,
William was the first to invoke a version of the maxim of choosing the
lesser of two evils. He contended in his exposition that what "obliges more
greatly is to be done (*faciendum est quod magis obligat*)."[124] With an appeal
to this principle, William concedes that in each case the two prongs of
the dilemma do oblige, but a difference in degree attends each prong,
and this difference justifies the selection of one over the other. By choosing
the prong that obliges more, one avoids the greater evil and only commits
the lesser evil. Since one is choosing a lesser evil, one has not escaped
moral wrongdoing. On the basis of his endorsement of the principle of the
lesser of two evils, it must be concluded that William endorses situations
of inescapable moral wrongdoing. As he never judges the agents in these
cases to have been guilty of a prior misdeed, it must be further concluded
that William allows the possibility that innocent agents find themselves in
such situations. In other words, since William does not present the *Usurer's
Money Dilemma* and the *Usurer's Wife Dilemma* as prior-fault dilemmas,
one is left to assume that neither the agent who receives the usurer's money
nor the woman who marries the usurer have committed culpable misdeeds
that generate the conflicts. The receiver of the usurer's money and the wife
of the usurer are innocent agents who are unable to avoid committing some
wrong, albeit a lesser wrong. William's analysis of these two dilemmas calls
into question the categorical rejection of unqualified perplexity that began
his account.

Similarly, Alexander invoked the principle of the lesser of two evils in
his account of three dilemmas: the *Simoniacal Priest at Mass Dilemma*,

---

[123] See Schenk, "*Perplexus supposito quodam*," 68–79.

[124] *Summa aurea*, 1054. See also *Summa aurea*, 1052: "always the less difficult is to be done, or that
which obliges more greatly (*semper minus difficile faciendum est, vel illud quod magis obligat*)."

the *Poor Parents Dilemma*, and the *Madman's Sword Dilemma*. It will be recalled that in analyzing these dilemmas Alexander postulated that "what obliges more greatly is to be adhered to (*quod plus obligat adhaerendum est*),"[125] and he used Gregory's principle that "When the mind is bound between greater and lesser evils, if there is not a way without evading sin, the lesser evils are to be chosen (*cum mens inter maiora et minora constringitur, si non sit sine peccato evadendi aditus, minora eligantur*)."[126] His adherence to the view that the agents in these cases should select the course of action that constitutes the lesser evil commits Alexander to the view that the agents in these cases do perform some evil, and cannot escape doing it, even though they can avoid greater evils. It is notable that of these three dilemmas, the *Simoniacal Priest Dilemma* appears to be a prior-fault dilemma but not a resolvable one. The agent in this case has committed a prior fault but the after-effects cannot be undone simply by repenting of the prior misdeed, as was the case with the *Fornicating Priest Dilemma*. So, it must be concluded that Alexander grants the existence of *irresolvable prior-fault dilemmas*. Alexander does not present the *Poor Parents Dilemma* and the *Madman's Sword Dilemma* as any kind of prior-fault dilemma, as the agents in these cases are depicted as both innocent and unable to fulfill their obligations.

Despite clear endorsements of the principle of the lesser evil in both *Summae*, neither work gives much specification regarding the kind of sin that is committed when the lesser evil is selected. That is, neither work offers the claim that an agent in a moral dilemma only sins venially by selecting the lesser evil. Presumably the lesser sin can attain the level of a serious or mortal sin in moral dilemmas consisting entirely of two quite grave options. In any event, neither work contends that the necessity to commit the lesser sin in a dilemma detracts from the seriousness of the sin committed.

2.6 FOUR TYPES OF MORAL DILEMMA

In sum, it can be concluded that William of Auxerre and the authors of the *Summa Halesiana* collectively defend four classes of moral dilemma. There are:

---

[125] *Summa Halesiana*, 394.
[126] *Summa Halesiana*, 395; Gregory the Great, *Moralia in Iob*, III: 1658; *Morals on the Book of Job*, III.2: 540.

(1) merely apparent moral dilemmas;
(2) resolvable prior-fault moral dilemmas;
(3) irresolvable prior-fault moral dilemmas; and
(4) innocent agent moral dilemmas.

The majority of the twenty cases from the *Summa aurea* and the *Summa Halesiana* fall under class no. 1, and they are not true moral dilemmas since the agents are not truly bound to perform wrongdoing. In such cases, there exist morally permissible alternatives that the agents simply overlook. Several cases are given by both works for class no. 2. In such cases, agents are able to remove the after-effects of a prior wrong to fulfill a present obligation, and such mitigation often involves repentance. The *Summa Halesiana* provides us with one representative case from class no. 3, and both works provide cases falling under class no. 4. Class no. 3 consists of those dilemmas for which the after-effects of a prior misdeed cannot be defused, so present obligations cannot be fulfilled. Both works advise agents to appeal to the principle of choosing the lesser evil for cases of classes no. 3 and no. 4, so that the wrongdoing of agents in those cases might be minimized to the greatest extent possible, but some degree of wrongdoing still is unavoidable. Even though there are early statements in both *summae* that deny inescapable moral wrongdoing, the arguments drift from these early categorical denials as the respective treatments progress. Despite early attempts to minimize the force of Gregory the Great's account of moral perplexity (such as William's contention that Gregory is speaking only hypothetically), it appears that both William and the authors of the *Summa Halesiana* are significantly indebted to Gregory and adopt his approach when dealing with cases of irresolvable prior-fault dilemmas and innocent agent dilemmas. Both works never quite free themselves from the position first articulated by Gregory the Great and later promoted by Gratian.

CHAPTER 3

Raymond Lull and moral ensnarement in the Vita coaetanea

At the venerable age of seventy-five, the long-bearded philosopher Raymond Lull (*c.* 1232–1316) boarded a ship from his home in Majorca and sailed across the Mediterranean Sea to the North African Saracen city of Bougie. Upon disembarking, Lull immediately went to the main square of the city and began shouting wildly in Arabic. The *Vita coaetanea* records his words as, "The Christian religion is true and holy and acceptable to God; the Saracen religion, however, is false and full of error, and this I am prepared to prove." The spectacle of a blaspheming foreigner drew the attention of the town's senior religious leader, who gave orders that Lull be brought before him. Shortly thereafter Lull subjected him to an exotic disquisition that employed various subtle Neoplatonic metaphysical distinctions. Baffled by this display, the religious leader ordered Lull's immediate imprisonment. The angry assembled crowd then seized Lull, beat the old man with fists and sticks, forcefully dragged him by his beard, and then locked him away in the sewer pit of a thieves' jail "where for some time he led a painful existence." After an incarceration for a year and a half, Lull was expelled from the city and placed on a ship for Genoa, but when it was ten miles offshore from the port of Pisa a violent storm arose and capsized it. While tossing him about, the storm managed to remove the greater part of Lull's clothing, but he was able to reach the shore in a small rowboat, mostly naked, but alive.[1]

---

[1] *Vita coaetanea*, §§36–8. The Latin text of Lull's *Vita coaetanea* (or, as it is sometimes called, the *Vita Beati Raymundi Lulli*) cited below is taken from the critical edition in *Opera Latina*, vol. VIII, ed. Hermogenes Harada, OFM, *Corpus Christianorum continuatio mediaevalis*, vol. XXXIV (Turnhout: Brepols, 1980), 272–309. The English translation is from Anthony Bonner, *Doctor Illuminatus: A Ramon Llull Reader* (Princeton University Press, 1993), 11–40, originally published in *Selected Works of Ramon Llull (1232–1316)*, ed. and trans. Anthony Bonner, 2 vols. (Princeton University Press, 1985), I: 13–48. The recent inclusion of Bonner's translation of the *Vita* as an appendix to Amador Vega, *Ramon Llull and the Secret of Life*, trans. James W. Heisig (New York: The Crossroad Publishing Company, 2002), 236–58, should be used with caution, since the second half of §11 appears to have been inadvertently omitted. This chapter adopts the spelling of the author's name as "Raymond

Like many of the ventures of Lull's life, this late apologetic trip was largely unsuccessful. Nevertheless, the Christian Neoplatonic philosopher Raymond Lull is an intriguing figure whose long life, extensive literary output, unconventional projects, and far-reaching influence among later medieval and Renaissance thinkers have long made him an object of study. The author of approximately 260 works, Lull is best known for his *Art* (*ars*), a complex technique that was intended to solve problems in metaphysics as well as convert Islamic and Jewish believers to the Christian faith. In the course of his extensive travels, Lull approached popes, kings, and sultans in an attempt to find endorsement and material support for his apologetic aims, and his efforts included lecturing at universities throughout Europe to defend his *Art*. His extraordinarily diverse literary corpus, written in Latin, Catalan, and Arabic, included poetic works and novels, and treatises on philosophy, theology, and nearly every other established discipline of the period.[2]

3.1 THE AUTHORSHIP OF THE *VITA COAETANEA*

Many details of Lull's remarkable life are preserved in his *Vita coaetanea* or *Contemporary Life* mentioned above, an unusual autobiographical work composed in 1311, five years before the philosopher's death. While *Vita* has been rightly characterized as "a document almost unique among the literature of medieval thought," one might judge that on the basis of its spiritual, philosophical, and theological merits it invites comparison to other classic testaments of the Middle Ages written by philosophers.[3] For instance, Lull's moving account of his spiritual conversion and his rejection of an earlier life of profligacy easily brings to mind the *Confessiones* of Augustine and the *Historia calamitatem* of Peter Abelard, while the work's apologetic and philosophical fervor bears comparison with Al-Ghazālī's memoir, *The Deliverance from Error*. Regardless of the merits of such comparisons, it cannot be doubted that Lull was an indefatigable figure whose ventures were emblematic of his wide-ranging concerns that spanned the active as well as contemplative dimensions of life. When recounting the central aims of his life's work in the *Vita*, Lull identified no fewer than

---

Lull" according to one version of the Latin orthography, rather than following other options such as "Ramon Llull" or "Raymond Lully," among others. For a discussion of the variants among the Latin, Spanish, and Catalan versions of Lull's first name and surname, see Bonner, *Doctor Illuminatus*, 9, n. 13.

[2] For a catalogue of Lull's works, see Bonner, *Selected Works*, II: 1257–304.

[3] Bonner, *Doctor Illuminatus*, 10.

five monumental projects. Shortly after his conversion, the *Vita* relates he dedicated himself to the first three: intending to establish houses of study where languages could be learned as an aid to converting non-Christians; planning to write one book, no less than "the best in the world (*melior de mundo*)"; and finally, resolving in due course to die a martyr's death.[4] Later in life he added the two goals of refuting Latin Averroism, a form of heterodox Aristotelianism, and unifying all Christian militant orders for the recapture of the Holy Land.[5] While in each of these goals Lull plainly failed, he did leave behind a complex literary corpus that has yet to be fully appreciated.[6]

The text of the *Vita* itself has an unusual history. Shortly after the philosopher's death, the Latin text was included in the *Electorium magnum*, a massive collection of Lull's works compiled by his disciple Thomas Le Myésier. The *Vita* was translated into Catalan in the early fourteenth century, and for many years the translation was considered by scholars to be the more authoritative version, but now the Latin version is recognized to be the original.[7] In its preface, Lull indicates the origin of the work, stating that at the urging of certain religious who were his friends he acceded to recounting his life events and permitting his words to be written down.[8] These religious were the Carthusian monks at the Abbey of Vauvert in Paris, and their role in the notation of the philosopher's words may explain why Lull's autobiography is written in the third person, a feature that at times has obscured its autobiographical character. Earlier uncertainty regarding the authorship of the *Vita* is reflected in its manner of inclusion among the Lullian biographical documents in the *Acta Sanctorum*, where the *Vita* is described as "having been written by a nameless contemporary (*ab Anonymo coaevo scripta*)."[9] Although it has not always been recognized as autobiographical, the *Vita* is generally now regarded as so, even though the literary quality and sophistication of the work have led some to speculate that the extant text of Lull's recollections may be a redaction by one of the Carthusian monks rather than an unaltered transcription of Lull's words. J. N. Hillgarth speaks of the *Vita* as "apparently 'touched up' by its monastic

---

[4] *Vita*, §6.   [5] *Vita*, §8, §39.

[6] Not all of Lull's works are available in modern editions. For Latin works, there is the *Opera Latina*, ed. Friedrich Stegmüller *et al.*, vols. I–V (Palma de Mallorca: Maioricensis Schola Lullistica, 1959–67), vols. VIff. (Turnhout: Brepols, 1975–), of which fifty-five volumes are planned.

[7] An English translation of the Catalan version of the *Vita* is *A Life of Ramón Lull*, trans. E. Allison Peers (London: Burns Oates and Washbourne, 1927), 1–45.

[8] *Vita*, §1.

[9] *Acta Sanctorum*, vol. VI, tom. V (Antwerp, 1709 [repr. Brussels: Culture et Civilisation, 1969]), 661–8, at 661.

author," yet "because of its date, it clearly possesses great authority."[10] Mark Johnston goes so far as to designate the work as "hagiographic,"[11] but such a characterization has been strongly contested by Miquel Batllori, who judges that such a designation belongs only to the embellished fourteenth-century Catalan translation.[12] Commentators on the *Vita* appear to be drawn in two conflicting directions when assessing its origin, privileging either Lull or the Carthusian monks in its composition.[13] Perhaps the recent description of it by Anthony Bonner as "a sort of autobiography" best characterizes its status in the estimation of present-day scholars.[14] Despite these differences, it should be emphasized that nearly all commentators take the *Vita* as the most authoritative text regarding Lull's activities, even if there is a range of views regarding the extent of biographical supplements to the autobiographical original.[15]

[10] J. N. Hillgarth, *Ramon Lull and Lullism in Fourteenth-Century France* (Oxford: Clarendon Press, 1971), I, 46. Hillgarth outlines the transmission of the text of the *Vita* in the manuscript tradition at 476–9. While staunchly defending the integrity of the *Vita* as an autobiographical document, Miquel Batllori identifies a further issue concerning the early editing of the Latin text, observing that "one does not know the writer or amanuensis who received the dictation from the lips of Ramon. He does not have to coincide, necessarily, with the one or ones who gave it the definitive literary form (*la forma rítmica definitiva*)." See Miquel Batllori, *Ramon Lull i el Lul·lisme, Obra Completa*, vol. II (Valéncia: Tres i Quatre, 1993), 70. See also Fernando Domínguez Reboiras, "Idea y estructura de la *Vita Raymundi Lulli*," *Estudios Lulianos* 27 (1987), 1–20, at 20.

[11] Mark D. Johnston, *The Evangelical Rhetoric of Ramon Llull: Lay Learning and Piety in the Christian West Around 1300* (New York: Oxford University Press, 1996), 5. Elsewhere Johnston speaks of the *Vita* as composed "perhaps from his own recollections." See Johnston, *The Spiritual Logic of Ramon Llull* (Oxford: Clarendon Press, 1987), 14.

[12] For a sustained discussion of the inappropriateness of that term "in the strict sense of the word (*en el sentit estricte de mot*)" or "in the pejorative sense of the epithet (*in el sentit pejoratiu de l'epítet*)," see Batllori, *Ramon Lull i el Lul·lisme*, 52–3, 70.

[13] Massimo Candellero, for instance, characterizes the *Vita* as "dictated by Lull to an anonymous disciple on urgent request of the hermits of Vauvert" while contending that it is a biography "commissioned" by Lull. See Candellero, "Un importante documento biografico Lulliano: La *Vita Coaetanea*," in *Atti del Convegno internazionale Ramon Llull, il lullismo internazionale, l'Italia. Omaggio a Miquel Batllori dell'Associazione Italiana di Studi Catalani. Napoli, Castel dell'Ovo, 30 e 31 marzo, 1 aprile 1989*, ed. Giuseppe Grilli (Naples: Istituto universitario orientale, 1992), 15–33, at 28 and 19.

[14] Anthony Bonner, *The Art and Logic of Ramon Llull: A User's Guide* (Leiden: Brill, 2007), 2. For a discussion of the range of approaches on the autobiographical question, see Amador Vega, *Ramon Llull and the Secret of Life*, 105–6, n. 5.

[15] Batllori adduces additional arguments in favor of its integrity as an autobiographical work. While conceding that "it is very true that no version of the original text has survived, as it was really dictated by Raymond Lull in his barbarous and approximate Latin, and that we only have the second redaction in a beautiful literary prose of monastic appearance," Batllori notes that the events depicted in the work can be confirmed by biographical documents contained in the prologues to other works by Lull (52). Additionally, Batllori emphasizes that the *Vita* does not relate the events of Lull's life after 1311. Were the work biographical, rather than autobiographical, it surely would have accounted for Lull's last five years and the circumstances of his death. Batllori explains that "the veridical character of the Latin text, dictated in Paris in 1311, is corroborated by the fact that the narration of the life of Raymond does not go beyond that date" (70). Elsewhere Batllori presents

The moral universe of the Vita coaetanea

Although not a philosophical treatise, the *Vita* presents in lively detail four occasions in which Lull considers himself trapped in a moral dilemma. In these situations Lull is frequently characterized as perplexed (*perplexus*). The *Vita* carefully describes the two prongs for each of the four moral dilemmas, explains Lull's evaluation of his options, and records his ultimate course of action. On the basis of evidence presented in this quartet of examples, the moral universe depicted in the *Vita* exhibits three striking characteristics relevant to the issue of inescapable moral wrongdoing:

i. The world ensnares unsuspecting agents into moral dilemmas;
ii. Petitionary prayer is the requisite solution for agents who find themselves in these situations; and,
iii. These moral dilemmas are resolvable only by divine intervention.

Since the *Vita* is not a formal treatise on philosophical or theological ethics, one must exercise caution when deriving theoretical claims from its content.[16] Its narrative style requires that characteristics (i–iii) be established inductively on the basis of elements Lull incorporated into the work. He was an octogenarian when he provided the autobiographical statement to the monastic scribe, so the work represents the philosopher's mature retrospective views. The three characteristics of: (i) ensnarement, (ii) petitionary prayer, and (iii) divine intervention are sufficiently repeated in the narrative of the work to allow for some substantive conclusions regarding Lull's views on the subject of moral dilemmas. In the *Vita*, Lull succeeds in expressing a sophisticated and distinctive medieval position on the issue of moral dilemmas, arguing for their existence and suggesting a strategy – albeit ultimately a theological one – for dealing with them when they arise.

3.2 THE CONVERSION DILEMMA

The early passages of the *Vita* quickly pass over the first thirty years of Lull's life, briefly noting that he served as a court official to the king

---

the argument with a slightly different emphasis, noting that "the seriousness of the anonymous Carthusian or Carthusians" who helped produce the *Vita* is exhibited by the fact that even though "the Carthusian monastery of Vavert became one of the centers for the irradiation of Lullism from the beginning of the fourteenth to well into the sixteenth century and beyond, it never dared to complete that autobiography dictated by Lull" (54). Thus, its unfinished character testifies to its authenticity as an autobiographical, rather than biographical, document.

[16] The *Vita* is a complex work admitting of a variety of approaches. For a reading of the work that emphasizes its spiritual dimensions, for example, see Mark D. Johnston, "Ramon Llull's Conversion to Penitence," *Mystics Quarterly* 16 (1990), 179–92. See also Llabrés Martorell, "La conversión del Bto. Ramón Llull, en sus aspectos histórico, sicológico y teológico," *Estudios Lulianos* 12 (1968), 161–73.

of Majorca and that he passed the time seeking vanities (*uanitates*) and engaging in lasciviousness (*lasciuia*).[17] This way of life was interrupted, however, when a strange series of visions began to visit him while he was composing love poetry. The *Vita* explains that on four evenings over the span of approximately two weeks, a vision of Christ crucified presented itself in mid-air in his room. Although Lull was quite frightened by each of the first three appearances of the vision, he responded by retiring to bed and falling asleep, only to awaken the next day and return to his affairs, ignoring the previous night's unusual occurrence. On the fourth visitation by this vision, however, Lull's fright increased and he was absolutely terrified, and he spent the entire night turning over these events in his mind and trying to determine what they signified.

Lull carefully summarizes his considerations concerning the visions by stating that his conscience (*conscientia*) gave two dictates to him, and these two jointly generate the first moral dilemma of the *Vita*. He explains:

> On the one hand, his conscience told him that [the visions] could only mean that he should abandon the world at once and from then on dedicate himself totally to the service of our Lord Jesus Christ. On the other hand, his conscience reminded him of the guilt of his former life and his unworthiness to serve Christ (*Hinc sibi quandoque dictabat conscientia, quod apparationes illae nihil aliud praetendebant, nisi quod ipse mox relicto mundo Domino Iesu Christo ex tunc integre deseruiret. Illinc uero sua conscientia ream se prius et indignam Christi seruitio acclamabat*).[18]

Here Lull reveals that he has discerned two dictates issuing from his conscience. First, conscience dictated (*dictabat*) that he should convert his life and serve God. Secondly, his conscience protested (*acclamabat*) that he was unworthy to serve God, and hence should not convert his life. The conflicting dictates of conscience generate a moral dilemma that can be expressed as a pair of contradictories {*a*, ~*a*}, where *a* stands for the obligation to abandon the world and follow God, and ~*a* stands for the obligation not to abandon the world and not to follow God. Consistent with medieval thinkers discussed in earlier chapters, Lull gives an account of perplexity where an agent is caught between a pair of impending obligations expressible as contradictories.

Lull presents putatively strong evidence on behalf of each of these two dictates of conscience. Evidence for *a* is simply the fourfold appearance of the vision of Christ over the roughly two-week period. Lull's dismissal of the vision in its first, second, and penultimate appearances reflects

[17] *Vita*, §3.   [18] *Vita*, §4.

an initial suspicion of its origin. Ultimately, however, Lull finds that the binding character of *a* is confirmed by the repeated supernatural appearance of the vision, presumably interpreted in light of the religious view that Christ's crucifixion was reparation for human moral failings, such as those constituting Lull's life of vanities and lasciviousness. Similarly, there is also strong evidence for ∼*a*, the second dictate of conscience. Lull's use of the term guilt (*reus*) and his reflection that he is unworthy (*indignus*) suggest that ∼*a* is grounded on a notion of sacrilege; to approach God unworthily would be more grave than any of Lull's previous moral failings of the flesh.

Moral dilemmas as sets of contradictories

The configuration of this dilemma deserves further scrutiny. Lull cannot avoid either *a* or ∼*a*, since these two contradictories together stand for an act and its omission. By doing nothing, Lull simply commits to ∼*a* and fails to respond to the obligation indicated by the vision. By performing *a*, Lull believes himself to commit a sacrilege. Either way, it seems, a moral failure occurs and Lull is perplexed. The perplexity in this case is not presented as simply a condition of unclarity regarding the respective future harms and benefits of two possible actions; presumably every action can be described in light of *pros* and *cons*, since one can find debating points for and against nearly every action that is intelligible. If Lull's situation were simply a dilemma of that sort, it would take the form of:

I do not know whether I should perform action x; and,

I do not know whether I should omit action x.

Such a simple dilemma of this sort is indeed a dilemma, but need not be a *moral* dilemma; there are often situations composed of two possible options where an agent happens to be unclear about which option deserves selection. These non-moral dilemmas are commonplace and need not warrant any serious moral consideration. Rather than experiencing a simple dilemma like those, Lull believes himself to be experiencing conflicting moral obligations that simultaneously make demands upon him. A dilemma is moral if real obligations impose upon him that cannot be set aside with the acquisition of further moral knowledge. A moral dilemma (in contrast to a simple dilemma) can be expressed as:

It is a moral failure to perform action y; and,

It is a moral failure to omit action y.

Lull's situation takes this form, assuming he has established the moral impermissibility of both prongs along with the obligation to do them. Thus, it is necessary to distinguish simple dilemmas where an agent is confused about options from moral dilemmas where the agent must choose between two obligatory yet incompatible alternatives. In short, simple dilemmas can be resolved with additional knowledge; true moral dilemmas cannot be.

Lull's reaction to this moral dilemma is to continue to examine the two options in the context of prayer. He explains:

Thus, alternately debating these points with himself and fervently praying to God, he spent the night without sleeping (*Sicque super his nunc secum disputans, nunc attentius Deum orans, laboriosam noctem illam duxit insomnem*).[19]

Lull's prayerful night-long *disputatio* yields a solution, but it is a supernatural one. The *Vita* relates that finally as a divine gift he was led to reflect on divine mercy, and on this basis he resolved to abandon the world and follow God. It appears that in prayer he was made aware that God would allow him to avoid sacrilege; through prayer he was given a route to avoid moral wrongdoing. The *Vita* notes that "at last, as a gift (*denique, dante*)" God intervened and Lull was able to escape the otherwise intractable dilemma.[20] The moral dilemma was presented as beyond Lull's power to escape, and its resolution required an extrinsic, gratuitous intervention by God.

Lull's contribution to thirteenth-century perplexed conscience debates

Lull's account of this first moral dilemma is striking for several reasons, not the least of which is its employment of the terminology common to twelfth- and thirteenth-century discussions of conscience by masters connected with the University of Paris. An increasing uniformity of expression in dealing with questions concerning conscience was partly secured with the widespread practice of commenting on Peter Lombard's *Sententiae* as an academic exercise, as Lombard's discussion of the will in distinction 39 of the second book of *Sententiae* became the *locus classicus* for scholastic theorizing on conscience, prompting many commentators to treat the issue of conflicts of conscience in a systematic way.[21] Lull's presentation of this first moral dilemma demonstrates that he was aware of the terms of such debates about conscience; perhaps his four visits to Paris prior to the composition of the *Vita* provided occasions for encountering texts on conscience

---

[19] *Vita*, §4.   [20] *Vita*, §4.
[21] The arguments of several such thinkers will be considered in the next two chapters.

by Parisian masters. Many commentators on Lombard theorized whether an agent could be perplexed (*perplexus*) when a judgment of conscience (*conscientia*) dictates (*dictat*) the performance of an action that is contrary to the natural law or a command of God. Even though there were wide disagreements about the nature of conscience among medieval commentators on the *Sententiae*, especially between members of the Dominican and Franciscan orders, there was near unanimity among commentators regarding what should be done in such cases.[22] In short, nearly all major thinkers agreed that it was necessary to set aside (*deponere, dimittere*) such a judgment of conscience, for it surely must be in error. For instance, such a position was defended by William of Auxerre as well as the authors of the *Summa Halesiana* at the beginnings of their respective treatments of perplexity, as was examined in the previous chapter.[23] It is noteworthy that Lull stands against this tradition in his account of conscience in the *Vita*, as he does not advocate the rejection of a dictate of conscience but suggests that agents await divine intervention after praying. His opposition to the traditional solution appears careful and deliberate. While employing the customary terms (e.g., *conscientia, perplexus, dictare*), Lull offers an unusual position. The judgments of conscience appear to be inviolable according to Lull, even when they oppose the law of God.

A repeated plot

Set forth at the beginning of Lull's autobiography, the first moral dilemma displays a structure that is repeated in other moral dilemmas described later in the *Vita*. Lull finds himself ensnared in a moral dilemma, becomes anguished with the recognition of his impotence to escape, turns to fervent prayer, and finally is saved with a divine intervention. Admittedly Lull is parsimonious in theorizing about this moral dilemma structure; the moral dilemmas and their resolutions are narrated historically rather than analytically. Despite this mode of presentation, conclusions regarding Lull's moral universe can be set forth on the basis of the recurrence of this structure. Several features of the structure in Lull's conversion story deserve comment. First, the ensnarement in the dilemma is entirely unforeseen by Lull; he had no reason to anticipate or predict the disruption of his nightly

---

[22] For an account that delineates the early competing interpretations of Franciscan and Dominican schools of thought, see Xavier G. Colavechio, O.Praem., *Erroneous Conscience and Obligations: A Study of the Teaching from the Summa Halesiana, Saint Bonaventure, Saint Albert the Great, and Saint Thomas Aquinas* (Washington, DC: The Catholic University of America Press, 1961).

[23] See *Summa aurea*, 1045; *Summa Halesiana*, 392.

routine by a vision of Christ crucified. Secondly, Lull appears genuinely concerned to avoid future moral wrongdoing once he is trapped in the dilemma. He displays an anguish that seems far removed from his carefree life of a courtier and poet. Thirdly, Lull's resort to prayer is intense; in this case as well as others, Lull is described as fervently praying at length in the context of reasoning or deliberating. Finally, the divine intervention occurs suddenly, the particulars of which are unanticipated by Lull.

3.3 *THE TEACHER–STUDENT DILEMMA*

Shortly after the presentation of the first moral dilemma in the *Vita*, Lull offers his second, and it is more complex. The *Vita* explains that Lull renounced his worldly ways, completed pilgrimages to various holy sites of Christendom, and resolved to prepare himself academically for a new life. Lull initially had planned to travel to Paris to pursue studies there, but was advised by the Dominican Raymond of Peñafort to remain in his homeland of Majorca.[24] In addition to remedying a deficient grasp of Latin, Lull began to study Arabic to train for his apologetic tasks, and he purchased a Saracen slave to be his tutor. A series of events involving his tutor-slave generates the background for the second dilemma of the work. The *Vita* narrates:

Nine years later it happened that, while Raymond was away, his Saracen slave blasphemed the name of Christ. Upon returning and finding out about it from those who had heard the blasphemy, Raymond, impelled by a great zeal for the Faith, hit the Saracen on the mouth, on the forehead, and in the face. As a result the Saracen became extremely embittered, and he began plotting the death of his master (*Deinde post annos nouem contigit, quod Saracenus ille, Raimundo quadam die absente, nomen Christi blasphemaret. Quod cum reuersus cognouit. Raimundus ab his, qui blasphemiam audiuerant, nimio fidei zelo motus percussit illum Saracenum in ore, fronte ac facie. Saracenus uero, rancore nimio inde concepto, ex tunc coepit mente tractare, quomodo dominum suum posset occidere*).[25]

The text of the *Vita* here notes that in Raymond's absence the slave blasphemed Christ, only to be punished on the master's return, and the motivation for the slave's subsequent homicidal intention is left unspecified apart from the mention of anger over being punished for blasphemy. More details, however, are present in some other texts. Lull's disciple, Thomas

---

[24] Raymond of Peñafort reportedly advised Thomas Aquinas to write the *Summa contra gentiles* (*Summary [of Theology] against the Pagans*). If true, Peñafort lies at the origin of two Christian apologetic initiatives of the thirteenth century.

[25] *Vita*, §11.

Le Myésier, mentioned above as the author of the *Electorium magnum*, also composed a digest of that work known as the *Electorium parvum* or *Breviculum*, which contained miniatures with dialogue featuring scenes between Lull and the Saracen. On the basis of these miniatures it can be inferred that an additional cause of the Saracen's murderous plans was the late discovery of Lull's intent to use the acquired knowledge of Arabic for the conversion of Muslims. In one scene from the *Electorium parvum* the Saracen explains, "I regret that I instructed you in Arabic! And why did I show you the Koran and Mohammed's law, which is true as we believe? You labor to assail it with necessary reasons! (*Doleo, quia arabicum te docui! Et quare Alcoranum et legem Macometi tibi ostendi ueram ut credimus? Rationibus necessariis niteris impugnare!*)"[26] This view of the Saracen's motivations is repeated in the account given by Carolus Bovillus (1479–1553) in his early sixteenth-century biography of Lull. In that text the Saracen is shown to be particularly distraught because, as Lull's tutor, he has been the source of Lull's knowledge of the language.[27]

The *Vita* and *Electorium parvum* are consistent in the rest of the details of the event that generate the dilemma: the Saracen slave grabbed a sword, shouted, "You are dead! (*tu mortuus es!*)," and wounded Lull seriously but not fatally.[28] After being subdued by Lull and tied up by house attendants, the Saracen was temporarily placed in a jail. The moral dilemma, Lull indicates in the *Vita*, concerned what exactly to do with the murderously intentioned Saracen slave.

---

[26] Thomas Le Myésier, *Breviculum seu Electorium parvum Thomae Migerii*, ed. Charles Lohr, Theodor Pindl-Büchel, and Walburga Büchel, *Corpus Christianorum continuatio mediaevalis*, vol. LXXVII. *Raimundi Lulli Opera Latina, Supplementum Lullianum*, vol. I (Turnhout: Brepols, 1990), 9–49, at 13. A facsimile edition of the *Electorium parvum* of the Badische Landesbibliothek, complete with color reproductions of the miniatures, is Thomas Le Myésier, *Electorium parvum seu Breviculum, Vollständiges Faksimile der Handschrift St. Peter perg. 92 der Badischen Landesbibliothek Karlsruhe, Kommentar zum Faksimile*, ed. Gerhard Römer and Gerhard Stamm, 2 vols. (Wiesbaden, 1988). A transcription of the Latin of the miniatures is given in J. N. Hillgarth, *Ramon Lull and Lullism*, 449–61, with text cited at 451.

[27] Bovillus writes, "The purchased Saracen who had taught Lull was fearful, lest Raymond's knowledge of the laws of the Muslims should become dangerous. He was the sole cause of Lull's speaking of Arabic, since Lull had demanded to receive the knowledge of the language of the Arabs from him (*Timensque ideo emptitius Saracenus, qui eum docuerat, ne Raemundi doctrina Mahumeticae legi perniciosa fieret praefertim cum solius praedicationis causa, Arabici sermonis peritia, ab eo se imbui postulasset*)." The text of the *Vita* of Bovillus is included in the *Acta Sanctorum*, 668–73, with the cited text at 671. The present interpretation of the Saracen's motives is supported by a brief and likely autobiographical story in Lull's *Felix*, 7.39: "In a certain land there was once a Christian who had a Saracen whom he trusted very much, and whom he did many favors; the Saracen, however, being against him because of his religion, was unable to bear him any good will, but rather was continually thinking how he could kill him." See *Selected Works*, I: 22, n. 22; and II: 788.

[28] *Breviculum seu Electorium parvum*, 13; *Vita*, §12.

Identifying the prongs of the dilemma

Lull indicates that he proceeded to weigh (*deliberare*) his options and there appeared to be only three relevant possibilities from which to choose.[29] Each of these options had a strong reason in its favor but simultaneously a strong reason against it. They are all judged by Lull to be impermissible, so they collectively constitute Lull's moral dilemma concerning how to deal with the slave. The first option was simply to kill the Saracen. Lull immediately rules out this option as being too grave (*severum*), for he judges himself to have an obligation to the Saracen for the previous years of dedicated instruction in Arabic. It can be assumed, therefore, that Lull experiences a strong obligation of piety toward his teacher that has not disappeared simply because this teacher has acquired a homicidal intention. So, in short, the first option of this moral dilemma can be set forth as the contradictory set of $\{b, \sim b\}$, where b is executing the Saracen slave and $\sim b$ is desisting from such an act. In Lull's estimation, b is impermissible because of the obligation of piety, and $\sim b$, if it alone is Lull's response toward the wayward slave, is impermissible because of the expectation of the slave's continued designs on Lull's life.

Lull mentions briefly the two remaining options he considered: he could simply free the Saracen slave (hereafter, c), thereby removing him from Lull's household, or he could continue to keep the slave as part of his household (hereafter, d), presumably under Lull's watchful eye. Options c and d are immediately ruled out, since Lull judges that "from then on the Saracen would not cease his murderous machinations (*quod ipse non cessaret ex tunc in mortem ipsius machinari*)."[30] The options of $\sim c$ and $\sim d$ are of course equally problematic, for they, by themselves, again do not impede the slave from future attempts on his life. No other options apart from b, c, and d and their contradictories arise in the course of Lull's considerations. He experiences an obligation to protect his life which warrants some action against the Saracen, while simultaneously he experiences an obligation of piety which prevents action toward that Saracen, "by whose teaching he now knew the language he had so wanted to learn, that is, Arabic (*quo docente sibi linguam multum optatam, scilicet arabicam, iam sciebat*)."[31]

These deliberations come to a close with Lull's judgment that he is in a moral dilemma. He states simply that he is perplexed (*perplexus*).[32] While the term *perplexus* here carries the epistemic sense of confusion about how to proceed, there is the foundational sense of *perplexus* that is more

---

[29] *Vita*, §12.   [30] *Vita*, §12.   [31] *Vita*, §12.   [32] *Vita*, §13.

significant for the present purpose: Lull believes himself to be ensnared or entrapped by the moral life. His perplexity is not simply presented as a subjective one; he judges that it results from impossible moral demands imposed upon him. Neither acting (b, c, d) nor not acting ($\sim b$, $\sim c$, $\sim d$) will free Lull from the commission of a moral failure, since he judges each option to involve a transgression of a moral obligation to himself or to his tutor. In his account, the epistemic quandary about how to act is caused by the world that has ensnared him in a situation of inescapable moral wrongdoing. In other words, there is no assumption of a secret unknown option that Lull could pursue if he simply had more knowledge. He is ensnared by the world, not by any ignorance about how to act.

Lull's explicit identification of the courses of action labeled here as c and d should not obscure that Lull's situation is still at its foundation a single dilemma composed of two contradictories. There are not three moral dilemmas, but only one: the dilemma here is between the contradictories of executing the homicidally intentioned slave (b) and not executing him ($\sim b$). The courses of action identified as freeing the slave (c) and keeping the slave in the household (d) are simply more particularized versions of ($\sim b$). There really is only one moral dilemma, that of executing or not executing the murder-minded Saracen. Lull's presentation, therefore, possesses a significant affinity with earlier thinkers considered previously, insofar as they examined dilemmatic cases of inescapable moral wrongdoing expressible as a single set of contradictories and leave unmentioned any more complex situations such as trilemmas or tetralemmas.

A divine intervention

A familiar pattern emerges in Lull's continued description of the second moral dilemma: he turns to prayer upon recognizing his inability to escape moral wrongdoing. The *Vita* states that "he went up to a certain abbey near there, where for three days he prayed fervently to God about this matter (*ascendit ad abbatiam quandam, quae prope erat, orans ibidem Dominum super hac re instantissime per tres dies*)."[33] This decision parallels, of course, Lull's earlier decision to spend a night in prayer after discovering the dilemma following the apparition of Christ crucified, since in both situations an inability to resolve his dilemma through rational deliberation alone leads Lull to seek divine assistance. To Lull's surprise, however, his

---

[33] *Vita*, §13.

three days of praying in the abbey do not lead to an immediate resolution. The *Vita* reports:

When the three days were over, astonished that the same perplexity still remained in his heart and that God, or so it seemed to him, had in no way listened to his prayers, he returned home full of sorrow (*Quibus completis, admirans, quod adhuc in corde suo praetacta perplexitate remanente, Dominus, ut sibi uidebatur, ipsius orationem nullatenus exaudisset, maestus ad domum suam rediit*).[34]

Subsequent to the praying, the perplexity (*perplexitas*) remains. Lull's astonishment at this fact presupposed a confidence that the moral dilemma would be resolved by petitionary prayer; his sorrow (*maestus*) testifies to his confident expectation that his prayers would elicit a resolution to his dilemma. On the way home, however, Lull visited the jail where the Saracen was temporarily being held and there he made an astonishing discovery: the Saracen had hanged himself by means of the rope with which he had been originally bound by Lull's house attendants.

Lull's response to discovering the unexpected suicide of the Saracen is instructive for confirming his view of moral dilemmas and their resolution by divine means. The *Vita* reports:

Raymond therefore joyfully gave thanks to God not only for keeping his hands innocent of the death of this Saracen, but also for freeing him from that terrible perplexity concerning which he had just recently so anxiously asked him for guidance (*Reddidit ergo Raimundus gratias Deo laetus, qui et a nece praedicti Saraceni seruauerat manus eius innoxias, et eum a perplexitate illa graui, pro qua paulo ante ipsum anxius exorauerat, liberauerat*).[35]

Several key features of this text deserve attention. To begin, this passage credits God with securing Lull from the situation of grave perplexity (*perplexitas grauis*). By the time Raymond turns to prayer, he does not expect an epistemic solution to his moral dilemma. That is, his *perplexitas* is not going to be resolved with more information or the uncovering of some unconsidered alternative that he might pursue on his own accord. Lull's judgment that he is *perplexus* leads him to cease searching for *ad intra* resolutions, and he believes that only an *ad extra* intervention by God will save him from moral wrongdoing. The *Vita* presents this and other morally dilemmatic situations as inescapable apart from such divine intervention.

---

[34] *Vita*, §13. The Catalan version of this scene from the *Vita* renders the dilemma more explicit: "he was in great fear and perplexity as to what he ought to do . . . [Lull] had prayed there for three days, and marvelled greatly that his spirit had no rest in either solution, whether in killing him or in letting him live, but was ever in the same perplexity." The translation here is from Peers, *A Life*, 10.

[35] *Vita*, §13.

There is nothing left for Lull to do in these situations to escape the dilemmas: unless God intervenes by interfering in the world and extricating Lull, the philosopher will be bound to perform some wrongdoing. Also, the passage above underscores the firmness with which Lull has adhered to the view that he held a pious obligation to his teacher of Arabic. Lull's rejoicing that his hands are blameless (*innoxia*) in the Saracen's death supports this position. Presumably Lull believed that if he had killed the slave himself, he would be blameworthy (*noxia*); that is, he would have been guilty of a moral failure.

Two objections

A present-day reader may have at least two objections to the *Teacher-Student Dilemma*. First, one might question whether the execution of the slave is truly the only sufficiently self-protective measure that Lull can pursue to save his life. At least, this assumption, absent a justification in the *Vita*, does not seem obviously warranted. Secondly, one might question the notion that Lull has a true moral obligation of piety toward the Saracen. Admittedly, a complex relationship obtains between tutor and student. On the one hand, Lull is the slave's civil master, since he purchased the Saracen who thereafter existed in a condition of servitude toward him; yet, on the other hand, the slave in one significant respect has exercised a position of authority over Lull, insofar as he has been Lull's teacher with regard to the Arabic language. The nine years under the Saracen's Arabic tutelage are not easily forgotten by Lull. Perhaps because of the widely accepted hierarchical conceptions of the universe and society, medieval philosophers and theologians at times examined the question of the obligations of an inferior when faced with the injustices of a superior. Lull's situation with his homicidal tutor parallels in some respects an unusual example given by Peter Abelard (1079–1142) in his *Ethics* (*Ethica*). There, Abelard prompts the reader to consider the case where an innocent man is pursued by his raging cruel master (*dominus*) with an unsheathed sword, and the man, as far as he can, attempts to avoid his own murder. In the end, however, the inferior cannot put off his death any longer, so he kills his superior. A present-day reader may be surprised to see Abelard defend the view that the inferior "did do wrong in consenting to an unjust killing which he should have undergone rather than have inflicted (*iniustae interfectioni quam eum potius ferre quam inferre oportuit*)."[36] According to Abelard, the obligation

---

[36] *Peter Abelard's Ethics*, ed. and trans. D. E. Luscombe (Oxford: Clarendon Press, 1971), 9.

of an inferior to a superior is not abrogated because of the superior's acquisition of a homicidal intention. Abelard explains: "because he consented
to a killing to which he ought not to have consented, this unjust consent
of his which preceded the killing was a sin (*quia in occisione consensit in
qua non debuit, hic eius iniustus consensus qui occisionem precessit, peccatum
fuit*)."[37] Lull appears to view the Saracen – even though he is a slave –
as his *dominus* of Arabic, and hence he cannot simply punish the Saracen
as he would punish other slaves. Later the *Vita* recounts Lull's discovery
that two of his hired servants were trying to poison him as part of a plan
to steal his belongings, and there Lull exhibits no hesitation in sending
them away.[38] Lull's relationship to the Saracen, therefore, is different in
kind from his other relationships to those in his household because of his
perceived obligation of piety that stems from the years of study under him.

A modern interpreter views the death of the Saracen as not only freeing
Lull from the obligations to his teacher but also as allowing him to be
autonomous in his future intellectual pursuits. Amador Vega remarks,
"The *Vita* relates the tragic episode of the Saracen's attempt to kill Lull and
of his subsequent suicide in prison. Thus discharged of all responsibility
toward the one who had taught him so much, Raymond makes his debut
as an author."[39] Moreover, one of the miniatures present in the *Electorium
parvum* by Thomas Le Myésier also supports the view that Lull believed
himself to be avoiding a moral failure with the unexpected death of the
Saracen, for one panel depicts Lull looking up and addressing the hanging
corpse of his former teacher with these stunning words,

Blessed be the Lord my God, who kept my hands blameless in your death, and
who kept me exempt from any conspiracy in your death (*Benedictus dominus Deus
meus, qui manus meas innoxias a morte tua liberauit et a consensu mortis tuae me
immunem conseruauit*).[40]

On all accounts, Lull's joyful reaction over being freed from his moral
dilemma hides any trace of sorrow over the passing of his teacher of nine
years. His jubilation over being released from impending inescapable moral
wrongdoing seems to have left no room for any personal feelings toward
the Saracen that might have survived the initial disclosure of the slave's
homicidal intention.

The resolution of this moral dilemma involving the Saracen has a similar
structure to the first dilemma examined above. Both dilemmas began with

---

[37] *Peter Abelard's Ethics*, 9.   [38] *Vita*, §34.
[39] Vega, *Ramon Llull and the Secret of Life*, 7.   [40] *Breviculum seu Electorium parvum*, 13.

Lull finding himself ensnared in a situation where he must act despite believing that all of the alternatives entail the commission of some moral wrong. Lull is confident after disputing with himself and deliberating among options that no hidden alternatives free from moral condemnation are left to be discovered. In his anguish over his impotence to escape imminent moral wrongdoing, Lull commits himself fervently to prayer with the expectation of immediate divine intervention. In both dilemmas, Lull is gratuitously allowed to escape the commission of an immoral act, and Lull recognizes the extrinsic character of his release from the dilemma. In the first dilemma, there is a divine intervention with a gift from God, and in the second, there is the providential suicide of the Saracen slave. The solutions are outside the range of Lull's actions and choices, and he attributes these solutions to God. In each situation, Lull exhibits confidence that his divine solicitations will free him from the moral dilemma in which he finds himself, but the manner by which his escape will be accomplished is unknown at the time of his prayerful entreaties.

3.4 THE DIVINE COMMAND DILEMMA

The third dilemma of the *Vita* concerns the preservation of Lull's famous *Art* (*ars*), the technique believed by him to have a broad use in Christian apologetics as well as metaphysics.[41] The *Vita* refers to the *Art* as a divine science (*scientia sancta*) given to Lull by God (*sibi datum a deo*) on a certain mountain near his home shortly after Lull's disavowal of worldly ways and his conversion to penitence (*conversio ad poenitentiam*).[42] The traditional date of this event is 1274, when Lull was forty-two years old and about to start his public apologetic project. He claimed to have received the form and method (*forma et modus*) of it by divine illumination.[43] The iterations of the *Art* throughout his extraordinarily numerous writings were attempts by Lull to make his vision suitable to various audiences; Lull complains in the *Vita* that he had to alter the presentation of it on several occasions in light of pedagogical concerns.[44] The fundamental aim of the *Art* was to

---

[41] For concise presentations of the *ars Lulliana, see* R. D. F. Pring-Mill, "The Analogical Structure of the Lullian Art," in *Islamic Philosophy and the Classical Tradition: Essays Presented by his Friends and Pupils to Richard Walzer on his seventieth Birthday*, ed. S. M. Stern, Albert Hourani, and Vivian Brown (Columbia, SC: University of South Carolina Press, 1973), 315–26; Robert Pring-Mill, "The Lullian 'Art of Finding Truth': A Medieval System of Inquiry," *Catalan Review* 4 (1990), 55–74; Charles H. Lohr, "Metaphysics," in *The Cambridge History of Renaissance Philosophy*, ed. Charles B. Schmitt *et al.* (Cambridge University Press, 1988), 537–638, at 539–48; and most recently, Bonner, *The Art and Logic of Ramon Llull: A User's Guide.*

[42] *Vita,* §20, §19, §1, and §20.   [43] *Vita,* §14.   [44] *Vita,* §19.

win converts to the Christian religion by demonstrating certain Christian doctrines such as the Trinity and the Incarnation, and various scenes in the *Vita* depict him as successful in winning converts.[45]

Lull's belief that he uniquely possessed a God-given instrument for the conversion and salvation of Jews and Muslims is a key to understanding his missionary purpose. This belief is also at the center of the third moral dilemma described in his autobiography. This moral dilemma was controversial; the portion of the *Vita* describing it was omitted from eighteenth-century editions, perhaps because, as one interpreter puts it, the event could be "considered doctrinally or psychologically embarrassing."[46] The unshortened *Vita* relates that during an early period of spiritual crisis Lull was staying at a Dominican house in Genoa, and he was twice visited by a supernatural vision that indicated he could be saved only by joining the Dominican order. While Lull saw the invitation to join the Dominicans as a solution to his spiritual despair, he considered that the order had not been receptive to his *Art*. The apologetic program established by Dominicans at that time was not reconcilable with the procedures of Lull's *Art*, and the philosopher was not blind to the essential differences of their respective apologetic methods.[47] In contrast, the Franciscan order had looked favorably upon the *Art*, even to the extent that the general of the Franciscans, Raymond Gaufredi, had authorized Lull to teach it at the order's houses in Italy. The third moral dilemma, therefore, pits Lull's personal salvation against the future salvation of untold numbers of Jews and Muslims who would presumably benefit from the *Art*. Raymond considered:

> on the one hand he would be damned unless he remained with the Dominicans, while on the other hand his *Art* and books would be lost unless he remained with the Franciscans (*hinc sui damnationem, nisi ipse cum Praedicatoribus, hinc Artis et librorum, quos fecerat, perditionem, nisi ipse cum fratribus Minoribus moreretur*).[48]

This dilemma is generated by Lull's belief that he has the simultaneous obligations to: (1) preserve the divinely received *Art* for the salvation of

[45] *Vita*, §19, §26, §27, §37. For a discussion of the alleged rationalism of Lull's theology, insofar as Lull speaks of being able to "prove" (*manifestare*, §19; *probare*, §37) articles of faith such as the Trinity and the Incarnation, see Hillgarth, *Ramon Lull and Lullism*, 19–24; Bonner, *Doctor Illuminatus*, 49, and most recently, Paul Richard Blum, *Philosophy of Religion in the Renaissance* (Farnham: Ashgate Publishing, 2010), 1–14, 179. While the *Vita* appears to privilege the use of the *Art* with regard to Muslims, Lull saw it as equally applicable in addressing Jews. See Harvey J. Hames, *The Art of Conversion: Christianity and Kabbalah in the Thirteenth Century* (Leiden: Brill, 2000), especially ch. 2: "The Jew in Llull's Eyes," 83–117.
[46] Bonner, *Doctor Illuminatus*, 27, n. 79. The portion of the *Vita* featuring this moral dilemma (§§21–4) is omitted, for instance, from the text present in the *Acta Sanctorum*.
[47] See Anthony Bonner, "Ramon Llull and the Dominicans," *Catalan Review* 4 (1990), 377–92.
[48] *Vita*, §23.

others; and (2) secure his own salvation. In this scenario, both options are impossible to pursue simultaneously; he cannot be both a Franciscan and a Dominican and gain the benefits that each order will bring. There are two horns to this dilemma: by joining the Dominicans to save himself, his *Art* will be lost and future converts ungained; by not joining the Dominicans to pursue the Franciscan habit he will spread the *Art* to save souls but bring about his personal damnation.[49] The dilemma is a strict disjunction composed of contradictories, and each contradictory contains a command whose obligatory force cannot be overridden by Lull. Each option appears to have an insurmountable reason in favor of it, so strong that not to perform it, in his view, would bring justifiable blame.

A lesser evil calculation

The decision Lull makes while ensnared in this moral dilemma sets it apart from the two previous dilemmas in a significant respect. The *Vita* relates that Lull loved God and others infinitely more than he loved himself, and therefore:

> Raymond chose (which was most admirable of him) his own eternal damnation rather than the loss of the *Art* which he knew he had received from God for the salvation of the many and especially for the honor of God himself (*elegit, quod erat supermirabile, damnationem sui ipsius aeternam potius, quam quod Ars praedicta, quam nouerat se recepisse a Deo ad multorum saluationem et Dei honorem praecipue, perderetur*).[50]

This decision to sacrifice his salvation for others is significant because by it Lull selects one of the two options that he judged to be morally impermissible: he resolves to join the Franciscans and thereby preserve his *Art* and save the souls of others. There is some historical question over the extent of Lull's adherence to the Franciscans, notwithstanding Lull's inclusion in the early seventeenth-century history of the order, the *Annales Minorum*, yet the *Vita* reports that Lull did request the Franciscan habit but that the guardian (*gardianus*) of the order agreed to bestow it upon Lull only when Lull was closer to death.[51] Nevertheless, the *Vita* is clear in

---

[49] Of this dilemma, Bonner comments that "in spite of the atmosphere of acute psychological crisis in which events take place, the opposition between the two orders in their attitude toward Llull and his Art could scarcely be clearer," in "Ramon Llull and the Dominicans," 389. For a discussion of this dilemma as a "psychopathological crisis," see Batllori, *Ramon Lull I el Lul·lisme*, 18–21.

[50] *Vita*, §23. See also §24.

[51] Luke Wadding, *Annales Minorum seu trium ordinum a S. Francisco institutorum*, 32 vols. (Clarae Aquae [Quaracchi]: Typographia Collegii S. Bonaventurae, 1931–5), IV: 477–9, VI: 223–4, VI: 259–69; *Vita*, §23.

maintaining that Lull chose the Franciscans and by doing so selected one of the two prongs of the moral dilemma. In previous episodes, the *Vita* showed Lull turning to prayer with the expectation that a divine intervention would free him from his perplexity. Here, however, he commits an act he believes to be inconsistent with his salvation and resolves to seek the habit of the Franciscans. Perhaps the reason he diverts from his normal response is the divine source of both prongs of the dilemma: the God who bestowed the *Art* upon him (with the attendant obligation to preserve it) is the God who now commands a course of action inconsistent with its preservation. The moral dilemma stems from an inconsistency of divine commands uniquely communicated to Lull. It seems as though Lull believes God can intervene to save him from moral ensnarement by the world, but God will not intervene to save Lull from God. The inconsistency appears to originate from two distinct communications by God, where the first was the bestowal of the *Art* on the mountaintop and the second was the vision indicating his salvation in the Dominicans. The *Vita* suggests that Lull judged the damnation of many souls to weigh more heavily on himself than his own, so it is arguable that his deliberation involves an implicit appeal to the principle of choosing the lesser of two evils. In light of the tradition discussed in the previous chapters such an interpretation cannot be ruled out. On any interpretation, however, it can be stated with confidence that Lull is opposed to any egoistic foundation to moral choices, since in his discernment of courses of action his very eternal salvation is judged to be less significant than the salvation of others.

Moral dilemmas and divine commands

In twentieth-century discussions of moral dilemmas some have argued that among major moral systems, pure command theories (including the divine and communitarian varieties) are distinctive in their ability to admit of the existence of moral dilemmas without being inconsistent. Alan Donagan has defended this view in the course of arguing that rationalist moral systems – such as the Kantian or Thomistic systems – cannot consistently allow moral dilemmas.[52] A pure command theory need not posit that the source of moral commands issues perfectly consistent edicts. Such a view is

---

[52] Alan Donagan, "Consistency in Rationalist Moral Systems," *The Journal of Philosophy* 81 (1984), 291–309, and "Moral Dilemmas, Genuine and Spurious: A Comparative Anatomy," *Ethics* 104 (1993). For an argument that divine command theory and moral dilemmas are incompatible, see Edmund N. Santurri, *Perplexity in the Moral Life: Philosophical and Theological Considerations* (Charlottesville: University of Virginia Press, 1987), esp. ch. 4: "Divine Commands and Moral Dilemmas," 117–55.

consistent with what is found in the *Vita*, as Lull views God as the source of both prongs of his third moral dilemma. The *Vita* explicitly likens the third moral dilemma to the situation of Abraham of the Hebraic tradition, who had been promised descendants by God and then commanded to sacrifice his only son Isaac.[53] The analogy between Abraham and Lull, though not explored in much detail in the *Vita*, does highlight certain common features between both figures. They each appear to receive seemingly inconsistent communications from God and are forced to make a choice. In the end, Abraham is willing to sacrifice his son. Lull, in contrast, does not appear willing to sacrifice his *Art*, but instead is willing to sacrifice his soul. Both Lull and Abraham appear willing to perform an action that appears morally impermissible. Abraham's willingness to sacrifice Isaac appears to violate a moral prohibition of murder, as both Immanuel Kant and Søren Kierkegaard famously noted, and Lull's pursuit of a Franciscan habit appears to violate the divine injunction to seek salvation within the Dominican order.[54]

After Lull selects one of the two impermissible actions of this dilemma by joining the Dominicans, there does come another divine intervention that brings this third moral dilemma of the *Vita* in line with the previous two. The intervention in this case takes the form of an additional illumination (*illustratio*) whereby the Holy Spirit restored in Lull the hope for salvation that had been long lacking in his mind.[55] The intervention is perhaps analogous to the angelic appearance that prevents Abraham from sacrificing Isaac at the last moment. In Lull's case, since the dilemma of strict contradictories is generated by two inconsistent commands from God, a resolution is possible only with a divine suspension of one of them. The *illustratio* of Lull's mind as a resolution to the dilemma parallels the description Lull had given earlier of his reception of his *Art*; on the mountaintop God had illuminated (*illustrauit*) his mind in bestowing the *Art*.[56]

3.5 THE KING'S EDICT DILEMMA

The fourth and final moral dilemma depicted in the *Vita* occurs shortly after the third in the course of the narrative. Leaving Genoa, Lull boarded

---

[53] *Vita*, §24.
[54] See Kant, *Reason within the Boundaries of Reason Alone*, 6:87, *The Conflict of the Faculties*, VII: 62–5. Translations of both works are present in Immanuel Kant, *Religion and Rational Theology* (Cambridge University Press, 1996). See also Søren Kierkegaard, *Fear and Trembling; Repetition*, trans. Howard V. Hong and Edna H. Hong (Princeton University Press, 1983).
[55] *Vita*, §25.   [56] *Vita*, §14.

a ship to Tunis and upon arriving at his destination began his missionary work. The *Vita* explains that by using the principles of the *Art* to speak of the attributes of God, Lull enjoyed some success in persuading some Muslims about certain Christian doctrines. A perceptive nobleman, however, discerned Lull's intention to destroy the Muslim faith of the Tunisians and advised the king about Lull's activities. As a result, Lull was imprisoned, beaten, and ordered to be expelled from Tunis. When he was placed on a ship ready to sail back to Genoa, the king issued an edict stating that if Lull should turn up again in the country he would suffer death by stoning. Lull then believed for the fourth time that he was in a situation of *perplexitas*: the new dilemma concerned whether to flee Tunis or remain. If he left the city, the "souls which he had already prepared for Christian worship would slide back into the trap of eternal damnation (*animas, quas iam disposuerat cultui christiano, in laqueum relabi damnationis aeternae*)," as Lull had not completed the arrangements for their baptisms; and if he did not leave, he would face the madness (*insania*) of the crowd that had previously beat him and were now prepared to enact the king's edict.[57] In finding himself in this dilemma Lull must have additionally feared the loss of his *Art* that his death would bring, rather than simply death itself, since he had identified martyrdom as one of his life goals shortly after his conversion.

A providential solution

The dilemma in this case takes the form of the contradictories of leaving or not leaving and each contradictory brings with it a likely terrible outcome. Lull believes that leaving will entail the eternal damnation of the Saracens who are awaiting baptism, and not leaving will secure his death and plunge the *Art* into oblivion, presumably with the resultant future loss of souls who would otherwise have escaped damnation by means of the *Art*. That Lull believes he has the simultaneous obligations to remain and leave is suggested by the *Vita*'s description of Lull as a "man of God ... afflicted by the pangs of the perplexity (*perplexitatis aculeo vir Dei ... afflictus*)."[58] The *perplexitas* here is presented as more than a simple epistemic perplexity where Lull knows not what to do; he believes he experiences simultaneously demands of both remaining and leaving.

At this point, given the structure of at least the first two moral dilemmas discussed above, one would expect Lull to turn to the standard procedure of praying fervently. There is no explicit mention, however, of a turn to

[57] *Vita*, §29.   [58] *Vita*, §29.

petitionary prayer, but the *Vita* describes an unusual sequence of events that is likely meant to be understood as a divine intervention. The *Vita* explains that there suddenly appeared at that time in Tunis a certain Christian, "similar to Raymond in bearing and dress (*in gestu et habitu similem Raimundo*)" traveling through the city.[59] This man was mistaken for Lull and seized by the Saracen crowd. During this time the real Lull escaped the boat leading him away from Tunis and secretly boarded another that was returning to the port of Tunis. The positioning of this story in the narration suggests that the crowd's mistake bought some time for Lull to continue his missionary activities there. Lull remained in Tunis for three weeks before determining he could do no further work given the current situation. The episode concludes with safe escapes by Lull and the Lull look-alike.

3.6 PRINCIPLES OF THE LULLIAN MORAL UNIVERSE: PROVIDENCE OR MORAL LUCK?

In light of the four moral dilemmas analyzed above, it is possible now to draw in outline some main features of the moral universe depicted in Lull's autobiographical statement. The *Vita* presents the world as a place that entraps agents into situations of moral wrongdoing from which such agents are simply unable by their powers to escape. The impotence exhibited by such agents is not because of defects in the agent's moral knowledge or perseverance, but is simply the result of a hostile moral world that on occasion lays impossibilities on unsuspecting agents. For example, in the dilemma featuring the Saracen with the homicidal intention, Lull is not presented as generating the dilemma by acts of prior wrongdoing, but rather he believes himself inexplicably unable to avoid committing a moral failure. He must act and believes in doing so he will either violate a moral obligation of piety toward a teacher or violate a moral obligation of protecting his existence. While Lull does, in the end, avoid the commission of both of these wrongs, it is only because of some unforeseeable turn of events, namely, the unanticipated suicide of the Saracen. Lull views his release from this dilemma, as with the others, as an act of divine providence that has supervened upon the natural order. Perhaps a less theological account of these four dilemmas might describe them in contemporary language as "moral luck."[60] On either account, there is no evidence that agents can

---

[59] *Vita*, §30.

[60] For a discussion of moral luck, see Bernard Williams, *Moral Luck: Philosophical Papers 1973–1980* (Cambridge University Press, 1982), 20–39; Thomas Nagel, *Mortal Questions* (New York: Cambridge

always expect to be delivered from dilemmas by way of divine intervention or moral luck, even though Lull appears to view petitionary prayer as a means of insuring a deliverance from moral dilemmas.

Another way of expressing this dilemma-laden feature of the Lullian moral world is to say that, according to the *Vita*, moral dilemmas are not simply subjective or epistemic, but they are objective or real. The possibility of being caught in a moral dilemma comes from how the world is structured, rather than from the subjective conditions of knowledge that an agent may have in a given situation. An increase in knowledge does not improve an agent's ability to avoid moral wrongdoing.

It was noted above that by employing the technical terms *perplexus* and *perplexitas* in his discussion of conflicts of conscience, Lull preserves the nomenclature of his predecessors as well as his thirteenth-century contemporaries who endeavored to theorize about conflicts of conscience. Even though Lull's solution to moral dilemmas involving conscience stands in stark contrast with those thinkers who argued that a judgment of conscience that dictates the performance of an action contrary to the natural law or a command of God should be set aside, there is general agreement about the terminology for formulating the issue. Ultimately, while presenting moral dilemmas as a feature of the moral life, Lull pursues a theological course by recommending petitionary prayer as a solution. Petitionary prayer does not defuse the dilemma; rather, the *Vita* presents the divine as extricating Lull from the dilemma by supernatural means. In the Lullian moral world, only divine extraction from dilemmas allows an agent to avoid moral wrongdoing; the examples of such interventions from the *Vita* are the providential death of the Saracen, the appearance of a Lull look-alike, and the bestowal of new infused communications by God that supersede prior divine commands. The necessity of these divine interventions in the moral life suggests that the moral universe in itself is not consistently ordered and must be constantly readjusted by God for an agent to be successful in the course of life. In this Lullian view, the world itself is disordered, not simply agents who may disorder themselves. Certainly the latter is possible, as Lull's early life attests. Three of the moral dilemmas described in the *Vita* are subsequent to Lull's conversion to penitence and thereby occur after his early life of profligacy. The divine interventions do not heal a fallen moral agent, but rather correct situations in the world that entrap moral agents.

At this point an objection to Lull's position on moral dilemmas is in order. One might be tempted to argue that Lull cannot consistently claim that moral dilemmas exist and at the same time endorse petitionary prayer as the recourse for perplexed agents. This objection adapts an argument found in twentieth-century discussions of moral dilemmas that holds that agents who believe themselves in moral dilemmas cannot consistently ask for advice when trapped in such situations, because advice is superfluous when wrongdoing is unavoidable. Terrance McConnell has argued that it is "irrational" for agents who believe themselves to be in moral dilemmas to seek advice on how to act, since on the assumption that moral dilemmas exist the only possible counsel is that the agent "ought to do each (or both) of two actions" constituting the dilemma.[61] In other words, if one believes oneself to be in a moral dilemma, one will never ask for counsel about which prong of the dilemma should be chosen, since advice can only take the form of recommending the impossible. This contemporary objection can be adapted and advanced against the view set forth in the *Vita* in the following way: if moral dilemmas exist, why is it rational to seek advice from God in the form of petitionary prayer? As a turn to petitionary prayer is Lull's standard recourse in the *Vita*, an answer to this objection is warranted.

In light of the preceding analyses of Lull's four moral dilemmas, two replies to this objection are possible. First, it can be said that the prominence of divine commands in generating Lull's moral dilemmas justifies seeking advice from God (i.e., praying), since the source of Lull's perceived moral obligations and the target of his petitionary prayers are identical: the God who commands inconsistent actions is the same God to whom Lull prays. In the case of the first and third dilemmas of the *Vita*, Lull escapes wrongdoing only with the promulgation of new divine commands that supersede previous commands. So, Lull's conception of the source of moral obligation warrants advice-seeking of a particular kind, namely, petitionary prayer. A second and more substantive reply to the objection against seeking advice is possible, one that is applicable regardless of whether one is seeking advice from human or divine counselors. Seeking advice need not be irrational for those trapped in moral dilemmas if the actions constituting the prongs of the dilemma differ in seriousness. While both actions of the prongs of the dilemma may be impermissible, they may not be actions of equal gravity. The Gregorian tradition of the lesser evil, examined in the previous

---

[61] Terrance C. McConnell, "Moral Dilemmas and Consistency in Ethics," *Canadian Journal of Philosophy* 8 (1978), 269–87, at 281.

chapters, suggests that advice-seeking by agents trapped in moral dilemmas is eminently rational, even though the advice offered will never free the agent from the commission of wrongdoing altogether. In light of the Gregorian tradition, advice could take two forms: the simple endorsement that the lesser evil should be chosen over the greater, and further, an identification of a lesser evil for a given moral dilemma.

The distinctiveness of Lull's position can be seen by contrasting his view with alternative theological views on the existence of moral dilemmas. First, Lull's position can be set against the view that moral dilemmas do exist as possibilities in the moral universe, but agents never experience them because a providential God protects human beings from them. On this view, the universe is replete with moral traps, but providence carefully directs every agent safely around them throughout the course of life. Peter Geach has defended this view by saying:

if God governs all events by his providence, he can see to it that circumstances in which a man is inculpably faced by a choice between forbidden acts do not occur. Of course such circumstances (with the clause "and there is no way out" written into their description) are consistently describable; but God's providence could ensure that they do not in fact arise.[62]

According to Geach, the moral life could lay impossibilities or conflicting moral demands on an agent, but never does, because of God's ongoing careful providence. Lull's position is not that of Geach, because Lull clearly sees himself as already lodged in moral dilemmas when he appeals for divine aid. On Geach's view, God's providence secures agents from ever experiencing moral dilemmas, whereas in Lull's moral universe God extricates agents who are already ensnared in them. Further, Lull's position can also be contrasted with the view that moral dilemmas exist but antecedent petitionary prayer inoculates agents from ever experiencing them. In this way, the petitionary prayer is not a solution for an experienced moral dilemma, but is a request that one not be placed in a dilemma in the first place. Again, Lull's position is not this one, since antecedent prayer does not protect Lull from ending up in moral dilemmas.

If Lull were simply saying that agents at times do not know how to act and should pray in such cases, he would merely be defending a long-standing traditional commonplace. Instead, Lull is offering a distinctive position on the question of moral dilemmas, since he defends the view

---

[62] Peter Geach, *God and the Soul* (New York: Schocken Books, 1969), 128. For a critique of this view, see Alan Donagan, *The Theory of Morality* (University of Chicago Press, 1977), 147–8.

that unsuspecting agents do get trapped in discrete situations of unavoidable moral wrongdoing as part of the moral life, and that such agents are impotent to extricate themselves from them. Lull never suggests that his experience of moral dilemmas is atypical for the moral life. He does not present himself as encountering a moral world different from that of others. As was discussed above, Lull is not hesitant to draw analogies between his experiences and biblical characters. In addition to the mention of Abraham, Lull compares his struggles to those experienced by Job, the prophet David, and the disciple Peter.[63] Ultimately Lull defends the view that only divine intrusions can spare agents from impending moral wrongdoing, and petitionary prayer will bring about such intrusions. By depicting the moral life in this way Lull's *Vita* carves out a distinctive position in the moral dilemma debate of the medieval period. He appeals to God as a *deus ex machina* who intervenes to protect an agent from a disordered moral universe that lays impossibilities upon agents. The Lullian moral universe is a broken one, so without petitionary prayer and the subsequent divine interventions, agents will face dilemmatic situations of inescapable moral wrongdoing. Human agents unwittingly find themselves ensnared in situations devoid of *ad intra* resolutions, and only *ad extra* intervention by the divine can save agents from moral wrongdoing.

[63] *Vita*, §20, §45. See the notes in Bonner, *Doctor Illuminatus*, 25.

CHAPTER 4

Thomas Aquinas, moral dilemmas, and a missing article from Quodlibet XII

A little more than two years before his death, Thomas Aquinas held his final quodlibetal disputation during Lent in 1272.[1] This event was one of the last official duties Aquinas performed as a master of theology during his second regency at the University of Paris, and by all indications it was a lively affair. It took place during a tumultuous period that led to a general strike at the university, but even if it had been conducted during a relatively normal academic period it would still have been an event not to be missed. Quodlibetal disputations were generally interesting, since they were unscripted debates open to the public, overseen by a master of a discipline, with topics for discussion not decided beforehand. Questions concerning anything (*de quolibet*) could be brought forward by anyone (*a quolibet*) in attendance.[2] The oral debate would be refined and sometimes put to writing, and the edited version served as the official record of the event. Given the quodlibetal format, the questions were unpredictable and often covered an exceedingly wide range of topics. One historian of the

---

[1] For the dating and context of the twelfth quodlibet, see René Antoine Gauthier, OP, "Introduction au Quodlibet XII," in *Quaestiones de quolibet*, in Thomas Aquinas, *Opera omnia* (Rome: Commissio Leonina, 1996), xxv.2: 152–60; Kevin White, "The *Quodlibeta* of Thomas Aquinas in the Context of his Work," in *Theological Quodlibeta in the Middle Ages*, ed. Christopher Schabel, 2 vols. (Leiden: Brill, 2006–07), 1: 49–133, at 102–10; and Simon Tugwell, OP, "The Life and Works of Thomas Aquinas," in *Albert and Thomas: Selected Writings* (Mahwah, NJ: Paulist Press, 1988), 201–67, at 318–19, n. 262. For the texts of Aquinas cited below, I have used the Leonine *Opera omnia* edition when possible. For works not yet available in the Leonine edition, I have used: *Scriptum super libros Sententiarum*, ed. P. Mandonnet and P. Maria Fabianus Moos, 4 vols. (Paris: Lethielleux, 1929–47); *Commentum in quartum librum Sententiarum*, in *Opera omnia*, vol. xi, ed. Stanislaus Fretté (Paris: Vivès, 1874); *Super epistolas S. Pauli lectura*, ed. Raphaelus Cai, OP, 8th edn, 2 vols. (Rome: Marietti, 1953); and *De correctione fraterna*, in *Quaestiones disputatae*, ed. P. Bazzi *et al.*, 9th edn, 2 vols. (Rome: Marietti, 1953) ii: 793–802.

[2] John F. Wippel, "Quodlibetal Questions, Chiefly in Theology Faculties," in *Les questions disputées et les questions quodlibétiques dans les facultés de théologie, de droit et de médecine*, by Bernardo Bazàn *et al.* (Turnhout: Brepols, 1985), 151–222, at 165–6; Jacqueline Hamesse, "Theological *Quaestiones Quodlibetales*," in *Theological Quodlibeta in the Middle Ages*, ed. Schabel, 1: 17–48, at 42. See also Leonard E. Boyle, "The Quodlibets of St. Thomas and Pastoral Care," *The Thomist* 37 (1974), 232–56, at 232.

quodlibetal genre has remarked that anyone who was willing to hold a quodlibetal disputation must have had "a presence of mind quite out of the common, and a competency almost universal in scope," and "many a master refused to risk himself at it."[3] In the words of a thirteenth-century Dominican witness to such events, quodlibetal disputations were "on anything at anyone's will (*de quolibet ad voluntatem cuiuslibet*)."[4] It is not surprising, therefore, that the questions put forward at Aquinas's last disputation did not disappoint. Some concerned issues in metaphysics (e.g., Can God make contradictories exist at the same time?), and others dealt with particulars of sacramental theology (e.g., Can a priest ever permissibly reveal a confession?).[5] There were a good number on ethical topics (e.g., Are the moral virtues connected?), and even the occasional odd questions difficult to categorize even on the most generous interpretation of thirteenth-century subject taxonomies, such as: "Is truth stronger than wine, a king, or a woman?"[6] For the present purpose, one article from this disputation – now commonly called *Quodlibet XII* – is of particular relevance because it pertains to the subject of moral dilemmas. At some point in the debate, someone (we know not who) asked "whether someone is able to be perplexed (*utrum aliquis possit esse perplexus*)."[7] That such a question was put to Aquinas is particularly significant because nowhere in the Thomistic corpus does Aquinas approach the concept of perplexity as a direct subject of inquiry. No article in the *Summa theologiae* is dedicated exclusively to the issue, and the only remarks on the topic are side comments that surface occasionally in the analyses of other issues.

Unfortunately, Aquinas's answer to this question on perplexity is not extant. Only the question survives, absent a reply, designated in modern editions simply as *De perplexitate*, question 22, article 3 of *Quodlibet XII*. Such difficulties plague other parts of *Quodlibet XII* as well, which on the whole appears less tidy than the received text of Aquinas's other quodlibetal disputations. On this basis, many commentators consider the text of *Quodlibet XII* to be a *reportatio* by one of Aquinas's students or at least

[3] P. Glorieux, *La littérature quodlibétique*, 2 vols. (Paris: J. Vrin, 1925–35), II: 10–11, quoted in M.-D. Chenu, OP, *Toward Understanding Saint Thomas*, trans. A.-M. Landry, OP and D. Hughes, OP (Chicago: Henry Regnery Company, 1964), 92–3.

[4] This designation is given by Humbert of Romans (*c.* 1200–77), the fifth master of the Dominican Order, in his *Instructiones de officiis ordinis*, c. 12, in *Opera de vita regulari*, ed. Joachim Joseph Berthier, 2 vols. (Rome: Typis A. Befani, 1888–89), II: 260.

[5] *Quaestiones de quolibet*, XII, q. 2, a. 1 (Editio Leonina, XXV.2: 399); *Quaestiones de quolibet*, XII, q. 10, a. 2 (Editio Leonina, XXV.2: 411).

[6] *Quaestiones de quolibet*, XII, q. 14, a. 1 (Editio Leonina, XXV.2: 416); *Quaestiones de quolibet*, XII, q. 13, a. 1 (Editio Leonina, XXV.2: 414).

[7] *Quaestiones de quolibet*, XII, q. 22, a. 3 (Editio Leonina, XXV.2: 429).

an unfinished work of Aquinas.[8] The editor of the Leonine edition of Aquinas's *quaestiones quodlibetales* argues that its rough form is because of Aquinas's departure from Paris for Italy immediately following Easter in April 1272 to attend in early June a chapter meeting in Florence of his Dominican province before going on to Naples. There Aquinas established a theological *studium generale* or Dominican house of studies for the study of sacred theology. Therefore, the reason for *Quodlibet XII*'s unfinished format is simply that "in these conditions, Aquinas had not the leisure to edit his dispute."[9]

Even though Aquinas's article on *perplexitas* does not survive, fortunately Aquinas's views on moral dilemmas can be gathered from those several discussions scattered throughout the Thomistic corpus. Resorting to such an approach is warranted because Aquinas does raise the issue with regularity in various works when treating of other subjects, such as whether an erroneous conscience binds or whether authorities can experience conflicting obligations when carrying out the duties of an office. By examining these other discussions carefully, Aquinas's answer to the question of whether someone is able to be morally perplexed can be discerned and confidently stated. Such a piecemeal approach is the best option in the absence of the text on perplexity for *Quodlibet XII*.

The present chapter examines those texts where Aquinas explicitly discusses the issue of moral perplexity. In addition to having this primarily exegetical orientation, the chapter also warrants a significant historiographical focus. Unlike the contributions of other medieval thinkers, the remarks of Aquinas on the topic of moral dilemmas have been a matter of some attention among present-day philosophers. Some have sought predecessors in establishing their own views. Others have turned to Aquinas as a foil for their positions. Since Aquinas has been used in both ways, there is little unanimity among twentieth-century interpreters concerning Aquinas's actual position on moral dilemmas. To interpret Aquinas correctly, the present chapter divides into five sections. Section 1 examines the views of a leading popularizer of several of Aquinas's texts. Section 2 divides the main texts of Aquinas on moral dilemmas into six groups. Next, section 3 evaluates several debates among contemporary philosophers. The penultimate section

---

[8] On the unfinished character of *Quodlibet XII*, see Leonard Boyle, "The Quodlibets of St. Thomas," 236; James A. Weisheipl, OP, *Friar Thomas D'Aquino: His Life, Thought, and Works*, 2nd edn (Washington, DC: The Catholic University of America Press, 1983), 367; Jean-Pierre Torrell, OP, *Saint Thomas Aquinas*, trans. Robert Royal, 2 vols. (Washington, DC: The Catholic University of America Press, 1996–2003), II: 209; and Gauthier, "Introduction au Quodlibet XII," 152–60.

[9] Gauthier, "Introduction au Quodlibet XII," 160.

addresses an issue left open by Aquinas, and the final one concludes the chapter with some remarks on a textual issue concerning Aquinas's missing article on *perplexitas*.

4.1 ALAN DONAGAN'S INTERPRETATION OF AQUINAS

In several works, including *The Theory of Morality*, the twentieth-century ethicist Alan Donagan contends that a moral system is internally consistent only on the condition that it precludes the possibility that a moral agent who has committed no prior wrong could end up in a situation where there is an inescapable conflict of duties or obligations.[10] In other words, a moral system is inconsistent if it allows for situations in which innocent agents find themselves in ethical situations commonly described as perplexities, dilemmas, predicaments, or quandaries. In setting forth his argument, Donagan repeatedly claims to be the beneficiary of a position found in the writings of Thomas Aquinas.[11] He appeals to Aquinas's distinction between perplexity *secundum quid* and perplexity *simpliciter*, where the former describes an individual experiencing a conflict of obligations arising from the prior commission of some morally impermissible action, and the latter describes an individual experiencing a conflict of obligations given no prior misdeed. Donagan claims that Aquinas and he agree that situations of perplexity *secundum quid* do exist, whereas situations of perplexity *simpliciter* do not. Further, Donagan claims that Aquinas agrees with his position that the existence of situations of perplexity *secundum quid* can never call into question the internal consistency of an ethical system. Despite tethering his position to four texts from the Thomistic corpus, Donagan has been criticized by several contemporary commentators who allege that he significantly distorts Aquinas's position on moral dilemmas in several ways.

Oddly, this contemporary dispute has focused almost exclusively on the four texts of Aquinas cited by Donagan (*Summa theologiae* I–II, q. 19, a. 6, ad 3; II–II, q. 62, a. 2, ad 2; III, q. 64, a. 6, ad 3; *De veritate*, q. 17, a. 4, ad 8). As this chapter will demonstrate, several other texts in Aquinas's writings present the distinction more thoroughly. This widespread practice of limiting the discussion exclusively to these four texts (or a subset of them) has

---

[10] Alan Donagan, *The Theory of Morality* (The University of Chicago Press, 1977), 144–53; "Consistency in Rationalist Moral Systems," *The Journal of Philosophy* 81 (1984), 291–309; and "Moral Dilemmas, Genuine and Spurious: A Comparative Anatomy," *Ethics* 104 (1993), 7–21.

[11] Donagan, *The Theory of Morality*, 144–5; "Consistency in Rationalist Moral Systems," 305–6; "Moral Dilemmas, Genuine and Spurious," 10.

caused some thinkers to misstate Aquinas's position.[12] Two factors explain the focus on these four canonical texts to the exclusion of other (arguably) more significant discussions of moral perplexity in the Thomistic corpus. To begin with, as mentioned above, no lengthy or sustained treatment of moral perplexity has survived in the writings of Aquinas. As a result, in order to discern Aquinas's doctrine of perplexity one is left to glean insights by examining his application of the distinction between the two kinds of perplexity in a wide variety of discussions throughout the corpus. The scattered use, however, of the distinction between perplexity *simpliciter* and perplexity *secundum quid* is alone not sufficient to account for the rather selective use of the four "canonical" texts by commentators. Turning to the second factor, it appears that most twentieth-century philosophers who broach Aquinas's discussions in their studies on moral dilemmas explicitly acknowledge a debt to Donagan for having brought to light the four texts.[13] Their dependence upon Donagan has shortchanged the range of texts that should be included in any analysis of Aquinas's position on the question of moral dilemmas.

Identifying Aquinas's true views on moral dilemmas has implications for understanding the larger issue of moral dilemma theory in the Middle Ages. There has been a significant increase in the number of contemporary philosophers who hold that innocent agents can indeed find themselves in genuine moral dilemmas and that any system that does not account for these occurrences is manifestly deficient.[14] The increase of proponents of

---

[12] They include: Kenneth E. Kirk, *Conscience and Its Problems: An Introduction to Casuistry* (London: Longmans, Green and Co., 1933 [repr. Louisville: Westminster John Knox Press, 1999]), 322; Georg Henrik von Wright, *An Essay in Deontic Logic and the General Theory of Action* (Amsterdam: North-Holland Publishing Company, 1968), 81; Donagan, *The Theory of Morality*, 254, "Consistency in Rationalist Moral Systems," 305, and "Moral Dilemmas, Genuine and Spurious," 10; Christopher W. Gowans, "The Debate on Moral Dilemmas," in *Moral Dilemmas*, ed. Christopher W. Gowans (New York: Oxford University Press, 1987), 3–33, at 31; Edmund N. Santurri, *Perplexity in the Moral Life: Philosophical and Theological Considerations* (Charlottesville: University Press of Virginia, 1987), 223; Walter Sinnott-Armstrong, *Moral Dilemmas* (Oxford: Blackwell, 1988), 235; Michael J. Zimmerman, "Lapses and Moral Dilemmas," *Philosophical Papers* 17 (1988), 103–12, at 108, 111; John O'Neill, "'The Same Thing Therefore Ought to Be and Ought not to Be': Anselm on Conflicting Oughts," *Heythrop Journal* 35 (1994), 312–14, at 314.

[13] See the preceding note above, with the exception of Kirk and von Wright. In *The Theory of Morality* (254) Donagan credits Kirk and von Wright for bringing to light the four passages dealing with perplexity. See Kirk, *Conscience and Its Problems*, 322 and von Wright, *An Essay in Deontic Logic*, 81. Von Wright credits a private discussion with Peter Geach to be the origin of the identification of the four texts (81).

[14] On the shift in recent discussions of moral perplexity, see Terrance C. McConnell, "Moral Dilemmas and Consistency in Ethics," *Canadian Journal of Philosophy* 8 (1978), 269–87, at 269–70; and Alasdair MacIntyre, "Moral Dilemmas," *Philosophy and Phenomenological Research* 50 (1990), 367–82, at 367–70.

such a position marks a shift away from the more traditional account of moral dilemmas. Immanuel Kant's denial that duties can conflict and John Stuart Mill's claim in *Utilitarianism* that moral conflicts can be solved by appeals to the notion of utility are perhaps the best-known examples from modern philosophy of the rejection of the existence of moral dilemmas.[15] As a few contemporary philosophers have begun to go farther back in the history of philosophy in search of predecessors for their positions, the meaning of some texts of Aquinas has become a source for disputes. In a significant sense the divide between Donagan and several of his opponents can be viewed as attempts on both sides of the moral perplexity debate to claim Aquinas as a philosophical ally. Thus, in answering the historical question as to the true doctrine of Aquinas on this issue one does contribute to the contemporary debate presently in progress. By taking all of Aquinas's texts on moral perplexity into account, including the canonical four, this chapter demonstrates that Aquinas unequivocally does deny the existence of cases of perplexity *simpliciter* and thereby cannot properly be allied with more recent trends in the moral perplexity debate. He does, however, provide a wide-ranging defense of the existence of prior-fault dilemmas, which he designates as situations of perplexity *secundum quid*.

4.2 THE THOMISTIC TEXTS

In the Thomistic corpus, there are eighteen texts that explicitly discuss situations where an agent appears to be perplexed (*perplexus*), that is, entangled in a moral dilemma. Collectively, these texts represent a wide range of genres from Aquinas's writing career: biblical commentaries, disputed questions, quodlibetal questions, as well as the major works of theological synthesis, including the commentary on the *Sententiae* of Peter Lombard and the *Summa theologiae*. These texts treating moral dilemmas also represent the complete span of Aquinas's writing career, since they occur in early, middle, and late works. Aquinas does not appear to have modified his view of moral dilemmas, as he remained committed to the distinction between the perplexity *simpliciter* of innocent agents and the perplexity *secundum quid* of guilty ones. Additionally, while the greater part of those texts pre-date Aquinas's *Quodlibet XII*, at least two were likely composed after this event.

---

[15] Texts illustrating the disavowal of conflicts of duty on the part of John Stuart Mill, Immanuel Kant, and others are assembled in *Moral Dilemmas*, ed. Gowans, 34–51, 52–61. For an analysis of the Kantian rejection of moral dilemmas, see Donagan, "Consistency in Rationalist Moral Systems," 291–309. Mill's position is examined in Robert W. Hoag, "Mill on Conflicting Moral Obligations," *Analysis* 43 (1983), 49–54.

Although all of these texts are scattered in a diversity of works written at different times and for different purposes, they are sufficiently embedded in the whole of the Thomistic corpus to allow one to draw some distinct conclusions regarding Aquinas's views on moral dilemmas, even in the absence of what would have been Aquinas's formal and definitive treatment of the issue in the unfinished *Quodlibet XII.*

These eighteen passages, taken together, present eighteen distinct examples of situations where an individual is believed to be perplexed or entangled in a moral dilemma. Sometimes the same example surfaces in several texts, but often an example is unique to one text. Aquinas never classifies these dilemmas according to the traditional division of spiritual and corporeal perplexity endorsed by William of Auxerre in the *Summa aurea* and by the authors of the *Summa Halesiana.* Instead, Aquinas is content to promote the *simpliciter/secundum quid* distinction. For the purposes of the present inquiry, these eighteen examples can be organized by type into six classes: *Malformed Conscience Dilemmas, Wayward Cleric Dilemmas, Evil Intention Dilemmas, Layperson Dilemmas, Infelicitous Oath Dilemmas,* and finally, *Hidden Option Dilemmas.*

Malformed Conscience Dilemmas

The largest of the six groups of moral dilemmas discussed by Aquinas consists of examples featuring an agent who possesses an ill-formed conscience dictating the performance of an act that is morally impermissible. Such an agent seems to have the irreconcilable obligations to follow the dictate of the ill-formed conscience and break a commandment or moral rule in doing so. As has been seen, the issue of moral perplexity stemming from an erroneous conscience was a topic analyzed by many medieval theologians and canonists of an earlier period well before Aquinas, and the topic continued to be discussed for centuries afterward.[16] In approaching Aquinas's analysis of this class of moral dilemmas, it may be helpful to note that

---

[16] The literature on the history of the problem of the ill-formed conscience is vast. Particularly noteworthy are: Odon Lottin, ed., *Psychologie et morale aux XIIᵉ et XIIIᵉ siècles,* 6 vols. (Louvain: Abbaye du Mont César, 1942–60), II: 354–406; Xavier G. Colavechio, O.Praem., *Erroneous Conscience and Obligations: A Study of the Teaching from the Summa Halesiana, Saint Bonaventure, Saint Albert the Great, and Saint Thomas Aquinas* (Washington, DC: The Catholic University of America Press, 1961); Michael G. Baylor, *Action and Person: Conscience in Late Scholasticism and the Young Luther* (Leiden: Brill, 1977), esp. chs. 2 and 3: "Conscience in the *Via Antiqua*: The Background to Aquinas," 20–69, and "Conscience in the *Via Moderna*: William of Ockham on Conscience," 70–118; and Richard Schenk, OP, *"Perplexus supposito quodam*: Notizen zu einem vergessenen Schlüsselbegriff thomanischer Gewissenslehre," *Recherches de Théologie et Philosophie médiévales* 57 (1990), 62–95. For more recent analyses, see Stéphan Geonget, *La notion de perplexité a la Renaissance* (Geneva:

Aquinas believes that to violate a dictate of conscience by a free act of the will, even if that conscience is ill-informed, is always to commit a sin.[17] To follow an erroneous conscience, however, can also be a sin.

In all, Thomas gives five distinct examples – some more unusual than others, but all unusual – where an agent is presented as *perplexus* because of a badly formed conscience:

1. A fornicator's conscience dictates that he must fornicate, but fornication is prohibited.[18]
2. A tyrant's conscience dictates that he must murder holy men, but doing so is evil.[19]
3. A heretic's conscience dictates that he must speak against the faith, but to do so is to incur a mortal sin.[20]
4. An unbeliever's conscience dictates that he must follow the Old Law and reject the New Law, but to do so is prohibited.[21]
5. A thief's conscience dictates that he must steal, but stealing is forbidden.[22]

With these five, Aquinas exhibits an assortment of individuals each of whom has adopted a particularly errant moral view and subsequently possesses a conscience that mandates the performance of a deed that is proscribed by the natural law, a divine command, or both. Each individual is judged *perplexus* in the sense of being entangled by seemingly inconsistent demands: one must always follow the dictates of conscience and one must always follow the commandments and the natural law. This entanglement also renders the agent confused, since the agent is thereby unsure about how to act in such cases. To take the first example, the fornicator believes himself to be under an obligation to fornicate, but fornication is prohibited expressly by a revealed Mosaic commandment and by medieval natural law theory. If the agent abides by his conscience and thereby

---

Librairie Droz, 2006), 215–51, and Takashi Shogimen, *Ockham and Political Discourse in the Late Middle Ages* (Cambridge University Press, 2007), 123–35.

[17] Aquinas stresses the serious obligation of agents to form their consciences properly. Regarding the formation of conscience he contends that "ignorance of the law is not an excuse (*ignorantia iuris non excusat*)" unless the ignorance is invincible, "as is the case in madness or insanity (*sicut . . . in furiosis et amentibus*)." Since agents are culpable for improperly formed consciences, it is incumbent upon them to form their consciences by taking into account genuine moral prohibitions. See *Quaestiones de quolibet*, III, q. 12, a. 2, ad 2 (Editio Leonina, XXV.2: 286), and *Super Galatas*, cap. 5, 1, §282 (Marietti, I: 626).

[18] See *In II librum Sententiarum*, d. 39, q. 3, a. 3, arg. 5, ad 5 (Mandonnet, 1001, 1004); *De veritate*, q. 17, a. 4, ad 8 (Editio Leonina, XXII.2: 526); and *Super Romanos*, cap. 14, 2, §1120 (Marietti, I: 208).

[19] See *In II librum Sententiarum*, d. 39, q. 3, a. 3, arg. 5, ad 5 (Mandonnet, 1001, 1004).

[20] See *Quaestiones de quolibet*, III, q. 12, a. 2, arg. 2, ad 2 (Editio Leonina, XXV.2: 285, 286).

[21] See *Super Galatas*, cap. 5, 1, §282 (Marietti, I: 626).

[22] See *Super Romanos*, cap. 14, 2, §1120 (Marietti, I: 208).

fornicates, he sins; and likewise if he ignores the dictate of conscience and omits to fornicate, he also sins. The two options are contradictories, so at least one is unable to be avoided. Admittedly the example is unusual, since presumably there are not many agents whose consciences insist upon obligatory fornication, but the example nonetheless vividly illustrates a possible situation of moral perplexity stemming from a malformed conscience. This example involving fornication was quite common in discussions of the obligatory character of conscience among thirteenth-century theologians, at times augmented so that an agent believed fornication to be necessary for salvation.[23] Perhaps the background of these discussions was Augustine of Hippo's account of certain pagan religious rites in the early chapters of his *De civitate Dei*. In any event, an agent with an ill-formed conscience commanding fornication seems bound to sin and thereby is characterized as *perplexus* by Aquinas.

Likewise, the examples involving the murderous tyrant, the heretical preacher, the unbeliever, and the thief are similarly constructed to illustrate seemingly inescapable situations of moral wrongdoing, since such agents possess consciences that mandate the commission of impermissible deeds. While Aquinas designates each agent as *perplexus*, since the omission and performance of those actions will necessarily result in sin, he does differentiate between the two senses of the term noted earlier. The agents are judged by Aquinas as not absolutely perplexed (*perplexus simpliciter*), but only qualifiedly or in a certain respect perplexed (*perplexus secundum quid*). Such agents are perplexed only insofar as their consciences are badly formed; had they not previously been negligent in forming their consciences they would not be perplexed. All is not lost, however, for the agents: Aquinas notes that they can reform their consciences and thereby avoid sin. A newly and properly formed conscience will recognize that there are no true obligations to fornicate, murder, preach heresy, reject the New Law, or steal, and hence the mandate of conscience evaporates with improved moral formation. The prong of the dilemma obliging an impermissible act disappears with additional moral formation, and the agent is released from the dilemma unscathed. Aquinas does not consider the agents in these cases to be inescapably perplexed, since in each case the agent is able to "put away the erroneous conscience (*conscientiam erroneam deponere*)"[24] or

---

[23] See, for example, the text of an anonymous thirteenth-century work, as well as one from Walter of Château-Thierry (d. 1249), both extracted in Lottin, *Psychologie et morale aux XIIᵉ et XIIIᵉ siècles*, II: 368, II: 371, II: 383.

[24] *In II librum Sententiarum*, d. 39, q. 3, a. 3, ad 5 (Mandonnet, 1004); *De veritate*, q. 17, a. 4, ad 8 (Editio Leonina, XXII.2: 526); *Quaestiones de quolibet*, III, q. 12, a. 2, ad 2 (Editio Leonina, XXV.2: 286); *Super Galatas*, cap. 5, 1, §282 (Marietti, I: 626).

"send away the erroneous conscience (*conscientiam erroneam dimittere*)"[25] and thereby avoid the commission of a sin. Thus, each agent is not *perplexus simpliciter*, but only *perplexus secundum quid*, with a way out of the moral entanglement.

Thomas Aquinas's solution to avoiding sin in moral dilemmas of the malformed conscience variety appears to be a straightforward one: agents should simply set aside their mistaken consciences and replace them with well-formed ones. Until such agents overcome their malformed consciences, they are in a condition of qualified perplexity. Aquinas's view implies that if agents ever discover their consciences to issue dictates that oppose the natural law or a divine command, then those agents have sufficient evidence to conclude that they have been negligent in forming their consciences, and so an examination of conscience is warranted. Present-day readers, however, may find Aquinas's solution to be problematic; it appears to call into question the integrity of the powers of moral discernment if an agent's reasoning can – and should – be so easily abandoned on occasions of perplexity. Aquinas's answer is, after all, that one should set aside a judgment of conscience upon encountering a moral dilemma. Such an evaluation of Aquinas's solution, however, is precipitous and can be avoided when Aquinas's view is placed within larger discussions of conscience that regularly concede human fallibility. What Aquinas is defending is not the abandonment of practical reason itself in the case of moral dilemmas, but the abandonment of a particular erroneous judgment of conscience. To say that conscience should be set aside is not to call into question the integrity of practical reason, but to contend that one can make errors in moral reasoning, and good evidence of prior errant moral reasoning is a judgment of conscience that mandates the performance of an act that is contrary to the natural law or an explicit command of God.

The position Aquinas defends concerning these *Malformed Conscience Dilemmas* is not original with him. As was considered earlier, it was present in William of Auxerre's *Summa aurea* and in the Franciscan *Summa Halesiana*, and can also be found in earlier medieval works.[26] Aquinas's

---

[25] *Super Romanos*, cap. 14, 2, §1120 (Marietti, 1: 208).

[26] For the presence of the expression "to set aside conscience (*deponere/dimittere conscientiam*)" in earlier thinkers, including Peter of Capua (d. 1214) and Peter of Poitiers (1130–1215), see Artur Michael Landgraf, "Der '*Casus perplexus*' in der Frühscholastik," *Collectanea Franciscana* 29 (1959), 74–86, at 75 and 78–9. For the *Summa aurea*, see William of Auxerre, *Summa aurea*, ed. Jean Ribaillier, 7 vols. (Paris: Editions du Centre National de la Recherche Scientifique, 1980–87), III.2: 1045: "[perplexity] is solved through the putting away of the erroneous conscience ([*perplexitas*] *solvitur per depositionem erronee conscientie*)." For the *Summa Halesiana*, see Alexander of Hales, *Summa theologica*, 4 vols. (Clarae Aquae [Quaracchi]: Typographia Collegii S. Bonaventurae, 1924–48),

immediate source for this view could be his teacher, Albert the Great (*c.* 1200–80), who in his early *Summa de creaturis* argued for the view that conscience is an act (*actus*) of practical reason. Albert contended that "conscience is a conclusion of practical reason from two premises, of which the major is from synderesis, and the minor from reason (*conscientia conclusio est rationis practicae ex duobus praemissis, quarum major est synderesis, et minor rationis*)."[27] According to Albert, therefore, conscience is a judgment drawn from a pair of premises, but the binding character of that judgment is always contingent upon having assumed true premises. In discussing the possibility that one might assume a faulty premise, Albert writes:

> If it should be argued that, according to this, someone will be perplexed (for if one obeys conscience one will sin, doing what is not right, or if one will not obey conscience, he will sin, acting against conscience), it should be said that one will not be perplexed, because one is able to put away conscience (*Si objiciatur, quod secundum hoc aliquis erit perplexus: sive enim sequatur conscientiam, peccabit faciendo non rectum: sive non sequatur eam, peccabit faciendo contra conscientiam. Dicendum est, quod not erit perplexus: quia potest deponere conscientiam*).[28]

Albert enjoins such agents to examine their minor premises, as they are often (*frequenter*) false, and when they are finally discerned to be false, agents are obliged to put away (*deponere*) any judgments based on them. Aquinas appears to accept, on the whole, this Albertist view concerning the erroneous conscience throughout his writings, and this context can preclude two possible misinterpretations of Aquinas's views. Aquinas does not hold that a particular judgment of conscience is to be followed unqualifiedly, and he does not hold that setting aside a particular judgment of conscience calls into question the integrity of moral reasoning as such.

Wayward Cleric Dilemmas

The second of the six groups of moral dilemmas in the Thomistic corpus comprises situations featuring clerics who appear simultaneously obliged to perform, and not perform, the duties of their religious offices. These clerics are perplexed because their religious offices require them to do

---

III: 388: "For if conscience dictates something should be done against the law of God, it is to be put away, and in this way one is released from the dilemma (*Si enim conscientia dictat aliquid faciendum contra legem Dei, deponenda est, et absolvitur homo ab huiusmodi vinculo*)."

[27] Albertus Magnus, *Summa de creaturis* II, q. 72, a. 1, sol., in *Opera omnia*, ed. Stephanus Borgnet, 38 vols. (Paris: Vivès, 1896), XXXV: 599.

[28] Albertus Magnus, *Summa de creaturis* II, q. 72, a. 2, q. 1, ad 1, in *Opera omnia*, XXXV: 601.

certain activities, but to do them happens to be proscribed in a particular
case because of the commission of prior sins. Aquinas's stock examples are:

6. It is incumbent upon a cleric to baptize others, but because of a serious sin he cannot baptize without committing an additional sin of
   irreverence.[29]

7. A priest who is in a sinful state because of the commission of a serious
   sin (e.g., fornication) still has an obligation to celebrate mass for those
   under his spiritual care, but to confect the Eucharist while in the state
   of mortal sin is prohibited.[30]

8. A priest has the obligation of fraternal correction, yet to rebuke others
   for their sins while being in a state of sin is itself sinful.[31]

Each of these examples features a priest who is *perplexus* because a prior
sin renders him unworthy to perform certain duties – specified here as the
dispensing of sacraments and fraternal correction – and if he fulfills these
obligations while in a state of sin, he will incur an additional sin. The
second of these three cases is identical to the *Fornicating Priest Dilemma*
treated by the authors of the *Summa aurea* and the *Summa Halesiana* and
appears to have developed into a stock example for medieval discussants of
perplexity.[32] Aquinas's Dominican contemporary, Raymond of Peñafort,
included it in his *Summa*, even considering whether it constituted two
dilemmas, since not only might the priest be said to be *perplexus* about
whether to continue with the mass, but likewise each parishioner might be
perplexus about whether to stay and hear it.[33] In cases 6–8 above, the clerics

---

[29] See *In IV librum Sententiarum*, d. 5, q. 2, a. 2, qc. 4, arg. 4, ad 4 (Moos, 217, 219); *Summa theologiae*
III, q. 64, a. 6, arg. 3, ad 3 (Editio Leonina, XII: 47, XII: 48).

[30] See *Super Romanos*, cap. 14, 2, §1120 (Marietti, I: 208); *Summa theologiae* III, q. 82, a. 10, arg. 2, ad
2 (Editio Leonina, XII: 269); *Quaestiones de quolibet*, III, q. 12, a. 2, ad 2 (Editio Leonina, XXV.2:
286); *In IV librum Sententiarum*, d. 12, q. 3, a. 2, qc. 2, ad 2 (Moos, 537); *In IV librum Sententiarum*,
d. 24, q. 1, a. 3, qc. 5, ad 1 (Fretté, 33).

[31] See *In IV librum Sententiarum*, d. 19, q. 2, a. 2, qc. 2, arg. 2, ad 2 (Moos, 990, 994).

[32] Additionally, see Bonaventure, *In librum quartum Sententiarum*, d. 13, dub. 1, in *Opera omnia*,
10 vols. (Quaracchi: Collegium S. Bonaventurae, 1882–1902), IV: 311.

[33] Raymond of Peñafort, *Summa*, lib. 3, *De scandalo, et perplexitate, et notorio*, §§6–7, in *Summa de
poenitentia et matrimonio cum glossis Ioannis de Friburgo* (Rome: Ioannes Tallinus Bibliopolus, 1603),
356: "Assume a priest is vested for mass and he then arrives at those words 'This is my body,' and then
some mortal sin of his conscience comes to mind, what will he do? If he proceeds, confecting and
eating the Eucharist, he sins mortally, because he eats and drinks judgment upon himself, etc. If he
should not confect, and feigns himself to confect, he seems to sin more gravely because he appears
to mock God and the people who he deceives . . . If, however, he abandons everything, he produces
a great scandal, and so he appears perplexed (*Pone sacerdotem indutum ad missam, et pervenit iam ad
illa verba: hoc est corpus, tunc occurrit conscientiae suae aliquod mortale, quod faciet? Si procedit, peccat
mortaliter conficiendo, et sumendo, quia iudicium sibi manducat, et bibit, etc. si non conficiat, et fingat
se conficere, gravius peccare videtur, quia Deo videtur illudere, et populo, quem decipit . . . si autem
ex toto dimittat, magnam scandalum generat, et ita videtur perplexus*)." In discussing the dilemma

are limited by their previous sins and seem to be simultaneously obliged to perform the religious duties of their office and not perform them. If they perform them, they sin, and if they omit them, they likewise sin. While Aquinas designates each of the agents in these cases as *perplexus*, he again invokes the distinction between two kinds of moral perplexity. Their perplexity is not absolute or unconditional, since it was only generated by a prior sin. In Aquinas's view, the prior sin precludes the possibility that these dilemmas are cases of perplexity *simpliciter*, they are only cases of perplexity *secundum quid*. Presumably each of the clerics in these examples could have avoided the sin that generated the dilemma. Unaddressed past moral failures have made the present obligations incapable of fulfillment in the given circumstances. The cause of the moral dilemma is the agent's own moral history, and the agent's prior sin seems to necessitate that the agent sin a second time.

Even though Aquinas designates these cases as instances of perplexity *secundum quid*, he identifies a route that allows each agent to avoid a second act of moral wrongdoing. The priests in such situations can simply repent and then complete the obligations of baptizing, saying mass, or correcting others without incurring an additional sin. Aquinas contends that the priest in each case "is not *perplexus simpliciter*, because he is able to repent (*nec tamen est simpliciter perplexus, quia potest poenitentiam agere*)."[34] Escaping the moral wrongdoing is contingent upon changing his circumstances. The priest must be willing "to turn back to God and repent (*ad Deum converti, et conteri*)"[35] and "to abandon the sin (*peccatum dimittere*)."[36] If the priest remains in sin, however, the avoidance of future wrongdoing is impossible and he will sin a second time. While Aquinas raises the possibility that a sinful priest bound to fraternal correction might avoid the dilemma by simply resigning from the office, such an escape does not seem to apply to all the examples.[37] If the priest refuses to repent or cannot resign, a

---

from the point of view of the *parochiani*, Peñafort specifies the priest's sin to be the presence of a "concubine in his house (*concubinam in domo*)" (357). Peñafort's discussion of this dilemma is referenced in the dictionary of canon and civil law of Albericus de Rosate (1290–1354/60). See the entry for "Perplexitas" in *Lexicon sive dictionarium utriusque iuris* (Pavia: Michael et Bernardinus de Garaldis, 1498).

[34] *Quaestiones de quolibet*, III, q. 12, a. 2, ad 2 (Editio Leonina, XXV.2: 286). See *Summa theologiae* III, q. 64, a. 6, arg. 3, ad 3 (Editio Leonina, XII: 47, XII: 48); *Summa theologiae* III, q. 82, a. 10, arg. 2, ad 2 (Editio Leonina, XII: 269).

[35] *In IV librum Sententiarum*, d. 12, q. 3, a. 2, qc. 2, ad 2 (Moos, 537). See *In IV librum Sententiarum*, d. 5, q. 2, a. 2, qc. 4, ad 4 (Moos, 217, 219).

[36] *In IV librum Sententiarum*, d. 24, q. 1, a. 3, qc. 5 ad 1 (Fretté, 33); *Summa theologiae* III, q. 82, a. 10, arg. 2, ad 2 (Editio Leonina, XII: 269); *In IV librum Sententiarum*, d. 19, q. 2, a. 2, qc. 2, arg. 2, ad 2 (Moos, 990, 994).

[37] *In IV librum Sententiarum*, d. 24, q. 1, a. 3, qc. 5, ad 1 (Fretté, 33); *In IV librum Sententiarum*, d. 19, q. 2, a. 2, qc. 2, arg. 2, ad 2 (Moos, 994).

second wrongdoing will not be avoided, since there will come a time when the priest must baptize, say mass, or correct those under his spiritual care. If he will not repent, he will be unable to avoid the commission of an additional moral wrong no matter what he does. He remains entangled by *secundum quid* perplexity as long as the sin remains unrepented. Raymond of Peñafort's above-mentioned account of the sinful priest is consistent with Aquinas's. Raymond notes that *perplexitas* "comes about at times from scandal and other sins (*provenit interdum ex scandalo, et aliis peccatis*)" and explains that to avoid another sin the priest

should repent and should turn back to God; also he should grieve, because he repents so late, and he should propose to confess as soon as he will be able to have the opportunity (*paeniteat, et convertat; doleat etiam, quia ita tarde paenitet, et proponat confiteri quam cito poterit habere opportunitatem*).[38]

With repentance, the priest can continue the mass without incurring an additional sin. Raymond seems to consider the dilemma of the perplexed parishioners to be merely apparent, as he notes that "very many doubts (*plurima dubia*)" are held in situations such as this one.[39]

Evil Intention Dilemmas

The next class of moral dilemmas is illustrated by one example set forth several times in the Thomistic corpus. Aquinas contends that the adoption of an evil or perverse intention (*intentio mala, intentio prava*) will render an agent incapable of avoiding further moral wrongdoing. Such an agent will be *perplexus* and will commit a moral failure as long as the intention remains. All such cases of perplexity are designated as instances of perplexity *secundum quid*, presumably because the antecedent adoption of an evil intention is voluntary on the part of the agent. Aquinas's repeated example is:

9. An agent who is obliged to give alms adopts an intention of vainglory (*gloria inanis*). If he gives alms under this intention, he sins. If he omits to give alms at all, he sins by not fulfilling his obligation to give alms.[40]

This example features an individual who adopts a posture of inordinately seeking the attention of others. Aquinas counts vainglory among the seven capital vices, noting it is a vice that causes other vices.[41] Having adopted

---

[38] Raymond of Peñafort, *Summa*, 35a, 356–7.   [39] Raymond of Peñafort, *Summa*, 357.

[40] See *De veritate*, q. 17, a. 4, ad 8 (Editio Leonina, xxii.2: 526); *Summa theologiae* i–ii, q. 19, a. 6, arg. 3, ad 3 (Editio Leonina, vi: 146, 147). See also *In II librum Sententiarum*, d. 39, q. 3, a. 3, arg. 5, ad 5 (Mandonnet, 1001, 1004).

[41] *Summa theologiae* ii–ii, q. 132, a. 4, corp. (Editio Leonina, x: 82–3).

this posture of vainglory, the agent appears unable to avoid further sin and is in a moral dilemma. If the agent gives alms under the vainglorious intention, then the agent sins. If the agent desists from giving alms to avoid that sin, then the agent commits a different sin. Aquinas considers the obligation of almsgiving or the performance of charitable works to be a requirement of justice, and he judges such acts to be obligatory for those who have the means.[42] This obligation is not suspended with the adoption of the vainglorious intention, but rather the intention renders the agent incapable of performing the act well. The agent appears obliged to give alms and not give alms at the same time, and since neither of these contradictories can be avoided, the agent seems bound to do wrong. Unsurprisingly, Aquinas designates this example as a case of perplexity *secundum quid*. Aquinas contends that sin is ultimately avoidable if the bad intention of vainglory is abandoned. Aquinas's analysis here is very similar to his account of the dilemmas of the malformed conscience variety, and at times he treats both cases together. The continued presence of either an evil intention or an erroneous conscience prevents an agent from keeping moral obligations fulfilled, but to abandon them allows an agent to avoid an additional wrong.

Layperson Dilemmas

The next group of Aquinas's moral dilemmas also consists of examples of agents who commit a prior wrong and thereby run into difficulty in fulfilling an obligation. This group of dilemmas shares similarities with the *Wayward Cleric Dilemmas* examined above, but a key difference lies in the source of their obligations. Whereas in the earlier group the obligations belonged to agents in virtue of a position in the church (as the reception of holy orders obliges priests to say mass or baptize), in *Layperson Dilemmas* the obligations pertain equally to all individuals insofar as they are members of the Christian community. The first example concerns the obligation of fraternal correction discussed above, but is considered simply insofar as it belongs to all and not just to clerics:

10. A man is obliged to fraternal correction, but to rebuke others for their sins while in a state of sin is itself sinful.[43]

A level of fraternal correction is considered by Thomas to be a moral precept binding on all members of a community, and yet to correct others'

---

[42] See, for example, *Summa theologiae* II–II, q. 32, a. 5, corp. (Editio Leonina, VIII: 253–4).
[43] *De correctione fraterna*, a. 1, ad 15 (Marietti, II: 797).

vices while possessing that vice is forbidden. As was seen above, those who have offices have a higher level of care for a community, and from those obligations of fraternal correction Aquinas suggested that a sinful cleric could avoid the dilemma simply by resigning from the office. Perhaps an instance of that case would be a confessor who becomes afflicted by a particular vice and then decides to resign from the spiritual guidance of an inferior who also struggles with that vice. Nevertheless, there is a basic level of fraternal correction that is obligatory for all members of a community, and such an obligation cannot be evaded by resigning from any office.[44] A layperson who persists in sin cannot evade this responsibility of correcting others, and the persistence in sin certainly does not free such an agent from this obligation. The agent seems perplexed insofar as he is obliged to engage in fraternal correction, and yet obliged not to correct others in virtue of his sin. He is only *perplexus*, however, as long as he persists in sin, because it is possible for him "to send away the sins, and thus correct others (*peccata dimittere, et sic corrigere*)."[45] Although Aquinas's comments on this example are quite brief, it is clear that someone who does not put away sin would then be in a situation of perplexity *secundum quid*, rather than perplexity *simpliciter*, because a prior sin is generating the dilemma.

Aquinas provides a second example of *Layperson Dilemmas*, one that has a similar structure to the first. He explains:

11. One is obliged to receive the Eucharist once a year according to the precept of the church, yet to take the Eucharist while in a state of serious sin is itself sinful.[46]

With this example Aquinas envisions an individual whose commission of a serious sin renders him unworthy to partake of the Eucharist at mass. To take communion while in a state of sin is an additional serious sin because it entails the commission of a sacrilege. One can imagine a scenario where a man finds himself at the last possible opportunity to fulfill his yearly obligation of receiving the Eucharist. At that point, he will either partake or not partake. If he partakes, he fulfills his obligation yet commits the sin of sacrilege. If he omits to partake, he avoids sacrilege but is guilty of violating the precept that commands the yearly reception of the Eucharist. Such an individual is in a moral dilemma, but the dilemma can be analyzed according to the twofold distinction concerning perplexity that is repeatedly defended by Aquinas. Regarding this example, Aquinas states

---

[44] Levels of obligation for fraternal correction are discussed in *Summa theologiae* II–II, q. 33, a. 3, corp. (Editio Leonina, VIII: 265).

[45] *De correctione fraterna*, a. 1, ad 15 (Marietti, II: 797).

[46] See *In IV librum Sententiarum*, d. 9, q. 1, a. 3, qc. 1, ad 3 (Moos, 377).

briefly that the individual is not *perplexus*, which means, in light of the other texts above, he is not *perplexus simpliciter*.[47] The agent is *perplexus secundum quid* rather than *perplexus simpliciter* because the agent can desist from sinning, offer repentance, and seek forgiveness. The difficulty in keeping the obligation to receive the Eucharist stems solely from the presumably voluntary prior misdeed that if avoided would allow the agent to keep the yearly obligation fulfilled.

Infelicitous Oath Dilemmas

Aquinas's penultimate group of moral dilemmas consists of cases where agents swear infelicitous oaths. In a pair of examples consistent with one promoted by Gratian in distinction 13 of the *Decretum*, Aquinas describes agents who swear oaths to commit crimes. The dilemmas are:

12. An agent swears an oath to commit adultery (*adulterium*), and then is caught between being an adulterer or a perjurer.[48]
13. An agent swears an oath to commit a homicide (*homicidium*), and then is caught between being a murderer or a perjurer.[49]

In these cases, each agent initially is described as being *perplexus* because each is unable to avoid choosing between two seemingly impermissible options. If an agent fulfills his oath and carries through with an adulterous or murderous plan, he avoids perjury but commits the grave sin of adultery or murder. If the agent desists from fulfilling the oath, he avoids adultery and murder but then sins as a perjurer. It was seen above that the Council of Toledo text appealed to the principle of choosing the lesser evil in such circumstances and identified the violation of the oath as the preferable option. The glossators on the *Decretum* concurred in advising that such an agent avoid fulfilling the oath, but they disagreed with the Council on the reason why that course of action was preferable. They did not justify abandoning the oath over the commission of adultery and homicide on the principle of the lesser evil, but rather contended that oaths regarding adultery and homicide are not obligatory and hence there is no dilemma. Aquinas's reply is similar to Gratian's glossators; he contends that such oaths are not binding because of their deficient subject matter, and so there is no real case of being *perplexus* here.[50] The agent who performs such an oath concerning the commission of adulterous or murderous acts does sin in swearing such an oath, as the agent thereby resolves to commit an evil,

---

[47] *In IV librum Sententiarum*, d. 9, q. 1, a. 3, qc. 1, ad 3 (Moos, 377).
[48] See *Summa theologiae* II–II, q. 98, a. 2, arg. 1, ad 1 (Editio Leonina, IX: 342).
[49] See *Summa theologiae* II–II, q. 98, a. 2, arg. 1, ad 1 (Editio Leonina, IX: 342).
[50] *Summa theologiae* II–II, q. 98, a. 2, ad 1 (Editio Leonina, IX: 342).

but there is no additional sin in not fulfilling the oath later, since the act fails as an oath and does not put the agent under any obligation to perform the deed. Hence, *Infelicitous Oath Dilemmas* are not genuine dilemmas according to Aquinas, as there is no situation of an agent who is *perplexus* in the sense of moral entanglement. For this reason, Aquinas does not appeal to the distinction between two kinds of perplexity for these cases, since the dilemmas are simply apparent.

Hidden Option Dilemmas

Like *Infelicitous Oath Dilemmas*, the final group of moral dilemmas also consists of situations where agents falsely believe themselves to be entangled by conflicting moral obligations. In these cases, there are many manifest impermissible courses of action yet at least one permissible course that remains unknown to the agents. These moral dilemmas are only apparent and fail to be moral dilemmas in a proper sense. The agents in such situations spend time deliberating among the impermissible courses of action but fail to discern a course that could allow them to keep all obligations fulfilled. Some of Aquinas's most exotic examples come from this last group. Occurring in the *Summa theologiae*, they all are presented in a similar way: an alleged situation of inescapable moral wrongdoing is set forth in an article's objection, and then in the reply to the objection Aquinas shows that the agent in each case is really not *perplexus* because there is at least one permissible (yet unforeseen) course of action.

Four of the five examples of this sort concern the celebration of the Eucharist. The first two are some of the more curious examples in all of Aquinas's writings:

14. A statute of the church requires that at mass a priest consume the contents of the chalice after consecration. Sometimes a fly, spider, or poisonous creature falls into the chalice, and if the priest drinks from the chalice he kills himself or tempts God.[51]

15. An evilly minded person places poison in the chalice after consecration, and if the priest drinks from the chalice he kills himself or tempts God.[52]

In these situations, a poisonous creature or a murderous individual renders the chalice unsuitable for consumption at mass. The first situation may recall a legend of Conrad of Constance, who is said to have consumed the contents of a chalice at mass after a poisonous spider fell into it, but was miraculously saved. Moreover, Aquinas's second example may also

[51] See *Summa theologiae* III, q. 83, a. 6, arg. 3, ad 3 (Editio Leonina, XII: 283, XII: 284).
[52] See *Summa theologiae* III, q. 83, a. 6, arg. 3, ad 3 (Editio Leonina, XII: 283, XII: 284).

recall an episode described in Peter Abelard's autobiographical work, the *Historia calamitatem*, where Abelard wrote about an attempt on his life consisting of poison placed in his chalice.[53] In both of Aquinas's examples, the priest appears to have an obligation to consume the contents of the chalice according to a statute of the church, but he cannot do so without possibly bringing about his own death or committing a sin of presumption in assuming that God will intervene with a miracle. Aquinas's introduction of the sin of presumption in this example provides a contrast to Raymond Lull's reflections on moral dilemmas considered previously, since the *Vita coaetanea* suggested that agents in moral dilemmas who prayed for assistance could experience a miraculous intervention. In contrast, Aquinas has no sympathy for such a view that expects miracles.

In these cases, the priest appears to be *perplexus*, since he seems unable to avoid sinning. Assuming that the occasion for the contamination of the chalice was not brought about by negligence on the part of the priest, the case cannot be classified as a situation of perplexity *simpliciter*. He is not at fault for the situation and nevertheless cannot avoid the options of either drinking or not drinking the contaminated elements of the chalice. While the avoidance of at least one of the contradictories of the contradictory set of consuming or not consuming is inescapable, Aquinas replies that the priest is not perplexed because a version of not consuming is permissible within church statutes. The priest should not consume the contents of the chalice until the creature is removed, and in the case of the deliberately poisoned chalice, the entire contents should be placed in a reliquary and the mass continued with new wine. Either of these two options allows the priest to fulfill all of his obligations and hence there is no true moral dilemma.

Aquinas gives a similar solution to avoiding sin with the next *Hidden Option* dilemma, and this one also concerns the celebration of the Eucharist:

16. A priest is obliged to consume the Eucharistic bread as well as contents of the chalice at mass to fulfill a complete sacrifice. During the mass, the priest notices that through the negligence of the server, water was not added to the chalice, or even perhaps wine. If the priest just consumes the Eucharistic bread, he will be guilty of performing an imperfect sacrifice. If he does not consume anything, then he has not fulfilled his obligation to consume at mass.[54]

---

[53] See J. T. Muckle, CSB, ed., "Abelard's Letter of Consolation to a Friend (*Historia calamitatem*)," *Mediaeval Studies* 12 (1950), 163–213, at 209, and Peter Abelard, *The Story of Abelard's Adversities*, trans. J. T. Muckle (Toronto: Pontifical Institute of Mediaeval Studies, 1964), at 76.

[54] See *Summa theologiae* III, q. 83, a. 6, arg. 4, ad 4 (Editio Leonina, XII: 283, XII: 284).

The priest here seems *perplexus* because, through no fault of his own, he appears to sin by performing an imperfect sacrifice or failing to consume under both species – bread and wine – at mass. There is negligence here, but it is entirely ascribable to the server rather than the priest. Thus, with respect to this priest, the situation cannot be designated as a prior misdeed or *secundum quid* case of perplexity. Again, Aquinas identifies numerous permissible courses of action tailored specifically to when the discovery is made and whether it is the water or the wine or both that are absent.[55] There is no perplexity in the sense of a moral dilemma of inescapable moral wrongdoing, since there are alternative courses of action possible that allow for the satisfaction of all impending obligations. There may be perplexity in the sense that the agent may not know how to proceed, but no agent is *perplexus* in the sense of being entangled by unfulfillable demands. Of course, Aquinas offers no guarantee that all agents will always have the knowledge to discern permissible courses of action for every situation. Similarly, there is never a guarantee that an agent has a properly formed conscience, as was seen above. It is incumbent upon agents to form their consciences properly, just as it is incumbent upon priests to know how to perform a sacrament in a variety of circumstances.[56]

The remaining two examples from this class of apparent moral dilemmas follow the pattern where Aquinas identifies permissible courses of action that were initially unforeseen by agents who mistakenly considered themselves to be perplexed:

17. A man is obliged to make restitution for the wrongdoing of taking away another's good name. He cannot, however, restore the other's good name without doing another wrong.[57]
18. A priest is obliged to consecrate the Eucharist, but an order of excommunication commands him not to do so. He appears to sin if he consecrates and sin if he does not.[58]

In these two cases, both agents are perplexed only in the epistemic sense of being unclear about how to proceed. There is no true perplexity of being entangled by a situation that imposes conflicting moral demands. It is significant that in both cases the agent has culpably performed some wrong. Aquinas does not proceed by designating either agent as *perplexus*

[55] *Summa theologiae* III, q. 83, a. 6, ad 4 (Editio Leonina, XII: 284).
[56] For a discussion of culpability, see Gregory Doolan, "The Relation of Culture and Ignorance to Culpability in Thomas Aquinas," *The Thomist* 63 (1999), 105–24, and Daniel McInerny, *The Difficult Good: A Thomistic Approach to Moral Conflict and Human Happiness* (New York: Fordham University Press, 2006), 141–3.
[57] See *Summa theologiae* II–II, q. 62, a. 2, arg. 2, ad 2 (Editio Leonina, IX: 42, IX: 43).
[58] See *Summa theologiae* III, q. 82, a. 10, arg. 2, ad 2 (Editio Leonina, XII: 269).

secundum quid in virtue of the agent's past misdeeds. His analysis is much simpler: neither agent is *perplexus* at all. In the case of the destroyer of another's good name, Aquinas notes that there are a variety of ways to make restitution to a victim, even if the original wrong cannot be righted. As Aquinas says elsewhere, compensatory restitution can be in the form of a variety of goods (such as money or honor), and the judgment of a good man should be sought as the standard of proportionate compensation.[59] With regard to the priest under a decree of excommunication who believes himself both obliged and not obliged to say mass, Aquinas remarks that there is no dilemma because the priestly obligation of saying mass lapses as soon as there is a decree of excommunication. The priest only mistakenly believes himself to be obliged to say mass in this case.

Now that all eighteen cases in the Thomistic corpus where an agent is at least provisionally designated as *perplexus* or in a moral dilemma have been examined, a few general principles can be noted. First, Aquinas regularly appealed to a conceptual distinction between perplexity *simpliciter* and perplexity *secundum quid*. Secondly, all of the examples of moral dilemmas considered genuine by Aquinas fell under the designation of perplexity *secundum quid*, where an agent's past misdeed limits the agent's future ability to keep moral obligations fulfilled. Each agent is indeed rendered *perplexus* or entangled, but the dilemma required a prior moral failure as a cause, such as fornication, an oath to commit murder, a vainglorious intention, a bad formation of conscience, and the like. In all, Aquinas identified no examples of perplexity *simpliciter*. As shall be exhibited shortly, Aquinas unequivocally denies that cases of perplexity *simpliciter* exist. Thirdly, even though Aquinas designates many cases as examples of perplexity *secundum quid*, he always identifies a route whereby an agent in the dilemma can avoid another moral wrongdoing, and this route usually involves repentance, conscience reformation, or putting away an evil intention. If the agent fails to take such a course of action, the agent will sin a second time.

4.3 TWENTIETH-CENTURY CONTROVERSIES

The topic of moral dilemmas became a much-discussed issue among some twentieth-century ethicists, some of whom have looked for both predecessors and foils to their own positions. Aquinas is the only medieval philosopher to have received significant attention among contemporary moral dilemma theorists, and as we have seen above, Alan Donagan's work has

---

[59] *Summa theologiae* II–II, q. 62, a. 2, arg. 2, ad 1 (Editio Leonina, IX: 43).

been largely responsible for popularizing Aquinas among those thinkers. Three points of Aquinas's doctrine have been contested by recent interpreters, and they each warrant consideration. These points are: whether Aquinas was interested in logical consistency; whether Aquinas allowed cases of perplexity *simpliciter*; and whether Aquinas really defended the existence of cases of perplexity *secundum quid*.

Logical consistency

In the eighteen cases examined above, the agents in cases I–II were considered by Aquinas to be true moral dilemmas, but they were dilemmas of the *secundum quid* variety. Aquinas was not troubled by the perplexity that is generated by a prior moral lapse, and he defended the existence of cases of perplexity *secundum quid* by noting:

> It is not *inconveniens* that, if some condition is presupposed, a man is not able to avoid sin (*non est inconveniens ut aliquo supposito, homo peccatum evitare non possit*).[60]

When it comes to offering an interpretation of what Aquinas means in this text and others by contending that it is not *inconveniens* for present moral transgressions to lead to future perplexities, Alan Donagan provides one account that has been controversial in recent philosophical literature. Donagan has maintained that the term *inconveniens* in this context carries the sense of "logically wrong" or "inconsistent."[61] He explains Aquinas's view as "it is a logical consequence of some sins that they entangle the sinner in situations in which he cannot but commit others."[62] By maintaining that *inconveniens* carries the sense of logical inconsistency, Donagan uses Aquinas as a key support for his larger claim that a moral system must be internally consistent, and that consistency is an essential characteristic of a legitimate moral system. On this view, any moral system that lays impossibilities upon innocent agents must be flawed. Some commentators, however, have opposed Donagan's rendering of *inconveniens* by claiming that the term does not carry such a strong logical meaning. The arguments of Donagan's detractors are worth examining. For instance, Edmund

---

[60] *De veritate*, q. 17, a. 4, ad 8 (Editio Leonina, XXII.2: 526). Parallel passages in discussions of moral perplexity include: *In II librum Sententiarum*, d. 39, q. 3, a. 3, ad. 5 (Mandonnet, 1004): "*sed quodam posito non est inconveniens, illo stante, aliquem perplexum fore*"; *Super Romanos*, cap. 14, 2, §1120 (Marietti, 1: 208): "*Nihil enim prohibet aliquem esse perplexum aliquo supposito.*"

[61] Donagan, "Consistency in Rationalist Moral Systems," 306.

[62] Donagan, *The Theory of Morality*, 145.

Santurri has claimed, "Donagan suggests that Aquinas's central concern is the preservation of consistency. Yet the textual support that Donagan provides for his reading is unconvincing."[63] Elsewhere he explains,

> Donagan's assumption that Aquinas's rejection of dilemmas is motivated by logical concerns appears to hinge on the former's translation of *inconveniens* . . . as "inconsistent." Yet the term *inconveniens*, as Aquinas uses it, need not denote strict logical inconsistency. On the contrary, it often means, more generally, unbecoming, unsuitable, unfitting, or incongruous.[64]

Another commentator has joined Santurri in opposing Donagan's rendering of *inconveniens*. William Mann contends:

> Defenders of the *secundum quid* thesis should not . . . rely on Donagan's claim that "Aquinas held that any moral system that allows for perplexity *simpliciter* must be inconsistent" . . . *Inconveniens* can sometimes be rendered as "inconsistent" when it occurs in medieval logical treatises, but in its garden-variety philosophical occurrences, it will bear no more weight than "unsuitable," "unfitting," "inappropriate," "discordant," or "awkward."[65]

It is uncontested that *inconveniens* can be translated in certain passages according to the suggestions given by Santurri and Mann.[66] Yet are there any reasons to follow Donagan's rendering of *inconveniens* as "logically wrong" in discussions of moral dilemmas? The insistence on the part of these two commentators to diminish the logical sense of the term, if proved to be true, would indeed do significant damage to Donagan's claimed intellectual ancestry in Aquinas regarding the issue of consistency for ethical systems. There is, however, strong evidence for Donagan's contested rendering of the term *inconveniens*.

A text occurring in a discussion of the obligatory character of conscience present in *Quodlibet III* can settle the matter. This text dates from the Easter season of 1270, which was during the middle period of Aquinas's second regency at the University of Paris.[67] In a passage there Aquinas distinguishes again between *perplexus simpliciter* and *perplexus secundum quid* in presenting one of the *Wayward Cleric Dilemmas* discussed above,

---

[63] Santurri, *Perplexity in the Moral Life*, 94. [64] Santurri, *Perplexity in the Moral Life*, 223, n. 27.

[65] William E. Mann, "Jephthah's Plight: Moral Dilemmas and Theism," *Philosophical Perspectives* 5 (1991), 617–47, at 634.

[66] See, for instance, Roy J. Deferrari, M. Inviolata Barry, CDP, and Ignatius McGuiness, OP, *A Lexicon of St. Thomas Aquinas* (Washington, DC: The Catholic University of America Press, 1948), 533; *A Latin-English Dictionary of St. Thomas Aquinas* (Boston: St. Paul Editions, 1986), 504–5; and P. G. W. Glare, *Oxford Latin Dictionary* (Oxford: Clarendon Press, 1982), 874.

[67] On the dating *of Quodlibet III*, see Torrell, 1: 211, and "Avant propos," in *Quaestiones de quolibet* XXV.1: IX*–X*, at IX*.

and then explains why the existence of cases of perplexity *secundum quid* should not be troubling:

> It is not *inconveniens*, however, that given a certain supposition, someone is *per-plexus*. Just as a priest who is obliged to chant, if he is in a state of sin, sins both by chanting and by not chanting, nevertheless he is not *perplexus simpliciter*, because he is able to repent and to chant without sin. Further, just as in syllogisms, one *inconveniens* being given, others arise, as is said in *Physics I* (*Non est autem inconue-niens quod, aliquo posito, aliquis homo sit perplexus, sicut sacerdos qui tenetur cantare, si sit in peccato, peccat cantando et non cantando, nec tamen est simpliciter perplexus, quia potest poenitenciam agere et absque peccato cantare; sicut etiam in sillogisticis, uno quodam inconuenienti dato, alia contingunt, ut dicitur in I Phisicorum*).[68]

Aquinas here notes that the existence of perplexity is not *inconveniens* when some condition is presupposed, as is the case in perplexity *secundum quid* situations. Having cited the example of a perplexed priest who can repent and then meet all of his obligations, Aquinas argues that perplexity *secundum quid* situations are like instances of faulty syllogistic reasoning. Given one move that is *inconveniens*, other things that are *inconveniens* will follow. Here it seems that the term *inconveniens* carries the sense of "illogical," for in this context Aquinas includes the term within logical nomenclature. The implication is that just as one should not expect the conclusions of a syllogistic argument to be reliable if errors are made in the beginning stages, so should one not expect future situations to be free from moral perplexity if moral errors have been made on prior occasions. The reference to *Physics* I at the end of the passage presents further evidence to support the rendering of *inconveniens* with a logical connotation. In commenting on an Aristotelian discussion in *Physics* I of the errant syllogizing of some Pre-Socratic philosophers, Aquinas adds, "it is not *inconveniens* that given one *inconveniens* others should follow (*non est autem inconveniens si uno inconvenienti dato alia sequantur*)."[69] A few lines later Aquinas repeats the point, saying, "It is not a serious matter, granting one *inconveniens*, others should follow (*non est grave si uno inconvenienti dato alia sequantur*)."[70] In short, the *Quodlibet III* passage and Aquinas's commentary on *Physics* I exhibit the term *inconveniens* in contexts of logical consistency.

There is strong evidence, therefore, for taking the term *inconveniens* to mean "inconsistent" according to the manner in which Donagan interprets

[68] *Quaestiones de quolibet*, III, q. 12, a. 2, ad 2 (Editio Leonina, XXV.2: 286).
[69] *Commentaria in octo libros Physicorum Aristotelis*, lib. 1, lec. 5 (Editio Leonina, II: 9).
[70] *Commentaria in octo libros Physicorum Aristotelis*, lib. 1, lec. 5 (Editio Leonina, II: 16).

Aquinas. The existence of *perplexus secundum quid* situations does not pose a threat to the internal logical consistency of moral systems. According to Aquinas's view, it is not only fitting, but is a logical consequence, that some prior moral lapses will generate future moral perplexities. To sin and to persist in the state of sin renders one incapable of meeting future moral obligations. As the existence of falsity in the conclusions of syllogisms does not call into question the consistency of logic if in the early stages of argument errors have been committed, in the same way prior moral wrongs that make future obligations impossible to meet do not vitiate the integrity of a moral system. The explicit parallel that Aquinas makes between logical reasoning and moral experience indicates that Aquinas does have the issue of consistency in mind with respect to ethics, and thus the several texts identified above add significant support to the interpretation of Aquinas by Donagan.[71]

Denials of perplexity simpliciter

The first eleven the of the eighteen examples of moral dilemmas discussed above were ultimately designated by Aquinas as perplexity *secundum quid* dilemmas, whereas the remaining seven were dismissed as merely apparent dilemmas, since there were morally permissible alternative courses of action available to agents in those cases. It is important to see that Aquinas identifies no cases of perplexity *simpliciter* in any of his writings. We have seen, however, that he often appeals to the concept of *perplexus simpliciter* when stating that a particular case does not fall under that designation. In a lengthy article, William Mann has contended that Aquinas does not reject the possibility of situations of perplexity *simpliciter*, and in doing so Mann has opposed the reading of Aquinas given by Donagan.[72] Mann's interpretation of Aquinas, if substantiated, would call into question Donagan's appeal to Aquinas for his thesis that a necessary condition of a satisfactory moral system is the preclusion of conflicts of duties for innocent agents. Mann formulates his objection to Donagan as follows:

---

[71] It is likely that Donagan saw the strength of such a parallel, but he does not offer a discussion of the matter. On two occasions he footnotes the following passage from the *Summa theologica*: "Just as in syllogistic arguments, granted one *inconveniens*, others necessarily follow; so in moral matters, given one *inconveniens*, others necessarily follow (*sicut in syllogisticis, uno inconvenienti dato, necesse est alia sequi, ita in moralibus, uno inconvenienti posito, ex necessitate alia sequuntur*)" (I–II, q. 19, a. 6, ad 3 (Editio Leonina, VI: 147). See Donagan, *The Theory of Morality*, 254; Donagan, "Moral Dilemmas, Genuine and Spurious," 10. The text from the *Quodlibet III* is stronger because it uses the terms *perplexus simpliciter* and *perplexus secundum quid*.

[72] Mann, "Jephthah's Plight," 626–34.

The thesis that all dilemmas are *secundum quid* . . . Aquinas does not hold . . . He does acknowledge that *some* dilemmas are *secundum quid* . . . Recent discussion of Aquinas's views cite four passages . . . [These] different examples are supposed to provide the data for the thesis that Aquinas believes that all dilemmas are dilemmas *secundum quid*.[73]

With a rhetorical flourish, Mann then adds, "Since the myth that Aquinas held the thesis has become pervasive in recent literature, it is high time to debunk it."[74] Mann fastens upon the peculiar feature common to nearly all recent interpreters of Aquinas on moral dilemmas, namely that they have focused exclusively on the four passages from Aquinas promoted by Donagan. Mann suggests that an examination of other passages from the Thomistic corpus will lead a reader to conclude that situations of perplexity *secundum quid* form only one class of moral dilemmas that Aquinas holds to exist, and other passages will show that Aquinas acknowledges the existence of perplexity *simpliciter* situations as well.

Evidence that Mann offers in defense of his view is taken from *Summa theologiae* III, q. 83, a. 6. The main texts he highlights there are the ones featuring dilemmas 14, 15, and 16 of the *Hidden Option* variety. With the analysis presented above, however, it was shown that Aquinas held those cases only to be apparent dilemmas and not real cases of moral perplexity, since the priest in each instance had at his disposal a morally permissible way to fulfill all of his obligations. Mann's contention that the priest is forced to do something that is "wrong in itself but that stems further worse results" does not represent a charitable interpretation of the text.[75] Rather than admitting that the situations described in the article's objections are genuine dilemmas, Aquinas shows in the replies that there are other alternatives open to the priest. In other words, the text falls short in establishing the claim that Aquinas acknowledges the existence of *perplexus simpliciter*.

Mann alleges that the strongest evidence for contending that Aquinas concedes the existence of perplexity *simpliciter* lies in Aquinas's treatment of the story of Jephthah in Judges 11:29–40. Jephthah vowed to sacrifice the first thing he saw upon returning home from victory in battle, and having returned home, his eyes alighted upon his daughter and thus he appears to have sacrificed her as an offering in accordance with his vow. Mann alleges, "I submit that Aquinas's treatment of Jephthah's plight recognizes it as a hard *simpliciter* dilemma."[76] Mann's interpretation of Aquinas on this issue is unsatisfying for the following reasons. First, one might argue that the

[73] Ibid., 626.   [74] Ibid.   [75] Ibid., 630.   [76] Ibid., 633.

situation of Jephthah would seem more properly to be a *secundum quid* perplexity given the rather problematic status of the oath, especially in light of our discussion of *Infelicitous Oath Dilemmas* above. Secondly, Aquinas clearly contends that an oath to do an evil act lacks binding force and fails to be a proper oath.[77] It is curious that Mann references this passage earlier in his article.[78] Thirdly, in his discussion of Jephthah, Aquinas cites Jerome who claims that the vow was "foolish (*stultus*)," and Aquinas then remarks that vows which have an "evil result (*malum eventum*)" should "not be kept (*non . . . observanda*)."[79] Fourthly, Aquinas does not use the term *perplexus* let alone *perplexus simpliciter* or *perplexus secundum quid* in his discussion of Jephthah. The evidence would seem to weigh against any admission on the part of Aquinas that Jephthah is in a case of perplexity *simpliciter*.[80]

Apart from providing alternative readings of the texts used by Mann, are there any other reasons to cast doubt upon Mann's interpretations? The most powerful evidence lies in several texts in the Thomistic corpus that have not been cited by Mann or Donagan's other detractors. Mann's suggestion, quoted above, that one should move to texts beyond the canonical four is good advice. In short, there are two texts where Aquinas explicitly denies the existence of situations of perplexity *simpliciter*. These texts, missed by Donagan, and by those who have followed Donagan, as well as by Mann, settle the issue definitively. It should be noted that no such denial of cases of perplexity *simpliciter* is found in the usual four texts upon which most commentators have based their views of Aquinas's discussion of perplexity. At most, in those four texts we find the denial that a particular instance is a case of perplexity *simpliciter*. Yet in two other texts Aquinas provides a universal denial that situations of perplexity *simpliciter* exist. Their rejection is short yet unequivocal. The first appears in the early commentary on the *Sententiae*:

No one is *perplexus simpliciter*, absolutely speaking, but given a certain supposition, it is not *inconveniens*, on that assumption, that someone would be *perplexus* (*simpliciter nullus perplexus est, absolute loquendo; sed quodam posito non est inconveniens, illo stante, aliquem perplexum fore*).[81]

---

[77] See *Summa theologiae* II–II, q. 98, a. 2, ad 2 (Editio Leonina IX: 343).
[78] For a discussion of Aquinas's text on oaths, see MacIntyre, "Moral Dilemmas," 380–1, and more recently, Daniel McInerny, *The Difficult Good*, 147.
[79] *Summa theologiae* II–II, q. 88, a. 2, ad 2.
[80] For a discussion of sixteenth- and seventeenth-century authors who did consider the case of Jephthah to be a situation of perplexity, see Geonget, *La notion de perplexité à la Renaissance*, 272–84.
[81] *In II librum Sententiarum*, d. 39, q. 3, a. 3, ad. 5 (Mandonnet, 1004).

The second denial of the existence of cases of perplexity *simpliciter* occurs in Aquinas's scriptural commentary on Romans, likely composed in Naples in 1272–7.[82] Again, Aquinas contends:

> For nothing prohibits someone to be *perplexus* given some supposition, although no one is *perplexus simpliciter* (*Nihil enim prohibet aliquem esse perplexum aliquo supposito, licet nullus sit perplexus simpliciter*).[83]

With these two texts – coming respectively from the beginning and the end of Aquinas's writing career – we find categorical denials of the very existence of situations of perplexity *simpliciter*. These two texts, absent from contemporary discussants of Aquinas on the issue of moral dilemmas, leave no ambiguity concerning Aquinas's view. While Aquinas distinguishes conceptually between *perplexus simpliciter* and *perplexus secundum quid*, he denies the actual existence of instances of the former, but argues for many instances of the latter. The only moral dilemmas that exist are those generated by an agent's prior misdeeds. In other words, innocent agents never experience moral dilemmas. These two texts, although not cited by Donagan, serve to vindicate his interpretation over the views of his detractors. Donagan was correct in assuming that Aquinas denies that cases of perplexity *simpliciter* exist.

It is worth noting that with the denial of the existence of moral dilem-mas for innocent agents, Aquinas becomes opposed to the view of his Majorcan contemporary, Raymond Lull, considered earlier. His *Vita coae-tanea* suggested that agents regularly find themselves ensnared and unable to escape moral wrongdoing without a miraculous divine intervention. To place Lull's position in Thomistic language, Lull defends the existence of cases of perplexity *simpliciter*, and recourse to petitionary prayer is the recommended procedure when such moral entanglements occur. Of the four moral dilemmas set forth in the *Vita*, it seems likely that the last three would be considered by Lull to be cases of absolute perplexity, with perhaps the first designated as *secundum quid* given that Lull's early life was committed to vanities. Therefore, Aquinas's position on moral dilemmas is not reconcilable with that of Lull. Aquinas's position is also irreconcil-able with those set forth by Gratian in distinction 13 of the *Decretum*. As Aquinas and Gratian have different views on the binding character of infe-licitous vows, and moreover, as the Gregorian example adduced by Gratian of the simoniacal cleric would clearly be characterized by Aquinas as a

---

[82] On the dating of this work, see Torrell, *Saint Thomas Aquinas*, 1: 340.
[83] *Super Romanos*, cap. 14, 2, §1120 (Marietti, 1: 208).

secundum quid dilemma because of the agent's prior wrong of bribery, their positions are opposed. Aquinas does have, however, close affinities with the glossators of the canon law tradition, evidenced by the gloss that claimed "In truth, however, there is no perplexity (*in veritate tamen perplexio nihil est*)."[84] This gloss is consistent with, if not identical to, Aquinas's denial of cases of perplexity *simpliciter*. Furthermore, as was seen, the glossators appear to have an implicit – though unformalized – view that those who think themselves to be in moral dilemmas should examine their past for misdeeds, a view that anticipates Aquinas's account of cases of perplexity *secundum quid*.

Denials of perplexity secundum quid

An anomaly among positions taken by readers of Aquinas has been one interpretation offered by Edmund Santurri, who has argued that despite Aquinas's use of the distinction of perplexity *simpliciter* and perplexity *secundum quid*, Aquinas's "intended position excludes the possibility of dilemmas *in any form*."[85] While examining the four canonical texts set forth by Donagan, Santurri gives particular attention to examples from the two groups of perplexity *secundum quid* identified above, namely, the perplexity experienced by an individual with an erroneously formed conscience and the perplexity experienced by a minister in a state of sin who is obliged to perform a sacrament. Santurri maintains that given that agents can change their consciences or repent of their sins, there really is no perplexity at all. Therefore, one should conclude that Aquinas does not endorse the existence of moral perplexity in any respect. According to Santurri, cases of perplexity *secundum quid* are merely apparent, given the option of repentance or the reformation of conscience.

On the whole, commentators have rejected Santurri's view.[86] What Santurri's interpretation fails to appreciate is the incontrovertible claim of Aquinas discussed above, namely, that given the commission of an impermissible action, situations of moral perplexity do arise. The state of perplexity of an agent in such a situation is not by any means illusory, for the agent will sin either by acting or not acting if the original wrong is not in some way rectified. Aquinas's treatment underscores the experiential

---

[84] *Glossa ordinaria*, XIII, d, 65, in Gratian, *The Treatise on Laws (Decretum DD. 1–20) with the Ordinary Gloss*, trans. Augustine Thompson, OP and James Gordley (Washington, DC: The Catholic University of America Press, 1993), 50.

[85] Santurri, *Perplexity in the Moral Life*, 94.

[86] See MacIntyre, "Moral Dilemmas," 381; Mann, "Jephthah's Plight," 627.

reality of perplexity *secundum quid* for agents who have committed prior transgressions. An initial transgression causes perplexity *secundum quid*, and the perplexity does remain unless some act to defuse the after-effects of the prior misdeed is performed. As William Mann has noted, Santurri presents a scenario where an individual who is experiencing perplexity *secundum quid* really is mistaken in thinking that there exists a state of perplexity.[87] Rather than being only two options of acting and not acting, both of which are sinful, according to Santurri's presentation there are really three equal options, two of which lead to sin and the third, which is permissible. Yet such an account by Santurri does not faithfully depict the details of Aquinas's discussions. To highlight the position of Aquinas in another way, one can note that if the individual does not discern what prior transgression has led to the dilemmatic situation in time, that individual will commit another wrong. This second wrong is a distinct moral failure, independent of the initial lapse that caused the dilemma. Nevertheless, the second sin is in some way caused by the first sin. Situations of perplexity *secundum quid* are truly dilemmas, because an agent in such cases will necessarily commit a second sin if nothing is done to alleviate the situation caused by the first sin. To highlight this point, one way of considering perplexity *secundum quid* dilemmas would be to call them "second sin" dilemmas, because the agent faces the prospect of sinning twice.

4.4 CAN AGENTS ALWAYS DEFUSE THE AFTER-EFFECTS OF PAST MORAL FAILURES?

It has now been established that Aquinas considers all real dilemmas to be of the perplexity *secundum quid* variety. He denies that instances of perplexity *simpliciter* exist, so innocent agents will never find themselves in true moral dilemmas. Setting aside the *Infelicitous Oath* and *Hidden Option* dilemmas that are judged by Aquinas to be merely apparent, one finds that the remaining moral dilemmas are of the perplexity *secundum quid* variety and fall under the classes of *Malformed Conscience Dilemmas, Wayward Cleric Dilemmas, Evil Intention Dilemmas,* and *Layperson Dilemmas.* In each of these cases, the dilemma is generated by a prior moral failure on the part of the agent. In light of the earlier consideration of moral dilemmas in the *Summa aurea* and the *Summa Halesiana,* it can be seen that Aquinas continues a medieval discussion of prior-fault dilemmas. It

---

[87] Mann, "Jephthah's Plight," 627.

is fitting to inquire into the distinctiveness of Aquinas's thirteenth-century contribution to theorizing about this particular kind of moral dilemma.

One significant difference between Aquinas's account of prior-fault dilemmas and the one found in the *Summa Halesiana* is that Aquinas does not present any prior-fault dilemmas where the bad effects of the prior misdeed cannot be defused. In the *Summa Halesiana*, the *Simoniacal Priest Dilemma* was presented as an irresolvable prior-fault dilemma, as the agent in such a case was presented as bound to choose between a greater and a lesser evil. Aquinas, however, presents all of his cases of prior-fault dilemmas as resolvable. Alasdair MacIntyre is correct in observing, "Aquinas never offers us an example of perplexity without also telling us how agents can resolve that perplexity."[88] Aquinas always identifies some way an agent can avoid moral wrongdoing in his eighteen examples of moral dilemmas, as the agent in each case must simply put away an evil intention, repent of a past sin, reform a malformed conscience, or discover a permissible yet presently unknown alternative. This feature of Aquinas's presentation has irked some interpreters.[89] A substantive unknown in Aquinas's account is whether Aquinas intends by the uniformity of his examples to imply that an agent in a prior-fault dilemma can *always* defuse the bad effects of the prior misdeed to avoid a second instance of moral wrongdoing. While the consistency of his examples seems to suggest it, the Thomistic corpus contains no general affirmation of this claim.

One way of approaching this question is by focusing on a key element that surfaces in Aquinas's remarks on *secundum quid* cases of perplexity. Aquinas notes that a certain supposition (*supposito quodam*) belongs to every *secundum quid* moral dilemma, and this point is worth a second look. Aquinas emphasizes this point in five texts:

No one is absolutely perplexed, absolutely speaking, but given a certain supposition, it is not inconsistent, on that assumption, that someone would be perplexed (*simpliciter nullus perplexus est, absolute loquendo; sed quodam posito non est inconveniens, illo stante, aliquem perplexum fore*).[90]

Nothing prohibits someone to be perplexed, given some supposition, although no one is absolutely perplexed (*Nihil enim prohibet aliquem esse perplexum aliquo supposito, licet nullus sit perplexus simpliciter*).[91]

---

[88] Alasdair MacIntyre, "Moral Dilemmas," 98.

[89] For example, Santurri, *Perplexity in the Moral Life*, 92–3, writes, "It is hardly satisfying to suggest that an agent with a mistaken conscience is not in a real dilemma because the error can be corrected." In "Moral Dilemmas," 98, MacIntyre holds a different view, stating, "Aquinas's answer is clear: to understand that one's conscience is in error is something possible at any moment for anyone."

[90] *In II librum Sententiarum*, d. 39, q. 3, a. 3 ad 5 (Mandonnet, 1004).

[91] *Super Romanos*, cap. 14, 2, §1120 (Marietti, 1: 208).

It is not inconsistent that given a certain supposition, someone is perplexed (*Non est autem inconueniens quod, aliquo posito, aliquis homo sit perplexus*).[92]

It is not inconsistent, under a certain supposition, that one is not able to avoid sin (*et hoc non est inconveniens ut aliquo supposito homo peccatum evitare non possit*).[93]

It is not inconsistent that someone is perplexed given a certain supposition (*Non est autem inconveniens quod sit perplexus supposito quodam*).[94]

In light of these texts, the issue can be reformulated as: is the "certain supposition (*quodam posito, supposito quodam, aliquod posito*)" present to all prior-fault dilemmas *always* able to be defused by the agents who are perplexed? All of Aquinas's examples suggest that such is the case, but Aquinas never explicitly says so. Donagan answers this question in the negative, contending, "it is possible, by breaking one moral prohibition, to entangle yourself in a situation in which, whatever you do, you must break another: that is, in which you are perplexed *secundum quid*."[95] Arguing for the existence of irresolvable cases of perplexity *secundum quid*, Donagan offers a recommendation in which one can detect the tradition of Gratian and the authors of early thirteenth-century *summae*: Donagan invokes the principle of *minima de mala eligenda* or "choose the lesser of two evils."[96]

Aquinas's general statements in the five texts are neutral on the issue of whether certain "harder" or irresolvable *secundum quid* dilemmas can exist. Any claim for their existence must always be contrasted with Aquinas's examples that all involve cases where agents ultimately can avoid moral wrongdoing with the aforementioned repentance, conscience reformation, or disposal of an evil intention. In short, it must be concluded that Aquinas's texts do not contain an explicit answer to the question of whether there are these harder or irresolvable *secundum quid* perplexity situations. Interpreters are bound to disagree depending on whether Aquinas's general statements regarding the *supposito quodam* are read in a certain light, or whether emphasis is given to the consistency of examples set forth by Aquinas. The texts on moral dilemmas appear to support both readings, and in the absence of an additional source of evidence it will be difficult to resolve the issue.[97] The ambiguity was inherited by the earliest Thomistic commentators who had the responsibility of providing a definite resolution, but that issue will be saved for the last chapter of this book.

[92] *Quaestiones de quolibet*, III, q. 12, a. 2, ad 2 (Editio Leonina, xxv.2: 286).
[93] *De veritate*, q. 17, a. 4, ad 8 (Editio Leonina, xxv.2: 526).
[94] *Summa theologiae* III, q. 64, a. 6, ad 3 (Editio Leonina, XII: 47, XII: 48).
[95] Donagan, *The Theory of Morality*, 152.   [96] See Donagan, *The Theory of Morality*, 152.
[97] Aquinas's designation that dilemmas can be generated by a "certain supposition" became influential among theorists in the fifteenth and sixteenth centuries. See Geonget, *La notion de perplexité a la Renaissance*, 250–1.

4.5 A TEXT FOR THE MISSING ARTICLE ON *PERPLEXITAS*

This chapter began by noting that what would have been Aquinas's definitive treatment on the subject of moral dilemmas is not available to us
because the relevant text from *Quodlibet XII* is not extant. Possessing only
the tantalizing title of *On Perplexity: Whether Someone is Able to be Perplexed*
(*De perplexitate, utrum aliquis possit esse perplexus*), one is left to reconstruct
Aquinas's view in a piecemeal fashion, examining those texts where Aquinas
raises the topic of moral dilemmas as a side issue when discussing other
subjects. The evidence, consisting of eighteen texts scattered throughout
the corpus, did yield many examples and categorical statements that allow
one to reconstruct, with some confidence, what Aquinas would have said
in the missing article. The account here would not be complete, however,
without mention of a disputed text attached to the Thomistic corpus on
the subject of moral dilemmas.

In the Biblioteca Medicea Laurenziana in Florence there is a manuscript
of Aquinas's quodlibetal questions where a text of the missing article on
moral dilemmas is presented. This manuscript has been associated with
the Dominican church Santa Maria Novella and dates from the fourteenth
century. The editors of the Leonine edition of Aquinas's works do not
consider the short text to be an authentic text by Aquinas, and the text
apparently exists only in this manuscript. Nevertheless, it is included as
an appendix to the critical edition.[98] Despite its questioned authenticity,
it warrants consideration, if only for its relevance as continued reflection
upon Aquinas's position. The main portion of the text is:

It should be said that perplexity is taken in two ways. First, with respect to
knowledge, and thus whoever doubts is perplexed. Second, with respect to ability,
and thus no one is *perplexus simpliciter*, because no one is in such a state that he
is not able to take care of his salvation; otherwise free will would be taken away.
Nevertheless, it is possible to be *perplexus secundum quid*, that is, accidentally.
Consider, for instance, someone who in no way is willing to forgo his mistress,
yet his obligation for celebrating mass is imminent. That person is thus *perplexus*
according to a certain supposition, because if he celebrates, he sins, and if he does
not celebrate, he likewise sins. Nevertheless, there can be a remedy: that he should
forsake his will. The one perplexed in knowledge, however, ought to seek the
wisdom of the wise man (*Dicendum quod perplexitas dupliciter accipitur: quantum
ad scire, et sic quicunque dubitat est perplexus; et quantum ad posse, et sic nullus
simpliciter perplexus, quia nullus est in statu tali quod non possit prouidere saluti
sue, alias tolleretur liberum arbitrium. Tamen secundum quid potest esse perplexus,*

---

[98] "Articuli additi in codici F," *Quaestiones de quolibet* (Editio Leonina, xxv.2: xvii–xviii).

scilicet in casu. Puta qui nullo modo uult dimittere concubinam et inminet sibi necessitas celebrandi, sic est perplexus supposito quodam, quia si celebrat, peccat, et si non celebrat, similiter. Tamen potest esse remedium, quod dimittat uoluntatem. Qui autem perplexus est in sciencia, debet requirere consilium sapientis).[99]

This passage begins by distinguishing two senses of perplexity: epistemic confusion and real moral entanglement. Anyone who is in doubt about any matter suffers from this first sense of perplexity, and there need not be any moral significance to the confusion that some people have about some things on occasion. The second sense of *perplexus* pertains to ability, and here the text broaches the issue of moral dilemmas. The text quickly issues a categorical denial of cases of *perplexus simpliciter*, and this denial is similar to the two that are present in the established Thomistic corpus. This text goes beyond the others, however, in explicitly arguing that the non-existence of such cases of perplexity *simpliciter* is required by free will (*liberum arbitrium*). If there were such a thing as perplexity *simpliciter*, the argument goes, human beings would not be free to determine their salvation (*salus*). The text then introduces the concept of perplexity *secundum quid* by giving an example from the *Wayward Cleric* variety discussed above. The text identifies the dismissal of the mistress as the manner in which the perplexed individual can avoid committing a second sin. The text closes with the view that those who are perplexed in the sense of epistemic confusion should seek the counsel of a wise person.

The value of this text, even if it is not Aquinas's own work but from the later Thomistic tradition, lies in its confirmation of the general interpretation of moral dilemmas set forth in this chapter. The text highlights the two classes of perplexity *simpliciter* and perplexity *secundum quid* distinguished by Aquinas, re-articulates a categorical denial of cases of perplexity *simpliciter*, defends the existence of perplexity *secundum quid* for non-innocent agents, and describes a situation where an agent entangled by a prior misdeed can still avoid committing a second sin. Of course it would have been delightful if the text had offered an opinion on the question of whether agents can escape all *secundum quid* dilemmas. Whether Aquinas would have offered a clearer answer to this question in the treatment of moral dilemmas during his Lenten quodlibets of 1272 remains unknown.

The present chapter has brought into the discussion of moral perplexity some Thomistic texts beyond the four consistently cited by Donagan and others. The inclusion of additional texts into the discussion has been primarily epexegetic, as the argument here has demonstrated that Donagan

---

[99] "Articuli additi in codici F," *Quaestiones de quolibet* (Editio Leonina, xxv.2: xviii).

on the whole interprets Aquinas correctly on this contentious issue among twentieth-century ethical theorists. Although Donagan based his interpretation of the Thomistic doctrine of perplexity on only four texts of the Angelic Doctor, he produced a sound interpretation of Aquinas's thought. This practice, however, engendered several difficulties for commentators who assumed that the four texts exhausted Aquinas's treatment of the subject. The aim of this chapter has been to bring the other relevant texts to light to confirm the interpretation of Aquinas by Donagan and to refute Donagan's detractors on several issues, including those of logical consistency, the denial of perplexity *simpliciter*, the affirmation of perplexity *secundum quid*, and obligations of one faced with a perplexity *secundum quid* situation. By doing so it has been shown that the more recent attempts by commentators to include Aquinas in the camp of those arguing for the existence of genuine moral perplexity for innocent agents will have to look elsewhere rather than to Thomas Aquinas for support. Better candidates for that genealogy include Gregory the Great, Gratian, William of Auxerre, and the Franciscan authors of the *Summa Halesiana*.

CHAPTER 5

Thomas Aquinas on failures of practical reasoning: Why synderesis doesn't inoculate agents against malformed conscience dilemmas

Among the truths designated by Thomas Aquinas as self-evident (*per se nota*) belongs a class of propositions promoted as the foundation for ethical reasoning.[1] Aquinas is confident that all agents possess at least a subset of these true propositions and regularly employ them in ethical decision-making.[2] He identifies the production of such basic ethical propositions or first principles with the habit of synderesis. This habit of synderesis for practical reasoning is parallel to the habit of understanding (*intellectus*) for speculative reasoning, as both habits supply self-evident first principles for arguments in their respective domains. Synderesis supplies general truths as major premises for practical syllogizing, and *intellectus* does the same for theoretical or speculative syllogizing. While Aquinas's best-known example of a self-evident principle of practical reasoning, "good is to be done and pursued, and evil is to be avoided (*bonum est faciendum et prosequendum, et malum vitandum*)," is famously asserted in the discussion of natural law in the *Summa theologiae* and subject to much discussion among twentieth-century Thomistic commentators, it is not the one to which Aquinas gives the most analysis throughout his writings.[3] Instead,

---

[1] For recent evaluations of the concept of self-evidence in Aquinas, see Luca Tuninetti, *Per Se Notum: Die logische Beschaffenheit des Selbstverständlichen im Denken des Thomas von Aquin* (Leiden: Brill, 1996), and M. V. Dougherty, "Thomas Aquinas on the Manifold Senses of Self-Evidence," *The Review of Metaphysics* 59 (2006), 601–30.

[2] Aquinas, *Summa contra gentiles*, III, cap. 47.6 (Editio Leonina, XIV: 128): "Now although different things are known, and different things believed to be true, by different people, yet some truths there are in which all men agree, such as first principles both of the speculative and of the practical intellect (*autem diversa a diversis cognoscuntur et creduntur vera, tamen quaedam sunt vera in quibus omnes homines concordant, sicut sunt prima principia intellectus tam speculativi quam practici*)." The English translation is from Thomas Aquinas, *The Summa contra Gentiles*, 4 vols. (London: Burns Oates and Washbourne, 1924–9), III.1: 110.

[3] *Summa theologiae* I–II, q. 94, a. 2, corp. (Editio Leonina, VII: 170). For discussions of competing interpretations of this principle, see Germain Grisez, "The First Principle of Practical Reason: A Commentary on the *Summa Theologiae*, 1–2, Question 94, Article 2," *Natural Law Forum* 10 (1965), 168–96; Vernon J. Bourke, "The Background of Aquinas' Synderesis Principle," in *Graceful Reason: Essays in Ancient and Medieval Philosophy Presented to Joseph Owens, CCSR* (Toronto: Pontifical

the first principle of practical reasoning most extensively discussed by Aquinas is "The commandments of God are to be obeyed." This principle, which for convenience can be referenced as the *Divine Command Principle* (hereafter, DCP), is defended in works throughout the span of Aquinas's writing career, yet it has largely been ignored by present-day commentators seeking to set forth Aquinas's philosophical ethics.

Aquinas's contention that all moral agents are supplied with at least some self-evident propositions of practical reasoning may lead one to question why agents are not shielded from moral dilemmas of the malformed conscience variety. Aquinas's answer can be stated succinctly: the errors of conscience do not come from the operation of synderesis, held to be infallible, but from the admixture of false premises unconnected with synderesis in the course of practical reasoning. Fortunately, Aquinas gives many examples of agents who succumb to this kind of error. Two of them deserve particular consideration here insofar as they are identical to the second and third of Aquinas's *Malformed Conscience Dilemmas* noted above. This chapter analyzes Aquinas's presentation of the DCP in practical reasoning, with particular attention to his discussion of agents who use the DCP but still find themselves in moral dilemmas of the *Malformed Conscience* variety. The chapter concludes with an overview of the medieval legacy of the view transmitted by Aquinas, with particular attention to the claim that agents who encounter this kind of moral dilemma should set aside (*deponere, dimittere*) their erroneous consciences.

5.1 THE DEFENSE OF THE DIVINE COMMAND PRINCIPLE

Aquinas's earliest discussions of the DCP occur in the second book of his commentary on the *Sententiae* of Peter Lombard. There, Aquinas describes it as self-evident in several passages treating of synderesis. In a representative text he states:

First principles, by which reason is directed in acting, are self-evident; and regarding these no error is possible, just as it is not possible to err regarding first principles in [scientific] demonstration. These naturally known principles of acting pertain to synderesis, such as "God is to be obeyed," and those similar to this (*prima principia, quibus ratio dirigitur in agendis, sunt per se nota; et circa ea non contingit errare, sicut nec contingit errare ipsum demonstrantem circa principia prima. Haec autem principia agendorum naturaliter cognita ad synderesim pertinent, sicut Deo esse obediendum, et similia).*[4]

Aquinas here contends that the human intellect is infallible with reference to the first principles of action, and a parallel is asserted between the role of self-evident principles of demonstration in speculative sciences and the role of practical self-evident principles in directing human action. As several scholars have noted, Aquinas often gives a priority to speculative or metaphysical self-evident propositions over practical or ethical self-evident propositions, insofar as he customarily discusses the latter only after having identified the former.[5] In the text above, Aquinas promotes a version of the DCP as an ethical self-evident principle provided by synderesis. By designating the proposition as self-evident, Aquinas implies it is knowable by reason; as such, it is considered to be a truth of the philosophical order rather than an article of faith. Admittedly this text does not specify precisely how this self-evident proposition will function in moral decision-making or moral science, but a fuller treatment will be forthcoming. That the habit of synderesis allows for the production of various forms of the DCP, along with other self-evident ethical propositions, is suggested in other texts from the same commentary. Aquinas explains:

It is requisite that practical reason be led by some self-evident principles, such as "evil is not to be done," "the precepts of God are to be obeyed," and others (*oportet quod ratio practica ab aliquibus principiis per se notis deducatur, ut quod est malum non esse faciendum, praeceptis Dei obediendum fore, et sic de aliis).*[6]

This text amplifies the role of synderesis insofar as another ethical self-evident principle is identified in addition to the DCP, namely, "evil is not to be done." This passage confirms that synderesis will be responsible for an agent's possession of a variety of self-evident ethical principles. It also suggests that the DCP is considered by Aquinas to serve a parallel role to the better known self-evident principle regarding the avoidance of evil noted above and famously defended in the discussion of law in the *Summa theologiae.*

There are two more formulations of the DCP in the commentary on the *Sententiae* that deserve mention. In a discussion of the existence of moral

---

[4] *In II librum Sententiarum*, d. 39, q. 3, a. 2, corp. (Mandonnet, 999).
[5] R. A. Armstrong, *Primary and Secondary Precepts in Thomistic Natural Law Teaching* (The Hague: Martinus Nijhoff, 1966), 34; Denis J. M. Bradley, *Aquinas on the Twofold Human Good* (Washington, DC: The Catholic University of America, 1997), 290; Ralph McInerny, *Aquinas on Human Action* (Washington, DC: The Catholic University of America, 1992), 206.
[6] *In II librum Sententiarum*, d. 24, q. 2, a. 3, corp. (Mandonnet, 610).

error, Aquinas raises the issue of whether the doctrine of the infallibility of synderesis might entail that moral error is impossible. If synderesis infallibly allows for the production of self-evident principles for directing practical reason, one may wonder about the means by which moral failure arises. Aquinas wishes to defend the infallibility of the habit of first principles while recognizing the frequency of moral failures by agents. To elucidate the issue, Aquinas proposes the example of a heretic who errantly believes that the swearing of oaths is impermissible:

> The heretic's conscience is mistaken when he believes that he ought not to take an oath, even in a lawful manner . . . not because he is mistaken with respect to the common principle that "nothing forbidden is to be done," but because he mistakenly believes that every oath is forbidden, which he accepts as if it were a principle (*conscientia haeretici decipitur dum credit se non debere jurare etiam pro causa legitima . . . non quia decipiatur in hoc communi principio, quod est, nullum illicitum esse faciendum; sed quia decipitur in hoc quod credit omne juramentum esse illicitum, quod quasi pro principio accipit*).[7]

With this discussion Aquinas contends that the heretic does not err with respect to the principle that what is forbidden (presumably by God) is to be avoided, but rather the heretic errs by falsely believing that certain activities (in this case, swearing) fall under that prohibition. This false belief concerning oaths is not derived from the DCP, but rather is logically independent from it. The heretic, on Aquinas's account, is correct in holding to the DCP, but his application of it to the particular activity of swearing is mistaken.

The Divine Command Principle in the practical syllogisms of erroneous consciences

After the commentary on the *Sententiae*, the next treatment of the DCP as self-evident occurs in *De veritate*, written *c.* 1256–9.[8] In discussions of synderesis, there Aquinas presents the DCP as self-evident using such formulations as: "obedience is to be given to God (*Deo esse oboediendum*),"[9]

---

[7] *In II librum Sententiarum*, d. 39, q. 3, a. 2, corp. (Mandonnet, 1000). See also *De veritate*, q. 17, a. 2, corp. (Editio Leonina, XXII.2: 520). This example is a common one in medieval discussions of conscience. See Walter of Bruges, *Quaestiones disputatae*, ed. E. Longpré, OFM (Louvain: Institut Supérieur de Philosophie de L'Université, 1928), q. XI, corp., 107.

[8] The translations from *De veritate* cited below are from *The Disputed Questions on Truth*, trans. Robert W. Mulligan, SJ, James V. McGlynn, SJ, and Robert W. Schmidt, SJ, 3 vols. (Chicago: Henry Regnery, 1952–4).

[9] *De veritate*, q. 16, a. 1, ad 9 (Editio Leonina, XXII.2: 506).

"submission is to be given to God (*Deo esse obsequendum*),"[10] "nothing prohibited by the law of God is to be done (*nihil prohibitum lege Dei esse faciendum*),"[11] and "it is evil not to believe what God has declared (*malum esse non credere his quae a Deo dicuntur*)."[12] In those instantiations of the DCP, synderesis provides the universal proposition that indicates obligation on the part of agents to follow the commandments of God. A more detailed account is given with these presentations of the DCP, for Aquinas provides examples of practical syllogisms that contain the DCP as a premise.[13] Several texts deserve mention. In the first, Aquinas proposes a practical syllogism representative of a judgment indicating the impermissibility of fornication:

If the judgment of synderesis expresses this statement: "nothing prohibited by the law of God is to be done," and if the knowledge of higher reason presents this minor premise: "sexual intercourse with this woman is forbidden by the law of God," the application of conscience will be made by concluding: "this intercourse is to be avoided" (*ut si ex iudicio synderesis proferatur, nihil prohibitum lege Dei est faciendum; et ex superioris rationis notitia assumatur, concubitum cum ista muliere esse contra legem Dei; fiet applicatio conscientiae concludendo, ab hoc concubitu esse abstinendum*).[14]

Expressed syllogistically, Aquinas's argument can be arranged as:

P1 Major (from synderesis):	"What is prohibited by the law of God is not to be done."
P2 Minor (from higher reason):	"This sexual intercourse with this woman is prohibited by the law of God."
C (act of conscience):	"This sexual intercourse with this woman is not to be done."

---

[10] *De veritate*, q. 16, a. 2, ad 2 (Editio Leonina, XXII.2: 509).

[11] *De veritate*, q. 17, a. 2, corp. (Editio Leonina, XXII.2: 520).

[12] *De veritate*, q. 16, a. 3, ad 2 (Editio Leonina, XXII.2: 511).

[13] On various recent approaches to Aquinas's view of practical syllogisms, see Daniel Westberg, *Right Practical Reason: Aristotle, Action, and Prudence in Aquinas* (Oxford: Clarendon Press, 1994), 149–55; Bradley, *Aquinas on the Twofold Human Good*, 155–7; Kevin L. Flannery, SJ, *Acts Amid Precepts: The Aristotelian Logical Structure of Thomas Aquinas's Moral Theory* (Washington, DC: The Catholic University of America Press, 2001), 5–12, 196–223; and Daniel McInerny, *The Difficult Good: A Thomistic Approach to Moral Conflict and Human Happiness* (New York: Fordham University Press, 2006), 92–6.

[14] *De veritate*, q. 17, a. 2, corp. This text has a parallel in *In II librum Sententiarum*, d. 24, q. 3, a. 3, corp. (Mandonnet, 624). In a discussion of the ways in which fornication is judged to be impermissible by an agent, Aquinas expresses the DCP as "everything prohibited by the law of God is to be avoided (*omne prohibitum legei Dei est vitandum*)."

In this practical syllogism, the major premise is the synderesis-supplied DCP. The DCP is a universal proposition that does not specify any determinate activity but merely states that activities that fall under divine prohibition are to be avoided. The minor premise, however, identifies a particular situation. In this practical syllogism, the minor term represents not a class of actions but an individual act, namely, intercourse with a particular woman.[15] The minor premise of this practical syllogism is not provided by synderesis, but is said to come from the agent's reasoning.[16] While synderesis provides premises that are universal and infallible, the minor premises adopted by an agent may or may not be true, and here Aquinas leaves room for the possibility of moral dilemmas of the malformed conscience variety.

The incorporation of a false minor premise into a judgment of conscience can also be exhibited, according to Aquinas, both in the practical syllogisms of heretics who omit to believe certain articles of faith, and in the practical syllogisms of men who martyred early Christians. Such examples are familiar, as they were the second and third of Aquinas's *Malformed Conscience Dilemmas* discussed in the previous chapter. Aquinas proposes that the respective agents in those cases follow practical syllogisms such as:

P1 Major (from synderesis):	"Only what God has dictated needs to be believed."
P2 Minor (from higher reason):	"God does not dictate X."
C (act of conscience):	"X need not be believed."[17]
P1 Major (from synderesis):	"Obedience to God is to be done."

---

[15] In *In II librum Sententiarum*, d. 24, q. 2. a. 4, corp. (Mandonnet, 613), Aquinas provides a similar syllogism, but the minor premise refers to adultery as such rather than a particular instance of adultery.

[16] The division of reason into *ratio superior* and *ratio inferior* originates in the writings of Augustine and has a long tradition in medieval ethical discussions. See Robert W. Mulligan, SJ, "*Ratio Inferior* and *Ratio Superior* in St. Albert and St. Thomas," *The Thomist* 19 (1956), 339–67, and "*Ratio Superior* and *Ratio Inferior*: The Historical Background," *The New Scholasticism* 29 (1955), 1–32. Mulligan contends that the distinction between higher and lower reason is, for Aquinas, "not a critical one," and that the distinction, when it appears in Aquinas's works, appears to be a deference to established philosophical parlance rather than a significant distinction (366). For a similar estimation, see Michael Bertram Crowe, *The Changing Profile of the Natural Law* (The Hague: Martinus Nijhoff, 1977), 159: "The distinction between *ratio superior* and *ratio inferior* . . . does not, in fact, appear to be of great importance." Aquinas defines higher and lower reason at *De veritate*, q. 15, a. 2, corp.

[17] *De veritate*, q. 16, a. 3, ad 2 (Editio Leonina, XXII.2: 511): "In heretics . . . the universal judgment of synderesis remains in them, since they judge it to be evil not to believe what God has said. But they err in higher reason, because they do not believe that God has said this (*in haereticis . . . in universali enim iudicium synderesis in eis manet, iudicant enim malum esse non credere his quae a Deo dicuntur; in hoc autem errant secundum rationem superiorem quod non credunt hoc esse a Deo dictum*)."

| P2 Minor (from higher reason): | "Obedience to God is the killing of Apostles." |
| C (act of conscience): | "The killing of Apostles is to be done."[18] |

In both of these practical syllogisms, synderesis provides a formulation of the DCP as the major premise, and with the adoption of a false minor premise a false conclusion is drawn. The first syllogism represents a judgment of a heretic, who, while not erring at the level of the DCP, does entertain a false minor premise regarding the content of what God dictates. In the second syllogism, another version of the DCP is supplied by synderesis as the major premise, but it is followed by a false minor premise asserting that the killing of the apostles is an act of obedience to God. In both cases, the false minor premise errantly specifies an application of the universal premise, adding content to the understanding of the major premise. Thus, by locating the source of moral error in faultily assumed minor premises, Aquinas seeks to account for moral failure while still maintaining the inerrancy of the natural habit of self-evident principles, that is, of synderesis.[19]

According to Aquinas's account of malformed conscience dilemmas, the adoption of the errant minor premise is generally considered the fault of the agent. For this reason, such dilemmas are classified by him as cases of perplexity *secundum quid* rather than as cases of perplexity *simpliciter*. The key for agents to avoid situations of perplexity *secundum quid* generated by erroneous consciences is the avoidance of false minor premises. When, nevertheless, an agent assumes a faulty minor premise, the solution to

---

[18] *De veritate*, q. 16, a. 2, ad 2 (Editio Leonina, XXII.2: 509): "Therefore, in that choice by which the murderers of the Apostles thought they were offering worship to God, the error did not come from the universal judgment of synderesis, that obedience should be offered to God, but from the false judgment of higher reason, which considered the killing of the Apostles as pleasing to God (*et ideo in illo arbitrio quo occisores apostolorum arbitrabantur se obsequium praestare Deo peccatum non proveniebat ex universali iudicio synderesis quod est Deo esse obsequendum, sed ex falso iudicio rationis superioris quae arbitrabatur occisionem apostolorum esse beneplacitam Deo*)." The inspiration for this example is John 16:2.

[19] Written approximately at the time of the writing of the *Prima secunda* of the *Summa theologiae*, *Quodlibet III* also contains a discussion of synderesis similar to that of the *De veritate*. Again the infallibility of the intellect with respect to ethical self-evident principles is defended and an account of moral error is presented as the acceptance of a false minor premise in the production of a practical syllogism. The example given by Aquinas is a familiar one, for Aquinas discusses the heretic who falsely believes that the swearing of oaths is impermissible. Aquinas defends the integrity of synderesis in the heretic, for in the judgment of such a person the major premise "nothing is to be done against divine precept (*nichil esse faciendum contra preceptum diuinum*)" is present (*Quaestiones de quolibet*, III, q. 12, a. 1, corp. (Editio Leonina, XXV.2: 284)).

avoiding further sin is its immediate abandonment when moral dilemmas arise.

Further endorsements in the Thomistic corpus

It is arguable that Aquinas's adoption of the DCP has not been fully appreciated by Thomistic commentators seeking to set forth Aquinas's moral theory. In his biblical commentaries Aquinas provides even more forceful endorsements of it as a necessary element of moral reasoning:

The act of conscience that something must be done is nothing other than a judgment that it would be against God's will not to do it (*habere conscientiam de re aliqua facienda, nihil aliud est quam aestimare quod faciat contra Deum, nisi illud faciat*).[20]

For no conscience dictates something to be done or avoided, except who believes this to be against or according to the law of God (*Non enim conscientia dictat aliquid esse faciendum vel vitandum, nisi quia credit hoc esse contra vel secundum legem Dei*).[21]

A similarly forceful statement can be found elsewhere in the Thomistic corpus:

Conscience does not oblige by virtue of its own power, but by virtue of divine precept; for conscience does not dictate that something is to be done for the reason that it seems to itself, but for this reason, because it is a commandment from God (*conscientia obligat non virtute propria, sed virtute praecepti divini: non enim conscientia dictat aliquid esse faciendum hac ratione, quia sibi videtur; sed hac ratione, quia a Deo praeceptum est*).[22]

These texts each assert that the experience of moral obligation is tied to the DCP. Aquinas opposes the notion that the experience of moral obligation is independent from a notion of divine commands. These texts suggest that the binding character of judgments of conscience presupposes that synderesis has provided the DCP. Without the DCP, agents will not experience the force of moral obligation in their practical reasoning. The DCP has yet to be examined seriously by those twentieth-century philosophers who have sought to extract from the Thomistic corpus an ethical system

---

[20] *Super Galatas*, cap. 5, 1, §282 (Marietti, I: 626).
[21] *Super Romanos*, cap. 14, 2, §1120 (Marietti, I: 208).
[22] *In II librum Sententiarum*, d. 39, q. 3, a. 3, ad 3 (Mandonnet, 1004). See *De veritate*, q. 17, a. 3, corp. (Editio Leonina, XXII.2: 522): "conscience is said to bind by the power of divine precept (*conscientia ligare dicitur in vi praecepti divini*)."

independent of any articles of faith or religious revelation, that is, a system that exclusively relies upon philosophical principles as a foundation.[23]

Aquinas's sustained consideration of practical syllogisms that express errantly formed judgments of conscience consisting of the DCP and a false minor premise exhibits the meaning of his often-repeated claim that agents in *Malformed Conscience Dilemmas* should "put away the erroneous conscience (*conscientiam erroneam deponere*)"[24] or "send away the erroneous conscience (*conscientiam erroneam dimittere*)."[25] With those recommendations, Aquinas is not advising morally perplexed agents to set aside their powers of moral evaluation or discernment, but rather he is indicating that the solution to avoiding further wrongdoing is the identification of minor premises that have corrupted moral decision-making. To a modern reader, Aquinas's texts might seem to advocate the abandonment of moral evaluation or discernment, but Aquinas is simply advising that a particular act or judgment of conscience be reevaluated. Aquinas's texts support only the dismissal of mistaken judgments, premised on faulty minor premises, not the abandonment of the powers of moral evaluation. In his examples, the judgment of conscience is mistaken because of a material error rather than a formal one; that is, the conclusion of an agent's act of moral reasoning is false because of the adoption of a false premise rather than a simple inferential mistake in reasoning. The latter, of course, is also an additional source of corruption in practical reasoning, but not one that Aquinas broaches in discussions of moral dilemmas.[26]

5.2 MALFORMED CONSCIENCE DILEMMAS AFTER AQUINAS

Much of thirteenth-century philosophy in general, and theorizing about conscience in particular, exhibits restrained creativity. Theorists philosophized with heavy deference to their predecessors while adding insights that

---

[23] For a range of evaluations concerning a purely philosophical Thomistic ethics, see Denis J. M. Bradley, *Aquinas on the Twofold Human Good* (Washington, DC: The Catholic University of America, 1997); David M. Gallagher, "The Role of God in the Philosophical Ethics of Thomas Aquinas," in *Was ist Philosophie im Mittelalter? Akten des X. Internationalen Kongresses für Mittelalterliche Philosophie*, ed. Jan A. Aertsen and Andreas Speer (Berlin: Walter de Gruyter, 1998), 1024–33, at 1027–8; and Brian P. Shanley, OP, *The Thomist Tradition* (Dordrecht: Kluwer Academic Publishers, 2002), 134–5.

[24] *In II librum Sententiarum*, d. 39, q. 3, a. 3, ad 5 (Mandonnet; *De veritate*, q. 17, a. 4, ad 8 (Editio Leonina, XXII.2: 526); *Quaestiones de quolibet*, III, q. 12, a. 2, ad 2 (Editio Leonina, XXV.2: 286); *Super Galatas*, cap. 5, 1, §282 (Marietti, I: 626).

[25] *Super Romanos*, cap. 14, 2, §1120 (Marietti, I: 208).

[26] See the discussions by Timothy C. Potts in "Conscience," in *The Cambridge History of Later Medieval Philosophy*, ed. Norman Kretzmann, Anthony Kenny, and Jan Pinborg (Cambridge University Press, 1982), 701, and *Conscience in Medieval Philosophy* (Cambridge University Press, 1980), 54.

expanded the ways problems were formulated and discussed. This feature is distinctively exhibited with the theorizing about perplexed conscience throughout the later Middle Ages and deserves consideration here.

Bonaventure

Also commenting on Peter Lombard's *Sententiae* in the mid-1250s in Paris was the Franciscan Bonaventure of Bagnoregio, who together with Aquinas later endured the mendicant controversy at the University of Paris, a situation that was finally resolved in 1257 when the two were admitted to the *consortium magistrorum* or consortium of masters at the university. Bonaventure and Aquinas each propounded similar solutions to the problem of the binding character of the malformed conscience while commenting on Lombard's work.[27] Bonaventure begins his discussion by asking, "Is a human being *perplexus* when conscience dictates one thing and divine law dictates the contrary (*utrum homo sit perplexus, quando conscientia dictat unum, et lex divina dictat contrarium*)?"[28] After discussing agents whose consciences are correctly formed, Bonaventure treats of those who have malformed consciences and concludes:

> It is clear that no one is caught in perplexity except temporarily, namely, for as long as the erroneous conscience remains. Yet one is not perplexed without qualification, in that one ought to set aside that conscience (*Patet etiam, quod nemo ex conscientia perplexus est nisi ad tempus, videlicet quamdiu conscientia manet; non tamen est perplexus simpliciter, pro eo quod debet illam conscientiam deponere*).[29]

Here Bonaventure uses the language that is consistent with discussions of mistaken conscience found in earlier thinkers, including William of Auxerre, the authors of the *Summa Halesiana*, and Albert. Bonaventure offers the categorical claim that agents in moral dilemmas generated by malformed consciences are not absolutely perplexed (*perplexus simpliciter*).

---

[27] The texts from Bonaventure's *In II librum Sententiarum* cited below are taken from the second volume of the *Opera omnia*, 10 vols. (Quaracchi: Collegium S. Bonaventurae, 1882–1902). The translation is that of A. S. McGrade, in *The Cambridge Translations of Medieval Philosophical Texts*. Volume II: *Ethics and Political Philosophy*, ed. Arthur Stephen McGrade, John Kilcullen, and Matthew Kempshall (Cambridge University Press, 2001), 169–99.

[28] Bonaventure, *In II librum Sententiarum*, d. 39, q. 3 (II: 906a, McGrade, 182).

[29] Bonaventure, *In II librum Sententiarum*, d. 39, q. 3 (II: 907b, McGrade, 185). See also pseudo-Bonaventure, *Compendium theologicae veritatis*, lib. 2, sec. 11, in Bonaventure, *Opera omnia*, ed. A. C. Peltier, 15 vols. (Paris: Vivès, 1864–71), VIII: 114: "perplexity is nothing absolutely; nevertheless someone is able to be perplexed according to an erroneous conscience, where put away, one will be freed (*perplexitas nihil est simpliciter; potest tamen quis esse perplexus secundum erroneam conscientiam, qua deposita, erit liberatus*)."

They are only perplexed for a time (*ad tempus*), that is, as long as agents persist in the errors generating the moral dilemmas. The solution to avoiding further sin is that agents must put away (*deponere*) their mistaken consciences; that is, the agents must locate the false minor premises and remove their commitment to them, since such premises corrupt acts of moral reasoning. As with Aquinas, Bonaventure's solution is not an abandonment of the agent's powers of moral discernment, but simply an injunction for the agent to discern where a faulty premise of reasoning has entered into practical syllogizing or moral reasoning. In the words of one present-day commentator on Bonaventure, "Self-education thus transforms an erroneous applied conscience into a correct applied conscience and permits an individual to follow his own conscience in good faith."[30]

Like Aquinas, Bonaventure also identifies the DCP as essential to moral reasoning, for he writes:

> Conscience is like a herald or messenger of God, and it does not command what it says from itself, but it commands, as it were, from God, like a herald proclaiming the edict of a king (*conscientia est sicut praeco Dei et nuntius, et quod dicit, non mandat ex se, sed mandat quasi ex Deo, sicut praeco, cum divulgat edictum regis*).[31]

According to Bonaventure, conscience adopts the principle that God's commands are to be obeyed, and this principle serves as the foundation for the experience of moral obligation. He explains his position further by arguing that conscience binds in one of two ways. If the premises of the judgment are true, conscience binds (*ligat*) to doing what it dictates. If there is a false premise that corrupts the judgment of conscience prescribing an act that is contrary to a divine command, then conscience binds (*ligat*) to setting itself aside.[32] This two-optioned binding of conscience preserves the obligation of agents always to follow the commands of God.

Bonaventure is somewhat more generous than Aquinas in offering explicit advice to those who might find themselves in situations of perplexity because of erroneous consciences. He counsels:

---

[30] Douglas Langston, "The Spark of Conscience: Bonaventure's View of Conscience and Synderesis," *Franciscan Studies* 53 (1993), 79–95, at 83. Throughout his analysis, Langston imports the term "applied conscience" to refer to the determination of conscience to a particular matter. Since at times Bonaventure describes conscience in a way similar to how Aquinas describes synderesis, Langston uses the term "potential conscience" to refer to the general infallible knowledge of moral truths possessed by conscience. See Langston, 80–1, and also Langston, *Conscience and Other Virtues* (University Park, PA: Pennsylvania State University Press, 2001), 26–7. See also Potts, "Conscience," 698–9 and *Conscience in Medieval Philosophy*, 41.

[31] Bonaventure, *In II librum Sententiarum*, d. 39, q. 3 (II: 907b, McGrade, 185).

[32] Bonaventure, *In II librum Sententiarum*, d. 39, q. 3 (II: 906b, McGrade, 182).

If we ourselves do not know how to judge matters, in that we do not know God's law, we ought to consult those who are wiser, or, if human counsel is lacking, turn to God in prayer (*et si nescit per se de illa iudicare, pro eo quod nescit legem Dei, debet sapientiores consulere, vel per orationem se ad Deum convertere, si humanum consilium deest*).[33]

In this text Bonaventure underscores that the formation of conscience may require that one defer to those who possess greater wisdom, and when wiser people are lacking, one should turn to prayer. This appeal to prayer is not the theological solution to dilemmas advocated by Raymond Lull, however. As was argued in Chapter 3, Lull presented a view in the *Vita coaetanea* where innocent agents are ensnared in moral dilemmas as part of the moral life, and the only escape is a divine intervention that extricates prayerful agents from such situations. Prayer does not offer an intrinsic solution to any dilemma, according to Lull, but simply prompts God to extract agents miraculously from dilemmatic situations. Bonaventure's turn to prayer here is quite different; it is simply a route to discerning the errors that cause consciences to be mistaken.

Peter of Tarentaise, Richard of Middleton, and Henry of Ghent

This solution of putting away an ill-formed judgment of conscience to avoid further sinning in a malformed conscience dilemma appears to have been widespread among medieval thinkers. It was clearly prevalent in the earlier part of the thirteenth century, as its proponents included William of Auxerre, the authors of the *Summa Halesiana*, and Albert the Great, and, as has been shown, later in the century it gained the support of Aquinas and Bonaventure. In the thirteenth century, it evolved into a fairly standard account, insofar as many of the most prominent thinkers of the age advocated this solution, despite many disagreements on other issues pertaining to conscience. In the late 1250s, Peter of Tarentaise (1224/5–76), a Dominican elevated to the papacy to become Innocent V, designated a section of his commentary on Lombard's *Sententiae* with the title *De perplexitate*. He notes there that an agent with an erroneous conscience "is not absolutely perplexed, because he is able to put away the conscience; but that conscience remaining, he is perplexed (*non est perplexus simpliciter, quia potest conscientiam deponere: sed perplexus est manente illa conscientia*)."[34] Similarly, the Franciscan Richard of Middleton (*c.* 1249–1302), a figure

---

[33] Bonaventure, *In II librum Sententiarum*, d. 39, q. 3 (II: 907b, McGrade, 185).

[34] Peter of Tarentaise, *In II Sententiarum*, d. 39, q. 3, a. 3, ad 5, in *In IV librum Sententiarum commentaria*, 4 vols. (Toulouse: Academiae Tolosanae Typographum, 1649–52 [repr. Ridgewood, NJ: The Gregg Press, 1964]), 2:329. See also John of Paris, *Super Sententias*, q. 97, d. 39, q. 2, in *Commentaire*

well acquainted with the work of Aquinas and Bonaventure, stated that an agent with an erroneous conscience "nevertheless is not able to be absolutely perplexed, because he is able to put away such a conscience, by that fact one is liberated from that perplexity (*tamen simpliciter perplexus esse non potest, quia talem conscientiam potest deponere, quo facto ab illa perplexitate liberatus est*)."[35] Richard adds that those who might be tempted to invoke the authority of Gratian to defend the view that an erroneous conscience can generate an inescapable moral dilemma or a situation of perplexity *simpliciter* should recall that "Master Gratian is reprehended in the apparatus (*in apparatu repraehenditur magister Gratianus*)," that is, the jurist's position has been refuted by the glossators of the *Glossa ordinaria*.[36]

Other contemporaries offered similar views. Henry of Ghent (*c.* 1217–93) discussed an agent with a perplexed conscience and concluded: "Therefore he is perplexed, so that it is necessary for him to sin, unless he puts away the error (*ergo perplexus est, ut necesse sit eum peccare, nisi errorem deponat*)."[37] The Franciscan Walter of Bruges (*c.* 1227–1307) provided much greater detail in a series of disputed questions on conscience. While considering an agent who is *perplexus* after the adoption of the shocking premise "God is evil," Walter judged, "it is not impossible that he should experience perplexity and multifaceted evil (*non est impossibile quod incurrat perplexitatem et multiplex malum*)."[38] Later, when discussing an agent who assumes the faulty premise that patricide is permissible, or the faulty premise that honoring of one's parents is illicit, Walter provides an analysis using language almost identical to Aquinas, saying that "nevertheless he is not absolutely perplexed, because he is able, and obliged, to put away that conscience (*nec tamen est perplexus simpliciter, quia potest et debet deponere illam*)."[39]

Giles of Rome and Augustinus Triumphus

In commenting on Lombard's *Sententiae* in the 1270s, Giles of Rome (1243/7–1316) contended that an agent with an erroneously formed

sur les Sentences, ed. Jean-Pierre Muller, OSB, 2 vols. (Rome: Herder, 1961–4), II: 225: "One is not perplexed, because one is able to send away the erroneous conscience (*Nec est perplexus, quia potest conscientiam errantem dimittere*)."

[35] Richard of Middleton, *In II Sententiarum*, d. 39, a. 2, q. 1, ad 2, in *Super quatuor libros Sententiarum*, 4 vols. (Brescia: Apud Vincentium Sabbium, 1591), II: 484.

[36] Richard of Middleton, *In II Sententiarum*, d. 39, a. 2, q. 1, ad 3, in *Super quatuor libros Sententiarum*, II: 484.

[37] Henry of Ghent, *Quodlibet I*, q. 18, sol., in *Opera omnia*, ser. 2 (Leuven University Press, 1979–), V: 155.

[38] Walter of Bruges, *Quaestiones disputatae*, q. XI, ad 3, 105, 110.

[39] Walter of Bruges, *Quaestiones disputatae*, q. XV, corp., 129–31, at 131.

conscience who appears bound to sin by either following or not following
its dictate "is not absolutely perplexed, because one is able to put away
the erroneous conscience (*non est perplexus simpliciter; quia potest conscien-
ciam erroneam deponere*)."[40] The agent in this case is only suffering from
qualified perplexity (*perplexio secundum quid*) and can, by sending away
the erroneous judgment of conscience, get "beyond the perplexity (*extra
perplexionem*)."[41] Giles's terminology here again is quite similar to his predecessors. The issue found new life in a discussion of papal authority,
when in his work *Summa de ecclesiastica potestate* (*Summa on Ecclesiastical
Power*), Augustinus Triumphus (1270/3–1328) considered whether a papal
command is more binding than an erroneous conscience. In formulating
his reply, Augustinus resurrects two of the malformed conscience dilemmas
discussed by Aquinas, namely, those featuring agents whose erroneous consciences dictate that they must fornicate or steal.[42] Augustinus considers
that in each case it seems that one will sin either by acting or not acting,
from which it seems that "one is perplexed and is, as it were, obligated
to the impossible (*perplexus est et quasi ad impossibile obligatus*)."[43] The
solution, of course, is a familiar one: such agents are able "to abandon the
perplexity (*perplexitatem . . . relinquere*)."[44] Augustinus explains: "To this it
is said that one is not perplexed without qualification, because one can and
ought to set aside an erroneous conscience at the command of the pope or a
superior (*ad quod dicitur quod simpliciter non est perplexus quia potest et debet
conscientiam erroneam deponere ad praeceptum pape vel superioris*)."[45] It is
evident, therefore, that the conceptual distinction between perplexity *simpliciter* and perplexity *secundum quid* transmitted by Aquinas is reinforced
by later thinkers.

John Duns Scotus, Peter Auriol, Thomas of Strasbourg, and Denis the Carthusian

Except for the presence of an unusual analogy, an otherwise similar solution
to avoiding sin in cases of perplexity involving ill-formed consciences is

[40] Giles of Rome, *Super secundo Sententiarum* (Venice: Lucas Venetus, 1482), d. 39, q. 3.
[41] Giles of Rome, *Super secundo Sententiarum*, d. 39, q. 3.
[42] The text from Augustinus Triumphus cited below is taken from Augustinus de Ancona, *Summa
de ecclesiastica potestate* (Rome: Domus Francisci de Cinquinis, 1479). The translation is that of
McGrade in *The Cambridge Translations of Medieval Philosophical Texts*. Volume II: *Ethics and
Political Philosophy*, 418–83.
[43] Augustinus Triumphus, *Summa de ecclesiastica potestate*, q. 63 (192, McGrade, 479).
[44] Augustinus Triumphus, *Summa de ecclesiastica potestate*, q. 63 (192, McGrade, 479).
[45] Augustinus Triumphus, *Summa de ecclesiastica potestate*, q. 63 (192, McGrade, 479).

presented by John Duns Scotus (1266–1308) in his commentary on Lombard. While discussing whether an agent sins to a greater extent by acting against an erroneous conscience than by acting according to it, Scotus posits that no agent is able to be absolved from a law of God. Borrowing an image from Augustine of Hippo, he contends that the relationship between the divine law and a judgment of conscience is analogous to the relationship between the command of an empress and the command of the empress's proconsul or procurator. In these situations, the divine law and the command of the empress bear the greater authority.[46] The agent who has the erroneous conscience "not only is obligated so that he does not act according to conscience, but so that he should put away that conscience; accordingly no one is able to be perplexed with respect to divine law (*non solum est obligatus ut non faciat secundum illam conscientiam, sed ut deponat illam; unde nullus potest esse perplexus in lege divina*)."[47] With the authority of Augustine, Scotus conceives of a dictate of conscience to be one of many obligations that can be serially ordered according to degrees of authority, where the dictates of a higher authority take precedence over a lower.[48]

While the view advising the setting aside of an erroneous conscience becomes standard medieval fare in discussions of conscience in the thirteenth century, it continues to receive greater analysis from later thinkers. Particularly noteworthy are the remarks by Peter Auriol (*c.* 1280–1322), who adds that for agents who are perplexed in this way, there is no real compulsion to choose between the contradictories. He asserts that if an agent were truly perplexed, then sin would be involuntary, and such a conclusion is inadmissible. A remedy (*remedium*) must be found, and he explains:

For there is to be a middle way between acting according to what the erroneous conscience dictates and not acting according to the erroneous conscience; that middle way, however, is to put away conscience (*Est enim dare medium inter agere, quod dictat conscientia erronea, et non agere secundum conscientiam erroneam, illud autem medium est deponere conscientiam*).[49]

---

[46] See John Duns Scotus, *Lectura in librum secundum Sententiarum*, d. 39, q. 3, in *Opera omnia* (Vatican City, 1950–), XIX: 386–7.

[47] Scotus, *Lectura in librum secundum Sententiarum*, d. 39, q. 3, in *Opera omnia*, XIX: 387.

[48] For an analysis of such an invocation of Augustine, see Durandus of St. Pourçain, *In II Sententiarum*, d. 39, q. 5, arg. 1, ad 1, in *In Petri Lombardi Sententias theologicas commentariorum libri IIII*, 2 vols. (Venice: Typographia Guerraea, 1571 [repr. Ridgewood, NJ: The Gregg Press, 1964]), I: 97.

[49] Peter Auriol, *Commentaria in secundum librum Sententiarum*, 2 vols. (Rome: Aloysius Zannetti, 1604–5), d. 39, q. 1, a. 1, 2:309.

Auriol's suggestion that a middle way (*medium*) exists between the contradictories of acting and not acting should not be understood as a denial
of the principle of excluded middle, but rather as the contention that a
moral dilemma of acting and not acting can be defused by removing the
erroneous judgment of conscience. The decision to put away an erroneous
conscience is not a decision to act against conscience, but is rather a way to
remove the choice between acting and not acting according to the dictate
of conscience.

It is worth noting that not all thinkers judge that agents who find
themselves in malformed conscience dilemmas are necessarily guilty of
negligence in the formation of their consciences. Thomas of Strasbourg
(d. 1357) contended that agents who are perplexed because of erroneous
consciences are not *perplexus simpliciter* because they can consult a variety
of sources to help them, such as a wise person, the instruction of sacred
scripture, or advice of others. He does not seem to identify malformed
conscience dilemmas with prior-fault dilemmas, as he suggests that there
are always available ways for agents to rectify their consciences, unless the
agents act pertinatiously (*pertinaciter*).[50]

A detailed and far-ranging précis of major medieval positions on the
question of whether an erroneous conscience binds was set forth by the
prolific thinker Denis the Carthusian (1402/3–72) in his commentary on
Lombard's *Sententiae*.[51] Denis catalogued various views, noting the general adherence to the position that erroneous consciences do not bind
unqualifiedly, as agents can set aside (*deponere, dimittere*) the error affect-
ing a judgment of conscience. Even the German Gabriel Biel (1420/5–95)
broached the subject of perplexity of conscience in his fifteenth-century
commentary, again defending the traditional view.[52] That such differently
minded thinkers propounded similar analyses of perplexed agents in their
respective commentaries on the *Sententiae* of Lombard testifies to the

---

[50] See Thomas of Strasbourg, *In II librum Sententiarum*, d. 39; Thomas de Argentina, *Commentaria in IIII libro Sententiarum* (Venice: Ziletti, 1564), 195v.

[51] See Denis the Carthusian, *In librum II Sententiarum*, d. 39, q. 3, in *Opera omnia*, 42 vols. (Montreuil, Tournai, and Parkminster: Typis Cartusiae S.M. de Pratis, 1896–1935), XXII: 523–8. See also Francisco Suárez's discussion "What It is to Put Away Conscience (*Deponere conscientiam quid sit*)," in *De bonitate et malitia humanorum actuum, Disputatio XII*, s. 4, §16, in Francisco Suárez, *Opera omnia*, 30 vols. (Paris: Vivès, 1856–78), IV: 446–7.

[52] Gabriel Biel, *Collectorium circa quattuor libros Sententiarum. Liber secundus*, ed. Wilfridus Werbeck and Udo Hofmann (Tübingen: J. C. B. Mohr, 1984), 666 (lib. 2, d. 39, q. 1, a. 3): "Truly he is not absolutely perplexed, because the way of escape is clear to him, namely, to put away the erroneous conscience. Because if he does not do it, by his own fault he is perplexed (*Verum non est simpliciter perplexus, quia patet sibi via evadendi, scilicet deponere conscientiam erroneam. Quod si non facit, ex sua culpa est perplexus*)."

influence of the commentary tradition on Lombard's textbook in theological studies for centuries.[53]

William of Ockham and The Odium Dei Dilemma

In light of the preceding discussion of the DCP and moral dilemmas of the perplexed conscience variety, it is fitting to mention the famous thought experiment of William of Ockham (*c.* 1285–1347) concerning an agent who might receive a divine command to hate God. Could God command hatred of God (*odium Dei*) of an agent, and could the fulfillment of such a command be meritorious? Ockham's affirmative answers to both questions were not well received in all quarters, as they were included among the theses condemned in Avignon in 1326.[54]

Ockham's thought experiment has garnered much attention in recent decades, invoked principally in discussions of whether Ockham is a divine command theorist.[55] If one focuses mainly on his political works, Ockham seems like a straightforward natural law theorist, particularly because in such texts he appears to champion right reason (*ratio recta*) as the authoritative guide for moral conduct and as the source of moral obligation. If, however, one focuses mainly on the earlier theological works, Ockham appears as a divine command theorist, insofar as he stresses that in virtue

---

[53] On the influence of this work, see Philipp W. Rosemann, *The Story of a Great Medieval Book: Peter Lombard's* Sentences (Peterborough: Broadview Press, 2007). See also *Mediaeval Commentaries on the* Sentences *of Peter Lombard*, vol. i, ed. G. R. Evans (Leiden: Brill, 2002); and *Mediaeval Commentaries on the* Sentences *of Peter Lombard*. vol. ii, ed. Philipp W. Rosemann (Leiden: Brill, 2010).

[54] The often-cited texts by Ockham on these issues include: *Quaestiones in librum quartum Sententiarum (Reportatio)*, ed. Rega Wood, Gedeon Gál, OFM, and Romualdo Green, OFM (St. Bonaventure, NY: St. Bonaventure University, 1984), q. 16, 352; *Quaestiones in librum secundum Sententiarum (Reportatio)*, ed. Gedeon Gál, OFM and Rega Wood (St. Bonaventure, NY: St. Bonaventure University, 1981), q. 15, 352–3. For the text of the censure at Avignon, see August Pelzer, "Les 51 articles de Guillaume Occam censurés, en Avignon, en 1326," *Revue d'histoire ecclésiastique* 18 (1922), 240–70, at 254. Ockham's position is re-affirmed in the summary of Ockham's principles *Tractatus de principiis theologiae*, in William of Ockham, *Opera dubia et spuria*, ed. E. M. Buytaert *et al.* (St. Bonaventure, NY: St. Bonaventure University, 1988), 509. For an English translation, see *A Compendium of Ockham's Teaching*, trans. Julian Davies, OFM (St. Bonaventure, NY: The Franciscan Institute, 1998), 9.

[55] The literature is vast. In addition to the works cited below, see Taina M. Holopainen, *William Ockham's Theory of the Foundations of Ethics* (Helsinki: Luther-Agricola-Society, 1991), 133–49; and Armand Maurer, *The Philosophy of William of Ockham in the Light of Its Principles* (Toronto: Pontifical Institute of Mediaeval Studies, 1999), 525–39. See also Thomas M. Osborne, Jr., "Ockham as a Divine-Command Theorist," *Religious Studies* 41 (2005), 1–22; Kevin McDonnell, "Does William of Ockham Have a Theory of Natural Law?" *Franciscan Studies* 34 (1974), 383–92; David W. Clark, "William of Ockham on Right Reason," *Speculum* 48 (1973), 13–36; David W. Clark, "Voluntarism and Rationalism in the Ethics of Ockham," *Franciscan Studies* 31 (1971), 72–87.

of God's absolute power (*potentia absoluta*) God could establish any act – including theft, adultery, and the above-mentioned *odium Dei* – as good and meritorious for salvation. Of course, Ockham notes that in the present state of affairs God has not established such acts as good. Theorizing about divine absolute power is simply a consideration of what God can or could have done, not what has been done, and in Ockham's view the only limitation to divine activity is the principle of non-contradiction. As Ockham frequently notes, God is not a debtor (*debitor*) to anyone, and there can be no restriction on the divine will other than what is self-contradictory. In the actual existing world, which is the expression of God's ordained power (*potentia ordinata*), the acts of theft, adultery, and hatred of God are proscribed, and hence they cannot at present be done meritoriously.

Ockham's thought experiment generates some problems. Would not an agent encountering such a command be in some kind of moral dilemma? Two difficulties might arise for the agent. First, the agent in such a situation could experience right reason and the divine commands to be issuing contradictory claims. In the words of one commentator, Ockham's view implies the possibility that "God could command the opposite of what right reason dictates, whether in general or in particular. Given such divine precepts, right reason would enjoin contradictory dictates."[56] On this view, right reason, informed by God's command, would recognize the obligation to obey God's command, but right reason would also recognize the disorder of such an act. The agent, therefore, would be cognitively perplexed and also morally perplexed, as the agent would experience the simultaneous obligations to hate and not hate God.

A second problem facing the agent in this *Odium Dei Dilemma* is considered in some detail by Francisco Suárez. He takes up Ockham's thought experiment when discussing whether God in virtue of his absolute power could grant dispensations from the natural law, and he identifies Ockham as the key figure among several who championed the affirmative view. Suárez argues that Ockham's general position has been rightly rejected as "false and absurd (*falsa et absurda*)" by other theologians, since "it is wholly repugnant to that which is essentially and intrinsically evil that it

---

[56] Marilyn McCord Adams, "Ockham on Will, Nature, and Morality," in *The Cambridge Companion to Ockham*, ed. Paul Vincent Spade (Cambridge University Press, 1999), 245–72, at 266. See also her contribution "William Ockham: Voluntarist or Naturalist?" in *Studies in Medieval Philosophy*, ed. John F. Wippel (Washington, DC: The Catholic University of America Press, 1987), 219–47, at 241: "[God] could enjoin acts of the species now labeled 'hatred of God,' 'fornication,' 'adultery,' 'theft.' And in this logically and metaphysically possible eventuality, right reason would lead to contradictory dictates." A similar view is defended in her article "The Structure of Ockham's Moral Theory," *Franciscan Studies* 46 (1986), 1–35, at 28.

should cease from being evil, since the nature of the thing cannot undergo change (*nihilominus prorsus repugnat ad id quod per se et intrinsece malum est, desinere esse malum, quia rei natura non potest mutari*)."[57] He continues by explaining that the mistaken foundation of Ockham's moral outlook is the assumption that external prohibition (*prohibitio extrinseca*) is the origin of evil for human acts.[58]

After making those general claims, Suárez then turns in particular to the example of the agent who receives a command to hate God. After noting that the very issuance of such a command would be incompatible with the attribute of divine goodness, he contends further that the agent receiving the command would be caught in a contradiction about how to act:

Furthermore, a certain contradiction would be involved in such a situation; for obedience to God is a virtual love of Him, and the obligation to obey springs, above all, from love; therefore, it would be contrary to reason that one should be bound by a precept to hold God Himself in hatred (*Item esset ibi quaedam contradictio: nam obedire Deo est quidam virtualis amor ejus, et obligatio ad obediendum praesertim nascitur ex amore; ergo repugnat obligari ex praecepto ad ipsummet Deum odio habendum*).[59]

The problem seems to be that for Ockham, love of God is the motivation of an agent to obey the commands of God, so if the agent were to obey the command to hate God, the agent would need to love and hate God at the same time. Surprisingly, Suárez's objection appears to repeat an objection that Ockham himself raises in another text.[60] Present-day commentators on Ockham have frequently remarked on the psychological and logical impossibility for an agent who receives a command of *odium Dei* to fulfill it. According to Philotheus Boehner, Ockham's own view is that there "would be a genuine perplexity or ethical antinomy. In such a case, the created will simply could not act. For if it obeys, and consequently hates God, it would love God."[61] In short, on this view it is not a contradiction

[57] Francisco Suárez, *De lege aeterna, naturali, et jure gentium*, cap. 15, in *Opera omnia*, 30 vols. (Paris: Vivès, 1856–78), v: 144–5. The English translation is from Francisco Suárez, *Selections from Three Works*, 2 vols. (Oxford: Clarendon Press, 1944), ii: 287–8.

[58] Suárez, *Opera omnia*, v: 145.   [59] Suárez, *Opera omnia*, v: 145 (*Selections*, 288).

[60] William of Ockham, *Quodlibeta septem*, ed. Joseph C. Wey, CSB (St. Bonaventure, NY: St. Bonaventure University, 1980), quod. 3, q. 14, 256. For an English translation, see *Quodlibetal Questions*, trans. Alfred J. Freddoso and Francis E. Kelley (New Haven: Yale University Press, 1991), 214. In this text, Ockham discusses whether God could command that an agent not love God for a time.

[61] Philotheus Boehner, OFM, "A Recent Presentation of Ockham's Philosophy," *Franciscan Studies* 9 (1949), 443–56, reprinted in Boehner, *Collected Articles on Ockham*, ed. Eligius M. Buytaert, OFM (St. Bonaventure: The Franciscan Institute, 1958), 136–56, at 153. See also Heiko Augustinus Oberman, *The Harvest of Medieval Theology: Gabriel Biel and Late Medieval Nominalism*, 3rd edn (Durham, NC: The Labyrinth Press, 1983), 92: "a man so commanded would be thoroughly

for God to command *odium Dei*, but it is impossible for an agent to fulfill it.

Among the approaches readers of Ockham have followed to account for the *Odium Dei Dilemma*, two stand out. First, there are those who simply assert that the contradiction facing the agent is simply a consequence of the unhappy blend of voluntaristic and rationalist elements in Ockham's thought, and therefore it is best to judge simply that Ockham's ethical views, unlike those in logic and epistemology, are "of questionable value" and "not wholly adequate."[62] Secondly, other commentators underscore that while in virtue of divine *potentia absoluta* an agent could in principle experience such a dilemma, being obliged to hate and love God simultaneously, in fact this possibility will never be realized.[63] On this account, the *Odium Dei Dilemma* remains an unactualized possibility, that is, a moral dilemma that could exist but never will. If it were to be actualized in the world, it seems, the *Odium Dei Dilemma* would seem to satisfy the conditions of a perplexity *simpliciter* moral dilemma of conscience, as such a situation would presumably involve an innocent agent, and the dictates of the agent's conscience could not be set aside according to the traditional advice offered by so many medieval theorists.

Ockham's followers, of course, inherited the *Odium Dei Dilemma*. It could not escape their notice as it provided a key touchstone in illustrating the lengths to which one who subscribes to a wide notion of *potentia absoluta* could be required to go. If the present moral order is truly contingent in all respects, it could be replaced with an entirely different moral order. Some followers of Ockham, such as the English Dominican Robert Holcot (*c.* 1290–1349), accepted Ockham's position in unmitigated form, arguing for the possibility that God could command *odium Dei* and that the agent's fulfillment of that command would be meritorious.[64] Others, like Gabriel Biel, were more cautious, underscoring that God could but

---

perplexed, for by obeying the will of God he would at the same time love God and not love God"; and Linwood Urban, "William of Ockham's Theological Ethics," *Franciscan Studies* 33 (1973), 310–50, at 348: "For the dilemma in which men are put is not just a psychological dilemma, but a logical one. For on Ockham's account, 'hating God because it is commanded' entails 'loving God,' and hence is contradictory." Lucan Freppert, OFM, *The Basis of Morality According to William Ockham* (Chicago: Franciscan Herald Press, 1988), 121–40, argues that Ockham might have changed his mind on the issue. Other discussants of the dilemma include Rega Wood, *Ockham on the Virtues* (West Lafayette: Purdue University Press, 1997), 270–1, and C. G. Normore, "Picking and Choosing: Anselm and Ockham on Choice," *Vivarium* 36 (1998), 23–39, at 36–8.

[62] Linwood Urban, "William of Ockham's Theological Ethics," 350.

[63] See Marilyn McCord Adams, "Ockham on Will, Nature, and Morality," 266.

[64] For a discussion of Holcot's view, see Leonard Kennedy, *The Philosophy of Robert Holcot, Fourteenth-Century Skeptic* (Lewiston: The Edwin Mellen Press, 1993), 75–80.

would not place an agent in such a situation.[65] For others, the *Odium Dei Dilemma* inspired general inquiries concerning norms and consistency in ethics, as the writings of Roger Roseth demonstrate.[66]

5.3 AQUINAS WITHIN THE TRADITION

In light of this excursus on *Malformed Conscience Dilemmas*, several conclusions can be drawn. First, while Aquinas strongly asserts that agents possess an infallibility with regard to certain basic self-evident ethical truths provided by synderesis, these truths only enter into practical reasoning as general major premises and need to be combined with minor premises to yield practical syllogisms or judgments of conscience. Since minor premises admit of falsity, there is no guarantee that conscience is correct in any given case. Agents experiencing malformed conscience dilemmas must locate their faulty premises to escape the commission of an additional moral failure. Secondly, there is general agreement among many prominent medieval thinkers that agents in malformed conscience dilemmas are not absolutely perplexed because there lies this possibility of locating the false minor premise. Finally, it can be seen that Aquinas endorses a position defended by the early thirteenth-century composers of theological *summae* and continued in the *Sententiae* commentary tradition well into the fifteenth century.

---

[65] An account of Biel's position is given by Oberman, *The Harvest of Medieval Theology*, 93–6.

[66] For the little that is known about Roseth's life, and for an assessment of the *Lectura super Sententias*, see Olli Hallamaa, "On the Limits of the Genre: Roger Roseth as a Reader of the *Sentences*," in *Mediaeval Commentaries on the* Sentences *of Peter Lombard*, vol. ii, ed. Philipp W. Rosemann (Leiden: Brill, 2010), 369–404. For a discussion of Roseth's expansion of Ockham's view, see Simo Knuuttila, *Modalities in Medieval Philosophy* (London: Routledge, 1993), 193–4; and Simo Knuuttila and Olli Hallamaa, "Roger Roseth and Medieval Deontic Logic," *Logique & Analyse* 149 (1995), 75–87, at 84–6.

CHAPTER 6

Moral dilemmas in the early Thomistic tradition: Johannes Capreolus and the Deceiving Demon Dilemma

A monument of the early history of Thomism is the wide-ranging *Arguments Defending the Theology of St. Thomas Aquinas* (*Defensiones theologiae Divi Thomae Aquinatis*) composed by the French Dominican Johannes Capreolus (1380–1444).[1] Capreolus authored this massive work to defend the philosophical and theological system of Thomas Aquinas against a barrage of criticisms offered by many theorists in the century and a half after Aquinas's death. In the course of 190 *quaestiones*, Capreolus presented objections from Peter Auriol, Duns Scotus, and Henry of Ghent, among others, and then furnished replies *ad mentem Thomae*. He began the work in 1407 at the University of Paris at the request of his Dominican superiors, finally bringing it to completion two and a half decades later in Rodez in 1432, but it was not printed for another half-century. The *Defensiones* stands as the earliest comprehensive presentation of Thomistic philosophical and theological thought, and in light of his achievement Capreolus bears the honorific title *Princeps Thomistarum* or "Prince of Thomists." In later decades Capreolus's masterwork became a sourcebook for Thomistic humanists of the Italian Renaissance as well as Catholic theologians of the Counter-Reformation.[2] The *Defensiones* is strongly polemical; in it Capreolus defends the doctrines of Aquinas while attacking those who have criticized various points of the Thomistic system. The force and energy that pervade the work have led one commentator to characterize Capreolus as "a good representative of the Thomist school at war."[3]

---

[1] Johannes Capreolus, *Defensiones theologiae Divi Thomae Aquinatis*, ed. Ceslaus Paban and Thomas Pègues, 7 vols. (Turin: Alfred Cattier, 1900–08). Unless otherwise noted, the translations from Capreolus below are my own.

[2] See Romanus Cessario, OP, *A Short History of Thomism* (Washington, DC: The Catholic University of America Press, 2005), 59–61, 68–9.

[3] Servais Pinckaers, OP, "La défense, par Capreolus, de la doctrine de Saint Thomas sur les vertus," in *Jean Capreolus en son temps (1380–1444)*, ed. Guy Bedouelle, Romanus Cessario, and Kevin White (Paris: Les Éditions du Cerf, 1997), 177–92, at 178. This chapter appears in English translation as "Capreolus's Defense of St. Thomas's Teaching on the Virtues," in John Capreolus, *On the Virtues*

At the beginning of the *Defensiones,* Capreolus states that he will be touting Aquinas's doctrines rather than presenting his own. The work largely comprises extracts from a wide range of authors, followed by texts from Aquinas's writings rearranged to form rebuttals to various criticisms. One interpreter has pointed out that this method insured that a "position of one's own was not necessary nor was it explicitly given" and that throughout the work Capreolus is "hiding... behind an authority."[4] Capreolus's methodological reflections in this regard bear some consideration, for he writes:

> My intention is to introduce nothing on my own, but only to relate opinions that seem to me to have been those of St. Thomas, and to introduce no proofs for the conclusions other than his own words, except rarely (*nihil de proprio intendo influere, sed solum opiniones quae mihi videntur de mente S. Thomae fuisse recitare, nec aliquas probationes ad conclusiones adducere praeter verba sua, nisi raro*).[5]

Such a project of defending Aquinas by interweaving passages from the Thomistic corpus to provide new answers to later detractors is an ambitious one, since the task presupposes a mastery of Aquinas's writings as well as a creativity for harnessing the resources of a philosophical and theological system to engage the problems of later ages.[6] While this method of using Aquinas's words to craft new responses may work well for issues that are treated somewhere in Aquinas's writings, it can be more challenging when used to address issues that are either not discussed by Aquinas at all or treated only incompletely.

The present chapter looks to Capreolus's *Defensiones* for assistance in answering the principal question left unresolved by Aquinas's explicit texts on moral dilemmas, namely, whether Aquinas's outlook can admit the possibility of irresolvable prior-fault dilemmas. Did Aquinas believe that there exists a subclass of prior-fault dilemmas where the ill-effects of the prior fault are so damaging that they cannot be defused by an agent, and

---

(Washington, DC: The Catholic University of America Press, 2001), xi–xxvi, and in a slightly abbreviated form as "Capreolus's Defense of Aquinas: A Medieval Debate about the Virtues and Gifts," in *The Pinckaers Reader: Renewing Thomistic Moral Theology,* ed. John Berkman and Craig Steven Titus (Washington, DC: The Catholic University of America Press, 2005), 304–20.

[4] Sigrid Müller, "The Ethics of John Capreolus and the 'Nominales'," *Verbum: Analecta Neolatina* 6 (2004), 301–14, at 304.

[5] Cited from: John Capreolus, *On the Virtues,* trans. Kevin White and Romanus Cessario, OP (Washington, DC: The Catholic University of America Press, 2001), xxix; Capreolus, *Defensiones,* 1: 1.

[6] The question whether Capreolus is a pure interpreter of Aquinas's doctrines on all points is one of the greatly explored topics for present-day approaches to Capreolus's work. For a discussion, see Edward P. Mahoney, "The Accomplishment of Jean Capreolus, O.P.," *The Thomist* 68 (2004), 601–32.

thereby the agent is unable to avoid a second moral failure? As examined earlier, Alan Donagan thought Aquinas believed such irresolvable prior-fault dilemmas to exist, whereas Alasdair MacIntyre expressed some doubt. The difficulty in answering this question definitively may stem from the absence of an authentic text for Aquinas's *De perplexitate* from *Quodlibet XII*, as was noted earlier. It is true that all of Aquinas's examples of prior-fault dilemmas display agents who can defuse the ill-effects of their past deeds. Aquinas described such agents as able to repent of their sins, put away evil intentions, or give up the faulty premises plaguing their moral judgments. With additional actions those agents could avoid a further sin. Despite his consistency of examples, however, Aquinas provided no categorical assertion that all prior-fault dilemmas were of that variety, and thus twentieth-century commentators have been divided on Aquinas's actual position.

The present inquiry is additionally justifiable in light of the increased interest among historians of philosophy who have attempted to assess Thomism as a consistent philosophical and theological system now in its eighth century.[7] As Capreolus is indisputably one of the most important exponents of early Thomism, his judgments on moral dilemmas bear much weight when seeking principles of the Thomistic system. The present chapter shows that in light of Capreolus's extensive discussion of moral dilemmas in the *Defensiones*, Thomistic ethics broadly understood does not admit the existence of irresolvable prior-fault dilemmas. To argue for this point, the discussion below divides into seven sections. First, the chapter discusses the medieval options available to agents who might find themselves in irresolvable prior-fault dilemmas. While the legal and literary traditions of the Middle Ages suggest a variety of strategies, the philosophical and theological traditions of the period on the whole privilege only two, namely, awaiting a miracle (as exhibited by Raymond Lull) or appealing to the principle of the lesser evil (as exhibited by many theorists). Secondly, the discussion turns to the context within which Capreolus deploys his discussion of moral dilemmas. Next, the chapter examines Capreolus's presentation of an unusual moral dilemma – designated here as the *Deceiving Demon Dilemma* – with particular attention to the employment of the

---

[7] In addition to Cessario, *A Short History of Thomism*, see also: Helen James John, *The Thomist Spectrum* (New York: Fordham University Press, 1966); Fergus Kerr, *After Aquinas: Versions of Thomism* (Oxford: Blackwell Publishers, 2002); Brian Shanley, OP, *The Thomist Tradition* (Dordrecht: Kluwer, 2002); Gerald A. McCool, SJ, *From Unity to Pluralism: The Internal Evolution of Thomism* (New York: Fordham University Press, 1992); and Gerald A. McCool, SJ, *The Neo-Thomists* (Milwaukee, WI: Marquette University Press, 2003). For a critical view, see Mark D. Jordan, *Rewritten Theology: Aquinas after His Readers* (Oxford: Blackwell Publishing, 2006), 3–7.

principle of the lesser evil. Various critiques Capreolus and other Thomists have leveled against the principle of the lesser evil are examined, and the chapter concludes by stating that Capreolus's rejection of the principle leaves no room for irresolvable prior-fault dilemmas within Thomism.

6.1 A REVIEW OF MORAL DILEMMA STRATEGIES

The preceding chapters have identified two distinctive options in the medieval philosophical and theological traditions for dealing with irresolvable moral dilemmas. The first is that agents should expect a miraculous divine intervention to save them from future moral wrongdoing when a moral dilemma that is otherwise inescapable arises. This option can be designated as the *Divine Intervention Resolution*, and Raymond Lull provided an exposition of it in his autobiographical *Vita coaetanea*. This option, however, has not escaped criticism. When Aquinas considered the case of a priest who is *perplexus* at mass upon discovering that his chalice has been poisoned, he rejected the view that the priest should drink it under the assumption that God will protect him, for the expectation that God will perform a miracle to disarm effects of the poison would be sinfully presumptuous.[8] Aquinas, therefore, does not endorse a *Divine Intervention Resolution* to moral dilemmas. The second and more frequently defended option for dealing with moral dilemmas offered by the medieval philosophical and theological traditions is an appeal to the principle of the lesser evil. This *Lesser Evil Resolution* found several adherents including Gregory the Great, Gratian, William of Auxerre, and the authors of the *Summa Halesiana*. This resolution did receive some criticism from the glossators on Gratian's *Decretum*. They found no need to endorse it as they considered all moral dilemmas to be spurious. According to the glossators, all purported dilemmas are simply the result of the foolishness of agents who are negligent in discerning and implementing morally permissible options. As wiser agents never experience dilemmas, any appeal to the *Lesser Evil Resolution* is superfluous.

While the *Divine Intervention* and the *Lesser Evil* resolutions have figured prominently in the preceding chapters, other traditions in post-medieval periods have explored additional possibilities, and they deserve brief mention as competing alternatives within wider discussions of moral dilemmas. In the secular legal tradition Gottfried Leibniz catalogued popular methods

[8] See *Summa theologiae* III, q. 83, a. 6, arg. 3, ad 3 (Editio Leonina, XII: 283, XII: 284) as well as the discussion in Chapter 4 above.

that judges use to resolve cases where there appear to be conflicting laws or equally opposing claims set forth by litigants. In his 1666 work, *On Perplexing Cases in Law* (*De casibus perplexis in jure*), Leibniz noted that judges facing these situations have traditionally resorted to a variety of extra-legal means, such as refraining from making a decision altogether to leave the *status quo*, using a random device (such as drawing lots or flipping a coin), making decisions based on mere preference, or even attempting some kind of compromise.[9] Leibniz criticized such judges, however, and rejected all of these extra-legal methods as unfitting. He argued that there are no unanswerable questions in law, as legal systems should provide a correct solution to all problems that arise in courts. Leibniz considered a judge who faces cases like these to be perplexed simply in an epistemic sense, as there are no true cases of irresolvable *perplexitas*, and a true under-standing of a legal system will allow a judge to render a correct verdict in all cases. Those extra-legal techniques for adjudicating conflicting or perplexing legal claims catalogued by Leibniz do not seem to have been championed by the medieval thinkers presently under consideration for use in resolving moral dilemmas. At least, the previously examined the-orists have not offered any endorsement of the view that agents should, for instance, flip a coin or defer to preference to pick between competing moral obligations. The medieval discussion closest to this view is William of Auxerre's supplementary account of the *Hermit Dilemma* examined ear-lier, where the agent was enjoined to consider God as a third party who will render a selection between morally impermissible alternatives.

In a recent book that focuses largely on legal and literary contexts, Stéphan Geonget identifies some further options available to perplexed agents – be they judges or simply moral agents – who find themselves seemingly caught in conflict situations. Using texts from François Rabelais (1494–1553), Michel de Montaigne (1533–92), and others, Geonget con-cludes that in addition to resorting to methods of chance (e.g., dice) or hoping for a miracle (i.e., the *Divine Intervention Resolution*), the literary and legal traditions at times enjoin agents who are perplexed to try other methods, such as:

- interpret and reconcile contradictory texts;
- give up judging the matter;
- privilege one party over the other in the absence of any justification;

---

[9] Gottfried Wilhelm Leibniz, *Disputatio de casibus perplexis in jure*, in *Sämtliche Schriften und Briefe* (Berlin, Darmstadt: Otto Reichl Verlag, 1930), VI.1: 231–56. For a discussion, see Hanina Ben-Menahem, "Leibniz on Hard Cases," *Archiv für Rechts- und Sozialphilosophie* 79 (1993), 198–215, at 202–3.

– choose a middle way and divide a contested good in two;
– resort to common opinion;
– invent a fictitious solution; or
– defer to the judgment of a prince.[10]

Most of these options relate best to agents who are judges of competing claims rather than agents who are in moral dilemmas, so they have limited applicability. A moral life filled with genuine moral dilemmas does not allow agents, for instance, to take abstentions in the way judges can recuse themselves from their cases. Further, moral dilemmas composed of strict contradictories don't allow for a true middle way, except perhaps in the loose sense defended by Peter Auriol mentioned previously. It seems unlikely, therefore, that Aquinas or others would have anticipated or endorsed any of these options from the secular legal or literary traditions in considering the possibility of prior-fault dilemmas. What remains, then, are the two options of the medieval philosophical and theological traditions: the *Divine Intervention* and the *Lesser Evil* resolutions. As Aquinas explicitly rejects the former, the latter remains to be considered.

The avenue to be followed here for exploring the question of whether Aquinas granted the existence of irresolvable prior-fault dilemmas is analyzing the degree to which a Thomistic ethical framework can incorporate the *Lesser Evil Resolution*. The texts of Capreolus provide a good test case for this inquiry for two reasons. First, as was seen above, Capreolus is indisputably an early authority of the Thomistic tradition. Secondly, Capreolus discusses in detail Aquinas's view of moral dilemmas while paying particular attention to the principle of the lesser evil.

6.2 DOING EVIL WHILE INTENDING GOOD

A word of explanation is necessary about Capreolus's presentation, as the format of Capreolus's *Defensiones* is unusual. As a question-commentary on Peter Lombard's *Sententiae*, it treats subjects according to the order of distinctions found in Lombard's work. While Capreolus is not unique in using the *Sententiae* as a pretext for investigating a wider range of issues rather than those explicitly mentioned by Lombard's text, the *Defensiones* does have the additional purpose of serving as an apology of Thomism. Each of the 190 *quaestiones* or investigations exhibits a consistent procedure. A *quaestio* begins with a brief introduction followed by three articles. In the first article, Capreolus sets forth *conclusiones* that present the view of

---

[10] Stéphan Gonget, *La notion de perplexité a la Renaissance* (Geneva: Librairie Droz, 2006), 61–158.

Aquinas on a particular issue, and these conclusions often contain substantive extracts from Aquinas's works. In the second article, Capreolus offers *objectiones* that oppose (or appear to oppose) Aquinas's view in some way, and these objections are taken from a variety of authorities who are usually identified by name. Finally, in the last article Capreolus provides a series of *solutiones* in which he attempts to defuse the preceding *objectiones*, and then the *quaestio* closes with the words, "Blessed be God. Amen (*Benedictus Deus. Amen*)." This tripartite structure of conclusions, objections, and solutions has been recognized as a "highly innovative contribution to the Parisian tradition of commentaries on the *Book of Sentences*" and "a new *genus* of academic literature."[11]

In concert with most medieval thinkers who examined moral dilemmas while commenting on Lombard's textbook, Capreolus broaches the subject in the context of Lombard's discussion of the will. His treatment in the *Defensiones* is occasioned by distinction 38 of the second book of the *Sententiae*, and Capreolus frames the issue as "Whether the goodness of the act of the will is from the end (*Utrum bonitas actus voluntatis sit ex fine*)."[12] Later in the text he rephrases the issue as whether the "intention of a right end excuses from sin (*intentio recti finis excusat a peccato*)."[13] In short, Capreolus considers whether an agent's performance of any action while willing a good end is sufficient to insulate an agent from moral wrongdoing. Capreolus answers decisively in the negative. Using texts from Aquinas, he contends that an agent who wills a good end can still commit a sin, as the final cause of an action alone is not sufficient to specify the action as good or bad. In the prefatory section of the *quaestio*, prior to setting forth the conclusions, objections, and solutions on this subject, Capreolus exhibits his position by offering a brief example:

To evangelize is good, and to eat is good; nevertheless to evangelize in order to eat is not good (*evangelizare bonum est, et manducare bonum est; et tamen evangelizare propter manducare non est bonum*).[14]

Presumably one who evangelizes for the sake of obtaining food commits a sin, even though food itself is a good. Capreolus argues further that for an act of the will to be good the agent must not only desire the right end, but the action itself must also be good. This issue is supported in great detail in the first article, where Capreolus adduces evidence (the *conclusiones*) from Aquinas's own commentary on the *Sententiae* and the *Summa theologiae*.

---

[11] White and Cessario, *On the Virtues*, xxviii; Müller, "The Ethics of John Capreolus," 305.
[12] Capreolus, *Defensiones*, IV: 435.   [13] Capreolus, *Defensiones*, IV: 437.
[14] Capreolus, *Defensiones*, IV: 435.

Capreolus uses extracts from these works to argue that "concerning the goodness of the act of the will the desire for the right end is required, yet is not sufficient (*ad bonitatem actus voluntatis requiritur appetitus recti finis, non tamen sufficit*)."[15] To illustrate this position, he introduces the example of an individual who is willing to steal for the sake of almsgiving. Such an individual – perhaps best conceived as a Robin Hood-like character – illustrates that the desire for a right end does not suffice for placing an act in its moral species, since stealing for the sake of aiding the poor is still stealing.

This technical discussion is the occasion for Capreolus to examine moral dilemmas. He provides an extended account of agents who become perplexed and then considers whether those agents can avoid wrongdoing simply by intending a good. The second article, consisting entirely of objections, proposes that perplexed agents can avoid wrongdoing; if they intend a good then they incur no moral fault. In the third article, consisting of solutions, Capreolus rejects these arguments and lays out a Thomistic view of moral dilemmas by appealing to texts of Aquinas and others. What Capreolus offers is more detailed and systematic than what is found in Aquinas's writings on moral dilemmas. His discussions are therefore quite valuable for considering a broader Thomistic outlook on the subject.

Capreolus's use of Thomistic texts on moral dilemmas

Capreolus does provide two substantive extracts from Thomas Aquinas's writings on the question of moral dilemmas. Framing the issue as "Whether concerning perplexity, there is some or none (*De perplexitate . . . utrum sit aliquid vel nihil*)," Capreolus advises that one consult a passage from the *Summa theologiae* and another from the *Scriptum super Sententiae*.[16] These texts jointly exhibit several key points of Aquinas's doctrine on moral dilemmas examined in Chapter 4 above. The first passage, extracted from *Summa theologiae* i–ii, q. 19, a. 6, describes a malformed conscience dilemma as well as an evil intention dilemma and offers the standard prescription that such agents should put away their erroneous premises or faulty intentions to avoid sinning further. The second passage, extracted from *In II Sententiarum* d. 39, q. 3, a. 3, ad 5, contains Aquinas's crucial denial of situations of perplexity *simpliciter*. After presenting these passages,

---

[15] Capreolus, *Defensiones*, iv: 435.
[16] Capreolus, *Defensiones*, iv: 440. The referenced passages are: Aquinas, *Summa theologiae* i–ii, q. 19, a. 6, ad 3 (Editio Leonina, vi: 147) and *In II librum Sententiarum*, d. 39, q. 3, a. 3, ad 5 (Mandonnet, 1004).

Capreolus also references a third from *De veritate* (q. 17, a. 4, ad 8), where Aquinas notes that malformed conscience dilemmas are simply *secundum quid* situations of perplexity.[17] Each of these three texts – the two that are extracted and one that is simply referenced – exhibits Aquinas's further claim that given a certain supposition (*supposito, quodam posito, aliquo supposito*) it will follow that an agent is *perplexus*. Capreolus uses these texts from Aquinas to establish concisely the main points of Aquinas's explicit doctrine on moral dilemmas. While the three are not exhaustive of Aquinas's treatment, they are representative of what Aquinas expressed on the subject. Incidentally, two of the three were included in the set of four canonical texts that dominated twentieth-century discussions of Aquinas's views on moral dilemmas. Capreolus's slightly shorter list, however, is a superior representation of Aquinas's doctrine insofar as it includes a passage exhibiting the categorical denial of cases of perplexity *simpliciter*.[18]

As was argued above, however, none of Aquinas's texts provides an explicit answer to the question of whether irresolvable prior-fault dilemmas exist. If Capreolus were only to restrict himself to citing passages from the Thomistic corpus, the *Defensiones* would have very little to say on this issue. Capreolus does, however, fortify his defense of Aquinas by incorporating extensive passages from the Italian Augustinian theologian Gregory of Rimini (1300–58). The extent of his borrowing from Gregory is staggering; for large sections Capreolus simply plays the role of an amanuensis to his predecessor.[19] The manner in which Capreolus presses Gregory of Rimini's arguments into service for a defense of Aquinas exhibits how, in Capreolus's view, early Thomism rejects the possibility of irresolvable prior-fault dilemmas. One further interpretive caveat must be noted: the texts that Capreolus borrows from Gregory of Rimini largely originate from an earlier source: the *De causa Dei contra Pelagium et de virtute causarum* (*On the Cause of God Against the Pelagians and on the Power of Causes*) composed by Gregory's contemporary Thomas Bradwardine (1290–1349). Bradwardine was an English theorist perhaps known more for his logical,

---

[17] Aquinas, *De veritate*, q. 17, a. 4, ad 8 (Editio Leonina, XXII.2: 526).

[18] Elsewhere in the *Defensiones* (VI: 115) Capreolus considers whether an evil minister (*minister malus*) can administer baptism without sin, and he extracts Aquinas's discussion of one of the *Wayward Cleric Dilemmas* from *Summa theologiae* III, q. 64, a. 6, ad 3 (Editio Leonina, XII: 48). There Aquinas denies that the minister is *perplexus simpliciter* and notes that an agent can be *perplexus* given the supposition that the agent remain in sin unrepentantly. That text from the *Summa theologiae* was also one of the four canonical texts cited by Donagan.

[19] Capreolus identifies Gregory of Rimini by name at the beginning of the second and third articles, and he notes he is taking the objections and replies from Gregory. In his selection of texts, Capreolus omits sentences at times and on occasion substitutes an interpretive paraphrase for Gregory's text.

scientific, and mathematical contributions than for moral philosophy. Late in life Bradwardine became Archbishop of Canterbury in July of 1349 only to perish of the plague the following month. Bradwardine's text was mined by Gregory of Rimini, and particularly relevant here is his appropriation of texts concerning moral dilemmas. The layered composition of Capreolus's presentation of Aquinas's account of moral dilemmas is intricate: under the pretext of a commentary on Lombard's *Sententiae* (itself a compilation of earlier theological and philosophical materials), Capreolus rearranges extracts from the Thomistic corpus to defend Thomas Aquinas against later detractors, supplementing his defense liberally with texts borrowed from Gregory of Rimini, who himself has taken from Thomas Bradwardine. What exists, therefore, is a defense of Aquinas on moral dilemmas that depends heavily on other thinkers to further an argument left unfinished in the Thomistic corpus.

6.3 THE *DECEIVING DEMON DILEMMA*

Having used Aquinas's texts in the first article to maintain that willing a good end is not sufficient to insulate an agent from moral wrongdoing, Capreolus sets forth arguments against this view in the second, and in doing so broaches the issue of moral dilemmas. The bulk of the discussion concerns an unusual moral dilemma involving an agent who is *perplexus* after being subjected to the scheming of the devil. Capreolus sets forth the basic facts of this *Deceiving Demon Dilemma* as:

> Someone without a prior fault is able to be so deceived by the devil that to him it altogether appears that, unless he should blaspheme or hate God, he necessarily will sin greatly. At that time, according to the judgment of most right reason, that man is obliged to blaspheme or hate God, lest he fall into great sin, because according to a common conception of the soul the lesser of two evils ought to be chosen (*aliquis, sine culpa sua praecedente, potest sic a diabolo decipi, ut sibi videatur omnino quod, nisi blasphemet aut odiat Deum, necessario plus peccabit. Iste tunc, secundam judicium rectissimae rationis, tenetur blasphemare Deum vel odire, ne incidat in majus peccatum: quoniam, secundum communem animi conceptionem, de duobus malis minus malum eligendum est).*[20]

This example is introduced primarily to defend the view that the existence of a good intention insures that an agent avoids sin. Several features deserve

---

[20] Capreolus, *Defensiones*, IV: 436; Gregory of Rimini, *Lectura super primum et secundum Sententiarum*, ed. A. Damasus Trapp, OSA, *et al.*, 6 vols. (Berlin: Walter de Gruyter, 1979–84), VI: 298; Thomas Bradwardine, *De causa Dei contra Pelagium et de virtute causarum*, ed. Henricus Savilius (London: Johannes Billius, 1618 [repr. Frankfurt am Main: Minerva GmbH, 1964]), 256b–c.

comment. To begin, the agent is described as entirely faultless in believing that unless he should blaspheme or hate God he will commit a grave sin. The respective gravity of the sins of blasphemy (*blasphemia*) and the hatred of God (*odium Dei*) were well-considered among medieval thinkers. For instance, Aquinas considered the former to be "a very grave sin (*peccatum maximum*)" and judged the latter to be the gravest of all sins.[21] The important stipulation in this example that the agent is innocent of any wrongdoing in believing such acts to be obligatory prevents an analysis of the situation as an instance of *secundum quid* or qualified perplexity in accordance with Aquinas's view of *Malformed Conscience Dilemmas*, for all of Aquinas's examples featured agents who had negligently omitted personal moral formation. This example stipulates that the agent's acquisition of a false belief pertaining to blasphemy and hatred of God has been secured principally through the machinations of the devil, who presumably has the resources to delude human beings about moral truths. The manner by which a demon might achieve such a state of mind in an agent is left unstated; the case simply postulates that the state of affairs is secured without any culpable act or omission by the agent. This postulation of the innocence of the agent seems opposed to a prevailing Christian view which held that any susceptibility to the deceptions of demons required an agent to have culpably invited such interference. An early defender of this view, John Cassian, had claimed "It is clear, then, that no one can be deceived by the devil except the person who has chosen to offer him the assent of his will (*constat ergo neminem posse a diabolo decipi, nisi illum qui praebere illi maluerit suae voluntatis assensum*)."[22] Of course, the idea that a demon can trick agents into accepting false views is not foreign to the general tradition of philosophizing, as René Descartes later famously appealed to the notion of a supremely powerful and malicious deceiver (*deceptor*) when he tested the indubitability of the *cogito*.[23] Here, however, Capreolus's appeal to a deceiving demon need not be seen as an anticipation of the elements of a Cartesian thought experiment, but rather is best viewed as an expansion of a theme of Gregory the Great, for that pope's treatment of moral dilemmas in the *Moralia* was conducted with the assumption that the

---

[21] Aquinas, *Summa theologiae* II–II, q. 13, a. 3, corp. (Editio Leonina, VIII: 110); *Summa theologiae* II–II, q. 34, a. 2, corp. (Editio Leonina, VIII: 275): "hatred of God is more grave than other sins (*odium Dei inter alia peccata est gravius*)."

[22] John Cassian, *Collationum* VII: 8, in *Patrologia Latina*, ed. J.-P. Migne, vol. XLVIX (Paris: 1874), 678a; *The Conferences*, trans. Boniface Ramsey (New York: Paulist Press, 1997), 254.

[23] René Descartes, *Meditationes de prima philosophia*, cap. 2, in *Oeuvres de Descartes*, ed. Charles Adam and Paul Tannery, 11 vols. (Paris: Librairie Philosophique J. Vrin, 1996), VII: 25.6; VII: 26.24.

devil (*Behemoth*) is the principal cause entangling agents into situations of perplexity.[24]

Even though the *Deceiving Demon Dilemma* has some obvious structural analogues with Ockham's *Odium Dei Dilemma*, key differences warrant consideration. The difficulties that Ockham himself, Suárez, and later commentators discussed – whether obedience to a command to hate God would be a contradiction – do not arise in Capreolus's presentation, since it need not be assumed that the agent in the *Deceiving Demon Dilemma* believes that God is commanding *odium Dei*. On the contrary, to the agent's mind there is an obligation to hate God, but it stems from the influence of the demon on the agent's right reason, not from any divine command. Moreover, the introduction of blasphemy as an alternative to hatred of God further distinguishes Capreolus's dilemma from that of Ockham. The *Deceiving Demon Dilemma*, therefore, cannot serve as a test case for examining divine *potentia absoluta*, and it has no bearing on voluntarist inquiries into foundations of moral obligation.

The agent in Capreolus's example decides to blaspheme or hate God after being led by the scheming devil to believe that doing so would be a lesser evil than not doing so. The facts of the case suggest that the agent's decision is a judgment of conscience that can be represented by the following practical syllogism:

P1 Major:	"The lesser of two evils ought to be chosen."
P2 Minor:	"To blaspheme or hate God is the lesser evil."
C (act of conscience):	"To blaspheme or hate God ought to be chosen."

Each of the premises constituting this practical syllogism has a distinct origin. The minor premise that designates the act of blaspheming or hating God as the lesser evil is said to come from the machinations of the devil. As examined in the preceding chapter, Aquinas and other scholastic thinkers emphasized that minor premises in acts of practical reasoning can be erroneous, as such premises lack the infallibility that attaches to any major premises supplied by the habit of synderesis. The major premise here is the principle of the lesser evil, and it is taken by the agent as true because it is assumed to be a "common conception of the soul (*communis animi conceptio*)." Such a characterization of this major premise deserves a closer look.

---

[24] Gregory the Great, *Moralia in Iob*, ed. Marcus Adriaen, 3 vols. (Turnhout: Brepols, 1979–85), III: 1656–8; *Morals on the Book of Job*, 3 vols. (Oxford: John Henry Parker, 1844–50), III.2: 538–40.

Is the principle of the lesser evil self-evident?

The expression *communis animi conceptio* is a synonym within medieval philosophy for *propositio per se nota*, that is, a self-evident proposition. The expression is a technical one with a long tradition in the history of philosophy. The Roman philosopher Boethius (*c.* 480–524/5) was likely responsible for making the expression an influential one among medieval philosophers, defining it in the *On the Hebdomads* (*De Hebdomadibus*) as "a proposition that anyone hearing it accepts (*enuntiatio quam quisque probat auditam*)."[25] Boethius added, however, that some such propositions are only understood by the learned (*docti*) and not by the ignorant multitude (*vulgus*). He considered the expression to be a synonym for *propositio per se nota*, and the interchangeability of these expressions is common among medieval writers.[26] Inspired by Boethius, Aquinas frequently argued that the truth of any self-evident proposition is immediately manifest to anyone who understands the subject and predicate terms forming the proposition, but if either of the terms is unknown then the proposition fails to be understood as self-evident.[27] Aquinas preserved Boethius's account by maintaining that while most people can understand the proposition "a whole is greater than its part" as self-evident, as the terms are not difficult to understand, only those who have some familiarity with metaphysics can grasp that the proposition "incorporeal substances do not take up space" is likewise self-evident.[28] In a representative text Aquinas explained:

Self-evident principles are such as are known as soon as the terms are understood, because the predicate is contained in the definition of the subject (*principia per se nota sunt illa quae statim, intellectis terminis, cognoscuntur, ex eo quod praedicatum ponitur in definitione subiecti*).[29]

---

[25] Boethius, *De hebdomadibus* I. See Boethius, *The Theological Tractates and the Consolation of Philosophy*, trans. H. F. Stewart, E. K. Rand, and S. J. Tester (Cambridge, MA: Harvard University Press, 1973), 38–51, at 40. For a discussion, see "Introduction" in Thomas Aquinas, *An Exposition of the On the Hebdomads of Boethius*, trans. Janice L. Schultz and Edward A. Sinan (Washington, DC: The Catholic University of America, 2001), at xxiv, n. 39: "The Boethian terminology *communis animi conceptio* . . . is a straight translation of the Stoic Greek expression *koinai ennoiai*."

[26] Boethius, *De topicis differentiis*, in *Patrologia Latina*, ed. J.-P. Migne, vol. 64 (Paris: Garnier, 1891), 1176c–d. Aquinas identifies the expressions as equivalent in his *Expositio libri Boetii De ebdomadibus* (Editio Leonina, L: 269). See *An Exposition of the On the Hebdomads*, 11. For a discussion, see G. R. Evans, "*Communis animi conceptio*: The Self-Evident Statement," *Archivum Latinitatis Medii Aevi* 41 (1979), 123–6.

[27] See M. V. Dougherty, "Thomas Aquinas on the Manifold Senses of Self-Evidence," *The Review of Metaphysics* 59 (2006), 601–30.

[28] For example, see *De veritate*, q. 10, a. 12, corp. (Editio Leonina, XXII.2: 341); *Summa theologiae* I, q. 2, a. 1, corp. (Editio Leonina, IV: 28); *Summa theologiae* I–II, q. 94, a. 2, corp. (Editio Leonina, VII: 169); *Expositio libri Boetii De ebdomadibus* (Editio Leonina, L: 269).

[29] *Summa theologiae* I, q. 17, a. 3, ad. 2 (Editio Leonina, IV: 222).

The self-certifying character of a *per se nota* proposition is guaranteed by the formal identity of the subject and predicate terms that constitute the proposition, but the recognition that a self-evident proposition is self-evident by any given person presupposes a knowledge of both terms of the proposition. By postulating in the *Deceiving Demon Dilemma* that the principle of the lesser evil is a common conception of the soul, Capreolus's example implies that it is a self-evident truth of moral reasoning. As examined above in Chapter 5, Aquinas assigns self-evident moral principles an important role in moral reasoning, as they are the major premises in many judgments of conscience. This example suggests that the principle of the lesser evil is one such principle, supplied by the habit of synderesis, to assist the agent in a judgment of practical reasoning. It is precisely this point that will later receive much criticism in the third article when Capreolus sets forth the solutions for the *quaestio*.

An invocation of authorities

To support the claim in the objections that the agent can blaspheme or hate God without sinning, Capreolus presents the customary medieval authorities who defended the existence of moral dilemmas. The standard texts from Gregory the Great, Gratian, and the Council of Toledo are displayed to support the view that agents can be in moral dilemmas and that in such cases they should choose the lesser evil.[30] As the arguments and examples of these authorities have been discussed in previous chapters, they need not be rehearsed here, except to note two points of Capreolus's presentation. First, Capreolus suggests that the *Deceiving Demon Dilemma* could be modified by substituting for the demon a religious superior who commands blasphemy or hatred of God.[31] With this adjustment the example becomes similar to the second case of perplexity that Gregory the Great introduced in the *Moralia* and that Gratian later promoted. Secondly, Capreolus's otherwise straightforward presentation of these authorities is altered by a notable assertion: Capreolus's *objectiones* postulate that a perplexed agent who appeals the principle of the lesser evil does not incur a sin in performing the lesser evil. The argument is:

Nor does it work if it is said that in such a case the agent nevertheless sins because he performs the lesser sin, as the cited authorities say: because no one sins while

---

[30] See Capreolus, *Defensiones*, IV: 436–7; Gregory of Rimini, *Lectura*, VI: 299–300; Bradwardine, *De causa Dei*, 256c–e.

[31] See Capreolus, *Defensiones*, IV: 436; Gregory of Rimini, *Lectura*, VI: 299; Bradwardine, *De causa Dei*, 256e.

doing what is necessary; such an agent does what is necessary to do. Further, no one sins while acting according to the altogether correct and universal judgment of the saints, the canon, and the general council (*Nec valet si dicatur quod in tali casu etiam peccat, quia facit minus peccatum, sicut dicunt auctoritates allegatae: quia nullus faciendo quod debet, peccat; talis autem facit quod debet. Nullus etiam faciendo secundum judicium rectissimum et commune Sanctorum, et canonis, et concilii generalis, peccat*).[32]

This argument claims that the agent does not sin in performing the lesser evil, as the inability to avoid wrongdoing creates a necessity to act and sin can never be necessary. To this point is added the familiar claim that the agent surely avoids sin by acting in accordance with moral authorities such as saints, canon law, and church council fathers who are said to endorse the principle of the lesser evil. The agent in a moral dilemma, the argument contends, does perform a lesser evil, but does not incur the guilt of sin in doing so. This analysis implies that an agent who appeals to the principle of choosing a lesser evil ends up performing an act that is objectively wrong, yet subjectively the agent is not guilty or accountable for the wrongdoing. Capreolus's argument here does have predecessors. In addition to its appearance in Gregory of Rimini's and Thomas Bradwardine's accounts, Raymond of Peñafort defended a similar view after discussing a variation of the *Wayward Cleric* type in his *Summa*. Peñafort explained:

You should say, therefore, that having examined the truth, perplexity is nothing; nor is someone able to be perplexed between two evils, that is, necessarily bound to the perpetration of some evil ... When, therefore, one is placed between two evils, either one is able to avoid one of them, or to do one of them without sin, and when it is requisite for me to do the other, I need to choose, in accordance with the counsel of Gregory, what in itself should be considered the lesser sin (*Dicas ergo, quod veritate inspecta nihil est perplexitas; nec potest aliquis esse perplexus inter duo mala, idest necessitate astrictus ad aliquod malum perpetrandum ... Cum ergo positus est inter duo mala, aut potest utrumque vitare, aut alterum facere sine peccato; et cum oportet me alterum facere, debeo eligere, iuxta consilium Gregorii, quod per se consideratum esset minus peccatum*).[33]

Peñafort's denial at the beginning of this quote that situations of perplexity exist should not be confused with the claim set forth by the glossators on Gratian's *Decretum* who had said that there is no perplexity. The glossators

---

[32] Capreolus, *Defensiones*, IV: 436; Gregory of Rimini, *Lectura*, VI: 299–300; Bradwardine, *De causa Dei*, 257c.

[33] Raymond of Peñafort, *Summa*, lib. 3, *De scandalo, et perplexitate, et notorio*, §6, in *Summa de poenitentia et matrimonio cum glossis Ioannis de Friburgo* (Rome: Ioannes Tallinus Bibliopolus, 1603), 356.

had argued that there are no situations of perplexity because the necessity to choose between impermissible options is simply an illusion generated by the foolishness of agents who fail to comprehend the range of alternatives in a given situation. In contrast, Peñafort's position here is that agents do encounter situations that necessitate a choice between morally impermissible alternatives, but that in choosing the lesser evil the agent does not incur the guilt of sin because the performance of some evil is unavoidable. The conjunction of an appeal to the principle of the lesser evil with a denial that an agent using the principle is guilty of a moral failure can be compared to more recent discussions in ethical theory. In analyzing Kant, for example, one commentator notes that for some contemporary defenders of moral dilemmas of the prior-fault variety, the

> "lesser evil" will have to be defined with a special spin, too, to avoid the implication that the agent is somewhat evil in choosing it. It will be, perhaps, the option that does less harm (an "evil") to others or the option that, were the agent not in the dilemma, would be a less grave offense than the other option.[34]

Such a qualification, consonant with the view of Peñafort as well as Capreolus's objection above, is an attempt to insulate the agent from the guilt of moral wrongdoing when choosing the lesser evil. Capreolus's objection claims further that this view is what Gregory the Great was really defending in the *Moralia*. As shall be seen, however, Capreolus modifies this position significantly by subjecting the principle of the lesser evil to greater scrutiny in the subsequent article. After citing a few texts from Augustine, Capreolus then closes this article of objections by stating that "From the preceding arguments it follows that the intention of a right end excuses from sin (*Ex praedictis sequitur quod intentio recti finis excusat a peccato*)."[35]

6.4 AN ATTACK ON THE PRINCIPLE OF THE LESSER EVIL

It must be remembered that the aforementioned arguments found in the second article are *objectiones* that do not represent the views ultimately espoused in the *Defensiones*. In the third and final article, Capreolus provides *solutiones* that seek not only to refute the objections constituting the previous article but also to affirm the position set forth in the first article,

---

[34] Thomas E. Hill, Jr., "Moral Dilemmas, Gaps, and Residues: A Kantian Perspective," in *Moral Dilemmas and Moral Theory*, ed. H. E. Mason (New York: Oxford University Press, 1996), 167–98, at 196, n. 24. See also Thomas E. Hill, Jr., *Respect, Pluralism, and Justice* (Oxford: Clarendon Press, 2000), 167.

[35] Capreolus, *Defensiones*, IV: 437.

namely, that the goodness of an act of the will is not simply from the end, as a good intention alone does not shield an agent from moral wrongdoing. The third article subjects the *Deceiving Demon Dilemma* to further scrutiny, and the analysis offered there is a blend of fairly traditional responses to the issue of a perplexed conscience plus a remarkable critique of the principle of the lesser evil. Again, throughout the discussion Capreolus incorporates large extracts from Gregory of Rimini.

By keeping in mind the medieval accounts of perplexed conscience dilemmas recounted in the previous chapters it becomes manifest that the arguments of this last *quaestio* are heavily indebted to Capreolus's thirteenth- and fourteenth-century predecessors. Capreolus returns to the *Deceiving Demon Dilemma* and presents the following quite traditional view:

> If such a case occurs, by no means is that man obliged to blaspheme or hate God; on the contrary he is obliged not to blaspheme and not to hate, because no one is obliged to conform himself to an erroneous conscience (*si detur talis casus, ille nequaquam tenetur blasphemare, nec odire Deum; immo tenetur non blasphemare et non odire, quia nullus tenetur se conformare erroneae conscientiae*).[36]

Here Capreolus is not arguing that conscience lacks the power to bind an agent to what it dictates, but rather that an erroneous judgment of conscience is not unqualifiedly binding insofar as its obligatory power can be disarmed with the identification of the errors that corrupt its conclusion. Capreolus explains further that "it does not follow that he ought to act against his conscience, because it is not the case that he ought to have such a conscience (*non sequitur quod debeat agere contra suam conscientiam, quia ipse non debet habere talem conscientiam*)."[37] He adds, "such a conscience is to be put away (*talis conscientia est deponenda*)."[38] These texts do not imply that agents who are perplexed because of an erroneous conscience are simply left to do nothing, abandon the moral life, or discard their powers of moral reasoning, but rather they should begin an inquiry into the source of their errors. It is clear that the statement that conscience is to be put away is simply shorthand for a strategy that enjoins agents to separate faulty minor premises that have been combined with self-evident major premises offered by the habit of synderesis. In setting forth these texts, Capreolus (by way of Gregory of Rimini) is presenting a fairly standard account for dealing with an erroneous conscience, at least by the standards of moral psychology of the late Middle Ages examined above. In the example here, the agent under

---

[36] Capreolus, *Defensiones*, IV: 437; Gregory of Rimini, *Lectura*, VI: 303.
[37] Capreolus, *Defensiones*, IV: 438.   [38] Capreolus, *Defensiones*, IV: 437.

the promptings of a demon assumed the false minor premise that judged blaspheming or hating God to be a lesser evil than not doing so.

The novelty of Capreolus's discussion, however, concerns the evaluation of the major premise "the lesser of two evils ought to be chosen" held by the agent of the *Deceiving Demon Dilemma*. The second article had asserted that this major premise was self-evident, insofar as it was designated as a common conception of the soul. This designation suggests that the premise is a first principle supplied by synderesis. Capreolus responds by arguing that the principle of the lesser evil is neither self-evident nor true, and it should never be followed when understood in its characteristic sense. At the beginning of an extensive critique he argues:

> That proposition, by which it is said that of two evils the lesser evil is to be chosen, if it should be taken in its characteristic sense, not only is it not itself a common conception of the soul, but it is unqualifiedly false, speaking always concerning the evil of fault (*ista propositio, qua dicitur quod de duobus malis, etc., si sumatur in sua proprietate, non solum ipsa non est communis animi conceptio, sed est simpliciter falsa, loquendo semper de malo culpae*).[39]

By denying that the principle of the lesser evil is a common conception of the soul, Capreolus judges that it is not an ethical proposition offered by the infallible habit of synderesis. While the Aristotelian and Thomistic traditions frequently argue that self-evident principles are unmistakably true to those who know the terms that constitute them, neither tradition holds that an agent is insulated from falsely believing that a proposition that is not self-evident is self-evident.[40] At times agents can mistakenly regard false propositions as well as true demonstrable propositions as self-evident. Capreolus, following Gregory of Rimini, contends that the agent in this example has made such a faulty assumption.

This criticism of the principle of the lesser evil, however, is restricted to an understanding of the principle in its characteristic sense (*in sua*

---

[39] See Capreolus, *Defensiones*, IV: 437; Gregory of Rimini, *Lectura*, VI: 303–4.
[40] Aquinas contends that the force of custom (*consuetudo*) leads some to accept as self-evident what merely has been habitually accepted as true. See *Summa contra Gentiles* I.II (Editio Leonina, XIII: 24). Additionally, in his commentaries on Aristotelian texts, Aquinas often identifies as the key error of many Pre-Socratic philosophers that they assumed as self-evident what is either false or in need of demonstration. See *Summa theologiae* I, q. 45, a. 2, arg. I, ad I (Editio Leonina, IV: 465, 466); *Sentencia libri De anima*, lib. I, lec. 6 (Editio Leonina, XLV.I: 28); *Commentaria in octo libros Physicorum Aristotelis*, lib. 3, lec. II (Editio Leonina, II: 136); *Sententia libri Metaphysicae*, lib. I, lec. 6, §109 (Marietti, 31). In other texts Aquinas contends that the Platonists erred with respect to the identification of *per se nota* principles. See *Sententia libri Metaphysicae*, lib. I, lec. 16, §247 (Marietti, 72). See also *In II librum Sententiarum*, d. 2, q. I, a. 2, corp. (Mandonnet, 67); *De potentia*, q. 3, a. I, arg. I, ad I (Marietti, 37, 39).

proprietate). Such a qualification suggests that the principle is capable of being understood in more than one way. The characteristic sense of the principle, according to Capreolus's account, assumes that the greater and lesser evils are moral evils, that is, evils of fault (*malae culpae*). Capreolus explains that a choice between moral evils is always impermissible, so that an agent should neither will nor intend either of them. He observes:

concerning two such evils neither is to be chosen; because each of them is evil, and as a consequence neither the more evil nor the less evil is to be chosen (*de talibus duobus malis neutrum est eligendum; quia utrumque est malum, et per consequens nec plus nec minus eligendum*).[41]

On this view, an endorsement of the principle of the lesser evil in its characteristic sense involves the will to do a moral evil, and presumably what is a moral evil should never be intended as an end. As context for such a view, one might recall that Aquinas identified the first precept of the natural law to be the self-evident principle "good is to be done and pursued, and evil is to be avoided (*bonum est faciendum et prosequendum, et malum vitandum*)," and the latter half of this proposition has traditionally been understood to forbid the willing of moral evils.[42] These texts maintain that it is never permissible to intend a moral evil as the end of an act of the will.

Capreolus holds, therefore, that any appeal to the principle of the lesser evil, when conceived as a procedure for selecting between moral evils, is not a permissible strategy for dealing with moral dilemmas insofar as it would require agents to intend evils. He suggests, however, that since the principle of the lesser evil is an equivocal expression, there may be permissible ways to use it if the terms are understood properly, as when the verb "choose" replaces the verb "avoid." He notes:

But it is quite true that with regard to two evils, the lesser evil is less to be avoided, and the greater evil is more greatly to be avoided (*Sed bene verum est quod de duobus malis minus malum est minus fugiendum, et majus est magis fugiendum*).[43]

The error of those who use the principle of the lesser evil in its characteristic sense is believing that because an action is less evil it can be considered good in contrast with the greater evil. The evaluation of evils in terms of more and less is not discounted by Capreolus, but he simply argues that

---

[41] See Capreolus, *Defensiones*, IV: 437; Gregory of Rimini, *Lectura*, VI: 304.
[42] Aquinas, *Summa theologiae* I–II, q. 94, a. 2, corp. (Editio Leonina, VII: 170).
[43] See Capreolus, *Defensiones*, IV: 437; Gregory of Rimini, *Lectura*, VI: 304. See Bradwardine, *De causa Dei*, 258d–e.

the most such an evaluation can offer is an insight into the degree to which particular evils should be fled or avoided. It is quite another thing to argue that on the basis of a qualitative evaluation of evils, the lesser evil should be *chosen*. Capreolus explains:

Because not only is it usefully advised to man that he should pursue good and should avoid evil, but also because, if he should not be able to avoid them, and concerning the two sins it should be necessary for him to go wrong in one of the two, he should avoid what is the greater evil; and this in a certain way is meant to choose the lesser evil (*Quia non solum utiliter consulitur homini quod agat bonum et vitet malum, sed etiam quod, si non possit vitare, et de duobus peccatis in alterum oporteat eum labi, vitet quod est majus malum; et hoc quodammodo dicitur eligere minus malum*).[44]

Here Capreolus explicitly states his precise view on the principle of the lesser evil. The principle can be used permissibly when it is understood simply as an injunction to avoid a greater evil. Capreolus's understanding of an avoidance of a greater evil must be different than a willingness to choose or consent to a lesser evil, as his earlier analysis presupposed that the agent in no way should will or intend any evil. Certainly the success of his analysis presupposes a distinction between choice and avoidance. In the case of the agent deceived by the devil, Capreolus maintains that the principle of the lesser evil in its characteristic sense would be of no help, as it would involve consenting to an evil. Moreover, Capreolus explains further that the only manner in which the principle of the lesser evil in its characteristic sense would be useful to the agent deceived by a demon would be on the assumption that "to blaspheme or to hate God were not an intrinsic evil, and that sometimes one would be able to do it well (*Deum blasphemare vel odire non sit per se malum, et quod aliquando possit bene fieri*)."[45] Of course, Capreolus is not willing to grant this assumption, as he views an act of blaspheming or hating God to be a per se evil that can never be done well and therefore can never be permissibly intended.

Capreolus and his source Gregory of Rimini are not the only thinkers to call into question the legitimacy of appeals to the lesser of two evils as a solution to the problem of moral dilemmas. Despite the frequency of such appeals by major thinkers such as Gregory the Great, Gratian, William of Auxerre, and the authors of the *Summa Halesiana*, it is possible to find

---

[44] See Capreolus, *Defensiones*, IV: 438; Gregory of Rimini, *Lectura*, VI: 305. See also Bonaventure, *In librum quartum Sententiarum*, d. 16, par. 1, art. 4, q. 2, cont. 5, in *Opera omnia*, 10 vols. (Quaracchi: Collegium S. Bonaventurae, 1882–1902), IV: 396.

[45] See Capreolus, IV: *Defensiones*, 439; Gregory of Rimini, *Lectura*, VI: 306.

earlier traces of resistance to this popular strategy. In the twelfth century, for instance, Peter of Poitiers (1130–1215) discussed a variation of the *Killers of Christ Dilemma* considered by the glossators on the *Decretum*, William of Auxerre among others, and Peter asserts an ecclesiological rejection of this principle, saying:

> Where perplexity happens, the church does not counsel that the lesser evil is to be done; but if a lesser or a greater happens to come about, the greater is more greatly to be avoided. Just as that doctor does not counsel for a sick person to consume ram's meat, but if he happens to eat either ram's meat or cow's meat, preferably the ram's meat, which harms less (*ubi incidit perplexio, non consulit Ecclesia minus malum esse faciendum; sed si contingat fieri minus vel majus, magis vitandum esse majus. Sicut iste medicus non consulit huic aegroto comedere carnes arietinas, sed si contigerit ipsum, vel arietinas, vel vaccinas comedere, potius arietinas quae minus nocent*).[46]

As with the account presented by Capreolus, Peter of Poitiers advocates a distinction between permissibly avoiding an evil and impermissibly intending an evil. This distinction requires, however, the dismantling of the claim that agents ever truly find themselves forced to choose between morally impermissible alternatives. That is, defenders of this view are required to deny that in a strict sense there are situations where agents involuntarily find themselves unable to fulfill all impending obligations.

6.5 QUESTIONING THE FACTS OF THE *DECEIVING DEMON DILEMMA*

Having observed Capreolus devote considerable attention to the *Deceiving Demon Dilemma*, one may be surprised to find that, before the *quaestio* is over, the Prince of Thomists ultimately denies that a demon could so trick an agent that the agent is blamelessly perplexed. At issue is whether an agent could really assume the false view that constitutes a minor premise and still remain innocent of any wrongdoing. Capreolus eventually reveals his doubt over this point, arguing that no agent without sin could come to believe that to blaspheme or hate God is preferable to not blaspheming or hating God. To stipulate as a fact of the case that an agent is innocent in adopting this view is simply to assume "one falsehood (*unum falsum*)."[47] Capreolus is not persuaded that an exercise of the powers of a demon could render the agent's acceptance of the minor premise entirely blameless. He asks,

---

[46] Peter of Poitiers, *Sententiarum libri quinque*, in *Patrologia Latina*, ed. J.-P. Migne, vol. CCXI (Paris, 1855), 1159c–d. For a discussion, see Artur Michael Landgraf, "Der '*Casus perplexus*' in der Frühscholastik," *Collectanea Franciscana* 29 (1959), 74–86, at 76.

[47] Capreolus, *Defensiones*, IV: 439; Gregory of Rimini, *Lectura*, VI: 307.

"For if it should not be a sin, what other error is to be called a sin? (*Si enim non esset culpa, quis alius error diceretur culpa?*)"[48] While thirteenth- and fourteenth-century theorists often underscored the limitations of demons to affect human intellects, reflection upon the absolute power (*potentia absoluta*) of God led many to postulate that God could in principle deceive human beings in innumerable ways.[49] In the end, Capreolus judges the *Deceiving Demon Dilemma* to be simply a prior-fault, erroneous conscience dilemma.

He explains that assisting any agent who might be subjected to the machinations of the devil are the Christian community and the moral and religious traditions. Capreolus observes:

Now however certain it is that such a man is thus perplexed, no saint, nor anyone, unless he is wicked or foolish, would counsel that one should blaspheme or hate God, but would counsel that such a conscience should be put away and abandoned (*Nunc autem certum est quod tali homini sic perplexo, nullus sanctus, nec aliquis, nisi nequam et impius aut stultus, consuleret quod Deum blasphemaret vel odiret; sed consuleret quod talem conscientiam erroneam deponeret et abjiceret*).[50]

The suggestion here that an agent so deceived by a demon would have to be foolish (*stultus*) is reminiscent of a line of argument offered by the glossators on Gratian's *Decretum*, for they had identified an agent's culpable foolishness to be the chief cause of situations of moral perplexity. The unanimity of saints is judged to be a sufficient bulwark against attempts by a devil to swindle an agent. This text also re-affirms the traditional solution to erroneous conscience dilemmas, as Capreolus contends that the judgment of an erroneous conscience should be set aside, presumably while the agent searches for the error that taints the integrity of the act of moral reasoning. Additional evidence that this line of argument is indebted to the earlier canon law tradition is Capreolus's reference elsewhere in the text to the *Glossa ordinaria*. Responding to the citation of Gratian that appeared in the presentation of authorities defending the lesser evil principle in the second article, Capreolus observes that Gratian's position is mistaken (*falsum*), and that Gratian should be reprehended "just as there his glossator rightly reprehends him, saying that Gratian badly maintained that case of perplexity (*sicut ibidem reprehendit eum glossator suus, et bene,*

---

[48] See Capreolus, *Defensiones*, IV: 439; Gregory of Rimini, *Lectura*, VI: 307.
[49] For a discussion of these points, see Dominik Perler, "Does God Deceive Us? Skeptical Hypotheses in Late Medieval Epistemology," in *Rethinking the History of Skepticism: The Missing Medieval Background*, ed. Henrik Lagerlund (Leiden: Brill, 2010), 71–192.
[50] See Capreolus, *Defensiones*, IV: 438; Gregory of Rimini, *Lectura*, VI: 306.

dicens eum male casum perplexitatis excepisse)."[51] Invoking this condemnation of Gratian is not unprecedented, as it is consistent with the remarks of Richard of Middleton noted earlier.

Capreolus's late contention that the agent in the *Deceiving Demon Dilemma* is not blameless appears sensitive to Aquinas's distinction between two kinds of perplexity. By judging the agent to be guilty rather than innocent in accepting the errant minor premise, the example moves from satisfying the conditions of a perplexity *simpliciter* dilemma to satisfying the conditions of a perplexity *secundum quid* dilemma. Such a transfer aligns Capreolus with Aquinas's view that there are no cases of absolute perplexity. Capreolus's acquaintance with the two kinds of dilemma is clear from his above-mentioned précis of Aquinas's position that began the *quaestio*, as one extract included Aquinas's explicit categorical denial that an agent is ever *perplexus simpliciter*, and another was one of Aquinas's discussions of the *Evil Intention* and *Malformed Conscience* dilemmas.[52]

6.6 THOMISTIC APPEALS TO THE PRINCIPLE OF THE LESSER EVIL

Capreolus clearly regards the principle of the lesser evil as admitting of more than one meaning. While he rejects the permissibility of appealing to its characteristic sense because doing so would require an agent to intend an evil, he concedes that the principle could be used legitimately if understood simply as a general injunction to avoid greater evils, presumably because doing so would not involve an act of willing or consenting to any evil. Further, Capreolus considers the principle of the lesser of two evils to be unnecessary for resolving moral dilemmas, at least insofar as he appears to endorse Aquinas's view that there are no situations of absolute perplexity. He ultimately reinterprets the *Deceiving Demon Dilemma* as a prior-fault dilemma where the agent can rectify the erroneous conscience by giving up the false major and minor premises enjoining the hatred or blasphemy of God. Capreolus contends that both premises are errant: the major premise is false when the principle of the lesser evil is taken in its characteristic sense, and the minor premise is obviously false to anyone who attends to the basic beliefs of Christian community or writings of the saints. So, Capreolus's considered view is that agents will not experience this dilemma as long as they do not culpably persist in maintaining these premises.

---

[51] See Capreolus, *Defensiones*, IV: 438; Gregory of Rimini, *Lectura*, VI: 305.
[52] See Capreolus, *Defensiones*, IV: 440.

Present-day interpreters of Aquinas have judged that the Angelic Doctor himself rejects the characteristic sense of the principle of the lesser evil as an adjudicating principle for moral decisions. John Finnis notes that Aquinas "firmly denies that one should seek to identify, and choose, the 'lesser evil,'" and in "every context in which a moral issue is to be resolved, Aquinas refuses the invitation to solve the issue by identifying the 'lesser evil'."[53] Even though Aquinas rejects the principle in its characteristic sense, as it enjoins an agent to intend an evil, its aforementioned equivocal character may lead one to ask whether the Thomistic tradition can embrace it in other ways. Aquinas does appeal to the principle in other senses. For instance, in situations designated by contemporary theorists as falling under the Thomistic doctrine of double effect, the foreseen but unintended bad consequences of alternative courses of action may be evaluated according to one sense of the principle. In short, a course of action should be rejected when its foreseen but unintended consequences are worse than those of an otherwise equivalent alternative course.[54] An example of such an appeal to the principle occurs in the short political work *On Kingship* (*De regno*), where Aquinas advises:

When a choice is to be made between two things, from both of which danger impends, surely that one should be chosen from which the lesser evil follows (*Cum autem inter duo ex quorum utroque periculum imminet eligere oportet, illud uidetur potissime eligendum ex quo sequitur minus malum*).[55]

The context of Aquinas's statement here is a consideration of forms of government in light of the evils that each form has a propensity to bring. This principle in the sense used here does not involve any intending of evil, but takes predicted bad side-effects into consideration in comparing the alternative courses of action. The evil or bad side-effects are beyond the intention (*praeter intentionem*) of the one who chooses, even though they

---

[53] John Finnis, *Moral Absolutes: Tradition, Revision, and Truth* (Washington, DC: The Catholic University of America Press, 1991), 56. See also John Finnis, *Aquinas: Moral, Political, and Legal Theory* (Oxford University Press, 1998), 167.

[54] The literature on the doctrine of double effect is vast. For an exposition of the doctrine in Aquinas's texts, see Joseph Mangan, SJ, "An Historical Analysis of the Principle of Double Effect," *Theological Studies* 10 (1949), 41–61; and T. A. Cavanaugh, *Double-Effect Reasoning: Doing Good and Avoiding Evil* (Oxford: Clarendon Press, 2006), 1–38.

[55] Aquinas, *De regno*, lib. 1, cap. 5 (Editio Leonina, XLII: 454); *On Kingship to the King of Cyprus*, trans. Gerald B. Phelan, rev. I. Eschmann, OP (Toronto: Pontifical Institute of Mediaeval Studies, 1982), 21. Shortly thereafter in the text, Aquinas presents another formulation of the principle of the lesser evil: "That from which great dangers follow more frequently is, it would seem, the more to be avoided (*illud magis fugiendum uidetur ex quo pluries sequi possunt magna pericula*)," (Editio Leonina, XLII: 454).

are foreknown. In accordance with the traditional doctrine of double-effect reasoning, the course of action with less evil unintended side-effects can be permissibly chosen in accordance with a restricted sense of the principle of the lesser evil.

Advising the lesser evil

One later Thomistic approach to the principle of choosing the lesser evil worthy of mention was examined by several sixteenth-century Thomistic commentators, not the least of which include the Dominicans Thomas de Vio (better known as Cajetan) (1469–1534), Domingo Soto (1494–1560), and Bartholomé de Medina (1527–81).[56] These heirs of the Thomistic tradition debated the permissibility of advising another, who is intent on doing evil, to substitute a lesser evil. In doing so, these Thomistic commentators gave new life to a controversy that continued well into the seventeenth and eighteenth centuries.[57] At issue was whether advising another to commit a lesser sin – either of degree or of kind – was ever itself sinful. Commonly discussed examples included whether someone who was intent on committing adultery should be persuaded to commit simple fornication instead, or whether someone who was intent on theft should be encouraged to spare a poor victim in preference to a rich one. Another example was whether someone who planned homicide should be persuaded to inflict a non-mortal injury instead. Central to these discussions was whether the one who persuades the other to commit a lesser evil is responsible for willing the lesser evil and thereby bears some culpability for the wrong done. At times, theorists approached the issue indirectly, by asking, for instance, if the person who has persuaded the thief to select a rich man rather than a poor man will owe the rich person restitution when the crime has been completed, as the rich man would never have suffered any harm had the thief never been enjoined to change victims. Frequently in the course of these discussions the question becomes whether the wrongdoer is persuaded to intend a different but lesser evil (e.g., as in substituting a beating for murder), or whether the wrongdoer is simply being persuaded to perform the same evil but to a lesser degree (e.g., get less drunk rather than more drunk). In an overview of ninety-nine philosophers and theologians from the sixteenth through early twentieth centuries, one commentator found that only

---

[56] The survey that follows is indebted to E. T. Hannigan, SJ, "Is It Ever Lawful to Advise the Lesser of Two Evils?" *Gregorianum* 30 (1949), 104–29.

[57] These discussions continued an analysis that surfaced in distinction 14 of Gratian's *Decretum* and in the *Venial Sin Dilemma* from the *Summa Halesiana*.

sixteen theorists rejected absolutely any appeals to the principle of the lesser evil in any form in discussing these cases, while the great majority favored some version of it.[58] This survey, however, predates the rise of the moral theory of proportionalism in the later part of the twentieth century, so it is not representative of present-day philosophical and theological moral theory. These long-standing debates underscore the continued reflection on the principle of the lesser evil as an expression admitting of more than one sense.

Twentieth-century interpretations of the principle of the lesser evil

The invocation of a restricted sense of the principle of the lesser evil within double-effect reasoning has had a long history since Aquinas. For instance, one finds the principle rejected in its characteristic sense (for reasons consistent with Capreolus's account) in standard twentieth-century handbooks of moral theology, then followed by an endorsement of an allowable sense. One such account, for instance, contends:

To choose the lesser of two evils is permissible if the lesser evil is not in itself a moral evil (sin), but a purely physical evil or the omission of something good or indifferent, from which in a specific case an accidental bad effect will follow, less serious, however, than that which another course would produce.[59]

On this view, where two courses of medicine have equal chances of curing a patient, the one with a lesser risk of side-effects is chosen over the more risky course. The principle of the lesser evil is operative in this case, but without requiring the intending of an evil, even though the lesser risk of side-effects is a foreknown evil that attaches to the selected course of medicine.[60]

The separation of senses of the principle of the lesser evil into permissible and impermissible senses also surfaced in significant debates involving

---

[58] Hannigan offers a numerical summary of his survey on the last page of his article.

[59] Ludovico Bender, OP, "Lesser Evil (Choice of)," in *Dictionary of Moral Theology*, ed. Francesco Roberti and Pietro Palazzini, trans. Henry J. Yannone (Westminster, MD: The Newman Press, 1962), 705–6, at 705. See also Ludger Honnefelder, "The Evaluation of Goods and the Estimation of Consequences: Aquinas on the Determination of the Morally Good," in *The Ethics of Aquinas*, ed. Stephen J. Pope (Washington, DC: Georgetown University Press, 2002), 426–36, at 433, who in reviewing the later Thomistic tradition emphasizes the variety of ways in which the term "lesser evil" has been understood: "In the case of otherwise equal circumstances and unavoidable harmful side-effects, one must choose the lesser of two evils over the larger, or the one of shorter duration over the long-term one, or the likely one over the certain, or the reversible over the irreversible, or that which affects few over that which affects all. This does *not* apply to morally bad actions, which must never be intended as such."

[60] See Bender, "Lesser Evil (Choice of)," 705.

more recent exponents of the Thomistic tradition. One of the twentieth century's most influential defenders of Thomism, Jacques Maritain, argued that the principle can be used in manifold ways, and he identified one sense as a necessary foundation for a mature political philosophy.[61] According to one interpreter, what Maritain means is that politicians must use the principle in order to "tolerate evils whose interdiction would lead to even greater evils."[62] A better-known controversy involving the principle concerned the above-mentioned moral theory of proportionalism, which held that the outcome of benefits and harms is the sole ground for determining the rightness or wrongness of actions.[63] The staunchest defenders of proportionalism resurrected the characteristic sense of the principle of the lesser evil, arguing that it is obviously true, and in doing so were reminiscent of the medieval allegation opposed by Capreolus that held the principle was a self-evident, common principle of the soul. In his defense of proportionalism, Richard McCormick asserted that for situations of moral conflict:

the rule of Christian reason, if we are governed by the *ordo bonorum*, is to choose the lesser evil. This general statement is, it would seem, beyond debate; for the only alternative is that in conflict situations we should choose the greater evil, which is patently absurd.[64]

Several philosophers often collectively designated as the "New Natural Law" thinkers, who are at least friendly to the Thomistic tradition if not members of it, subjected the proportionalist appeal to the principle of the lesser evil to fairly detailed analysis and criticism. They argued against McCormick and others by contending that the principle is impermissible when understood in its characteristic sense and that its claims to self-evidence are illusory.[65] Finnis explained, "it can *seem* plausible to say, as proportionalists do, that moral problems (or some moral problems) can be

---

[61] Jacques Maritain, *Integral Humanism*, trans. Joseph W. Evans (South Bend, IN: University of Notre Dame Press, 1973), 222: "In fact men most often use badly the principle of the lesser evil, because they see in it the pretext to do nothing for justice. This principle is, however, an essentially ethical principle, like the principle of justice to be pursued."

[62] M. Susan Power, *Jacques Maritain (1882–1973): Christian Democrat, and the Quest for a New Commonwealth* (Lewiston, NY: The Edwin Mellen Press, 1992), 111.

[63] For the classic articles, see *Proportionalism: For and Against*, ed. Christopher Kaczor (Milwaukee, WI: Marquette University Press, 2000). For an analysis, see Christopher Kaczor, *Proportionalism and the Natural Law Tradition* (Washington, DC: The Catholic University of America Press, 2002).

[64] Richard A. McCormick, SJ, *Ambiguity in Moral Choice* (Milwaukee, WI: Marquette University Press, 1973), 76.

[65] John Finnis, *Fundamentals of Ethics* (Washington, DC: Georgetown University Press, 1983), esp. chap. 4: "Utilitarianism, Consequentialism, Proportionalism ... or Ethics?" 80–108; Germain Grisez, "Against Consequentialism," *American Journal of Jurisprudence* 23 (1978), 21–72; Germain

resolved by the maxim 'choose the lesser evil'. Proportionalism persuades because its methodological maxim seems *self-evident.*"[66] Reminiscent of Capreolus, the New Natural Law theorists judge that the principle is neither self-evident nor true. They hold further that it cannot serve as a method for deciding among courses of action because goods are varied and incommensurate.[67] Recognizing, however, that the principle of the lesser evil has long been a moral maxim from at least the time of Cicero, they do concede that the principle is allowable in one sense: "if you are determined to act unreasonably, do not go the whole hog – if you are set on wrongdoing, at least restrict your wrong; the less serious your wrongdoing, the better."[68] On this line of thinking, the principle does not serve as a method for deciding among competing courses of action, but simply enjoins agents who are determined to act impermissibly at least to minimize their wrongdoing.

6.7 THOMISM AND IRRESOLVABLE PRIOR-FAULT DILEMMAS

This chapter began by noting that Aquinas left unanswered the question of whether there exist irresolvable prior-fault moral dilemmas. The texts of Aquinas were silent on the issue of whether agents might commit prior misdeeds that are so disordering that their ill-effects cannot be defused and the agents are thereby unable to avoid a second future moral wrongdoing. This chapter proposed that an answer to this question might be found by examining the remarks on moral dilemmas by Capreolus, an early and authoritative voice of the Thomistic school. Capreolus considered the question of moral dilemmas in some detail, largely focusing on a curious moral dilemma featuring an agent who is tricked by a demon. When the facts of this dilemma were set forth, one feature originally postulated was that

---

Grisez, *Christian Moral Principles* (Quincy, IL: Franciscan Press, 1983), especially chapter 6, "Critique of the Proportionalist Method of Moral Judgment," 141–71.

[66] John Finnis, *Fundamentals of Ethics*, 93.

[67] Grisez, "Against Consequentialism," 27: "First, the seemingly obvious statement that it is right to bring about the greater good or the lesser evil assumes what is not obvious, namely, that goodness is measurable and that diverse forms of it are commensurable. If there are nonmeasurable goods, toward which human acts should be oriented, then acting only in view of measurable goods will mean ignoring goods which cannot be measured but should not be ignored. If the consequences of one act include several goods and evils, how can one tell which good is the greater, which is the lesser?"

[68] John Finnis, *Fundamentals of Ethics*, 90. Germain Grisez, *Difficult Moral Questions* (Quincy, IL: Franciscan Press, 1997), 829, notes that "one may persuade someone determined to do a grave evil, which one cannot prevent, to do instead a less grave evil – for example, having fruitlessly tried to dissuade a suicidal man from jumping out a window above a crowded sidewalk, one might call his attention to a window overlooking a deserted alley and urge him at least to spare others."

the agent was blameless in coming to hold the false view enjoining hatred or blasphemy of God. This assumption of innocence appeared to preclude an interpretation of it strictly on the lines of Aquinas's view of *Malformed Conscience Dilemmas*, because Aquinas generally considers agents to be culpable when consciences are ill-formed. This assumption of innocence also suggested that the dilemma should be considered a perplexity *simpliciter* situation rather than a perplexity *secundum quid* situation. Later, however, Capreolus ultimately expressed doubt concerning the purported innocence of any agents who might find themselves in such perplexity.

Capreolus's consideration of the *Deceiving Demon Dilemma* can provide an argument for resolving the contested question of whether classical Thomism grants the existence of irresolvable prior-fault dilemmas. The central point of Capreolus's analysis was a critique of the principle of the lesser evil. Capreolus maintained that the principle afforded no help for agents in allegedly irresolvable moral dilemmas when the principle is understood in its characteristic sense as a choice between moral evils. There is reason to believe that such a rejection of the principle of the lesser evil is a faithful expression of Aquinas's moral philosophy, in part because the rejection coheres with Aquinas's commitment to the self-evident first precept of the natural law. Further, as was shown above, present-day heirs of the Thomistic tradition largely reject the principle in its characteristic sense.

Aquinas's medieval predecessors who defended irresolvable moral dilemmas tended to advise one of two options for agents in moral dilemmas, designated here as the *Divine Intervention* and the *Lesser Evil* resolutions. Neither, it appears, can be consistently incorporated into a Thomistic system. On this basis, then, it is plausible to conclude that Aquinas does not allow the existence of irresolvable prior-fault dilemmas. This argument, of course, is merely an ancillary one, as the principal argument against irresolvable prior-fault dilemmas in the Thomistic corpus is that all of Aquinas's examples allow for some further action by agents whereby they can defuse the ill-effects of their prior misdeeds in time to avoid an additional wrongdoing. That this inductive argument has been unpersuasive to some contemporary commentators has required an inquiry for an additional argument. Given that Aquinas's texts can be marshaled both against and in favor of irresolvable prior-fault dilemmas, this new argument can tip the scale in one direction.

Another way of approaching the evidence is to focus on Aquinas's consistency in never appealing to the principle of the lesser evil in any discussions of moral dilemmas. Aquinas's silence on this principle in these contexts may simply reflect that he judges doing so would be superfluous. Appeals to the principle are unnecessary for one who contends that there are no cases of perplexity *simpliciter* and that additional wrongdoing in cases of perplexity *secundum quid* are defusable by some further action. Of course, Aquinas's silence on the principle of the lesser evil in these discussions may also be for a more fundamental reason. He may simply endorse the one transmitted by Capreolus: the principle in its characteristic sense is, to use the expression of the *Defensiones*, "unqualifiedly false (*simpliciter falsa*)."

Conclusion

The systematic investigation of whether moral dilemmas exist is often seen as an achievement of modern or contemporary philosophy, but it is in medieval philosophy that the subject is first substantively analyzed. The narrative here has offered a sampling of these medieval debates, and along the way the principle of the lesser evil has emerged as central to these discussions. The foremost defenders of the existence of moral dilemmas in the Middle Ages invoked the principle as a guide for action, arguing that agents should strive to minimize wrongdoing when its complete avoidance is impossible. Counted among the defenders of both the existence of moral dilemmas and the permissibility of the principle of the lesser evil are some of the great thinkers of the medieval period, including Gratian, William of Auxerre, and the Franciscan authors of the *Summa Halesiana*, among others. Throughout these debates, the authority of Gregory the Great was evident, as he continued to cast a long shadow throughout discussions of moral dilemmas even to the time of Capreolus in the fifteenth century.

Not all medieval moral theorists were promoters of moral dilemmas, however. The glossators on Gratian's *Decretum* denied their existence, offering arguments similar to Aquinas's later denial of situations of perplexity *simpliciter*. Absent from Aquinas's presentation, however, was the glossators' forceful assertion that dilemmas are simply illusory and merely the result of the foolishness of moral agents. Aquinas's most distinctive contribution to medieval moral dilemma theory was his strict separation of innocent-agent dilemmas from prior-fault dilemmas. While he denied the existence of the former, he frequently discussed cases of the latter. Of course, many of the examples of moral dilemmas discussed by medieval theorists preceding Aquinas could, in retrospect, be categorized according to these two classes, but Aquinas formalized the distinction by consistently separating cases of perplexity *secundum quid* from alleged cases of perplexity *simpliciter*. This achievement transformed later medieval theorizing, particularly in discussions of moral dilemmas involving dictates of conscience. Aquinas's distinction also appears to have supplanted the earlier customary division of moral dilemmas into the classes of spiritual perplexity and corporeal perplexity championed by William of Auxerre in the *Summa aurea* and by the authors of the *Summa Halesiana*.

The account given here has also revealed the unmistakable influence of the canon law tradition upon medieval theorizing on moral dilemmas. The promotion of the existence of moral dilemmas by Gratian in his *Decretum*, and the subsequent mutiny against the Master by the glossators, each provided extremities for the array of views in later debates. Gratian and his glossators were consistently cited and discussed by both friends and foes of moral dilemmas for centuries thereafter.

The principle of the lesser evil touted by defenders of moral dilemmas in the Middle Ages did not exhaust the advice dispensed by them. Raymond Lull offered an unusual theological recommendation by suggesting that agents who find themselves unable to avoid moral transgressions should pray and expect a divine intervention. Aquinas appears to have been aware of this type of response, since in one text he dismissed such an approach as sinfully presumptuous.

Given the extensive theorizing on moral dilemmas in the Middle Ages, particularly in the period of 1150–1450, one may justly ask why the insights of the medieval period on the subject were lost to later philosophy. At least, one may question why the history of moral dilemma theory has generally omitted these contributions. A possible answer worth exploring lies in the tendency of late scholastic moral thought of the sixteenth and seventeenth centuries to privilege the epistemic sense of *perplexitas* as the key issue in moral theory, and this practice arguably eclipsed the medieval theorizing on moral dilemmas. The problem of moral uncertainty in decision-making mushroomed into a major theme – if not the major theme – of the moral theory of that later time, particularly with the contributions of such thinkers as Cajetan, Francisco de Vitoria (1485–1546), Domingo Soto, Bartholomé de Medina, among others.[1] The increased interest in the subjective conditions of moral decision-making in late scholasticism continued without abatement throughout the development of early modern casuistry. In that period, the traditional examples of moral dilemmas from the medieval tradition reappeared, but with a new emphasis: they were not seen primarily as examples of moral dilemmas, but rather as case

---

[1] Latin texts from these thinkers on this topic are excerpted in J. de Blic, "Barthélémy de Medina et les origines du probabilisme," *Ephemerides Theologicae Louvanienses* 7 (1930), 46–83.

studies illustrating that agents can be faced with moral uncertainty. In these discussions, the foundational sense of *perplexitas* as moral entanglement was subsumed by an interest in *perplexitas* as moral confusion.

The flashpoint for this controversy of late scholasticism concerned the extent to which agents could permissibly depend on the moral opinions of others when the need to act in situations of moral uncertainty was imminent. The best-known achievement of this period was the doctrine of probabilism, a theory that held that confused agents could follow any moral opinion without sin, as long as the opinion was approved by a significant moral authority.[2] While the view that authoritative opinions have a privileged place in moral philosophy was not new, in the sixteenth century it was argued that in cases of doubt any action was permissible provided its performance was sanctioned by a probable opinion (*opinio probabilis*). An opinion was generally considered to be probable if it enjoyed the endorsement of some reputable authority, but what attestation could make an opinion sufficiently reputable was often a matter of dispute. Candidates ranged from Church Fathers, to church councils, to saints, to even a single theologian. In this context, the probability of an opinion was tied to an extrinsic criterion, as probability depended upon the endorsement of a qualified authority rather than the soundness of arguments supporting it. With this extrinsic criterion, both a proposition and its contradictory could simultaneously be probable, given the plurality

---

[2] Studies of probabilism from more recent decades include: Julia A. Fleming, *Defending Probabilism: The Moral Theology of Juan Caramuel* (Washington, DC: Georgetown University Press, 2007); Rudolf Schüssler, "On the Anatomy of Probabilism," in *Moral Philosophy on the Threshold of Modernity*, ed. Jill Kraye and Risto Saarinen (Dordrecht: Springer Verlag, 2005), 91–113; James Franklin, *The Science of Conjecture: Evidence and Probability before Pascal* (Baltimore: The Johns Hopkins University Press, 2001), 64–76; Servais Pinckaers, OP, *The Sources of Christian Ethics*, trans. Mary Thomas Noble, OP (Washington, DC: The Catholic University of America Press, 1995), 266–7, 273–7; Ilkka Kantola, *Probability and Moral Uncertainty in Late Medieval and Early Modern Times* (Helsinki: Luther-Agricola-Society, 1994); John Mahoney, *The Making of Moral Theology: A Study of the Roman Catholic Tradition* (Oxford: Clarendon Press, 1987), 135–43, 227–9. The classic study remains Thomas Deman, "Probabilisme," in *Dictionnaire de Théologie Catholique*, ed. A. Vacant, E. Mangenot, and E. Amann, 15 vols. (Paris: Librairie Letouzey et Ané, 1930–50), XIIIA: 417–619.

Kantola's *Probability and Moral Uncertainty* is particularly important because it argues for the compatibility of medieval and early modern notions of probability while stressing the Aristotelian background to the medieval notions. Portions of Kantola's study were published without attribution to constitute the greater part of M. W. F. Stone, "The Origins of Probabilism in Late Scholastic Moral Thought: A Prolegomenon to Further Study," *Recherches de Théologie et Philosophie médiévales* 67 (2000), 114–57. The journal issued a retraction of the article in "A Note from the Editorial Board," *Recherches de Théologie et Philosophie médiévales* 76 (2009), v–vi. See also M. V. Dougherty, Pernille Harsting, and Russell L. Friedman, "40 Cases of Plagiarism," *Bulletin de Philosophie Médiévale* 51 (2009), 350–91.

of ways in which ordinary opinions could be transformed into authoritative (i.e., probable) ones with the discovery of suitable endorsers. The philosophical background of this view of probable opinions was Aristotle's contention that there exists a subclass of philosophically relevant opinions. Those opinions, designated as *endoxa*, acquired their privileged status in the Aristotelian sciences (including ethics) by being endorsed by everyone, the majority, or the wise.[3] Both on Aristotle's criterion for *endoxa* and on the later criterion for *opiniones probabiles*, an opinion could become an authoritative guide for action simply by acquiring one of a wide variety of endorsements.

Unsurprisingly, the possibility that any moral opinion whatsoever could eventually warrant a designation as probable according to this extrinsic criterion was tempting for some theorists of late scholasticism. In the words of one modern commentator, the "implicit invitation . . . to justify the most bizarre of moral opinions as 'probable' . . . was a challenge which did not go unaccepted."[4] Defenders of probabilism found themselves commonly designated as laxists, while opponents of probabilism in turn were labeled as rigorists. At the center of their debates was an analysis of cases, reincarnated from medieval moral dilemma discussions.

The Dominican theologian Medina gave the most famous expression to the doctrine of probabilism. In his 1577 commentary on Aquinas's *Summa theologiae* he contended, "It seems to me that if an opinion is probable, it is permissible to follow it, even though the opposite be more probable (*mihi videtur quod si est opinio probabilis, licitum est eam sequi, licet opposita probabilior sit*)."[5] This statement was revolutionary, primarily because it rejected the standard medieval view that held an agent was obliged to follow the more probable opinion in any situation of moral uncertainty. With probabilism, the age-old tension in moral theory between freedom of the will and conformity to law found a victor: probabilism privileged the freedom of the individual conscience over the limitations imposed by law. This victory, however, did not last long. The sustained criticism of probabilism came not only from the theorists who detected laxity in the probabilistic framework, but also in the form of ecclesiastical

---

[3] In *Topica* 1.1 100b20–2, Aristotle defines *endoxa* as those opinions that "are accepted by everyone or by the majority or by the wise – i.e. by all, or by the majority, or by the most notable and reputable of them." The Aristotelian background to the probabilism of high scholasticism is analyzed by Kantola in *Probability and Moral Uncertainty*, 15–19, 26, 179. Kantola notes that Boethius translated Aristotle's term *endoxon* as *opinio probabilis*.

[4] Mahoney, *The Making of Moral Theology*, 138.   [5] J. de Blic, "Barthélémy de Medina," 71.

condemnations and popular criticism. Those church condemnations issued from the somber pen of the pope,[6] and the most famous popular refutation issued from the witty pen of Blaise Pascal (1623–62), who relentlessly attacked Jesuit defenders of probabilism in his *Provincial Letters*.[7]

While it is rightly held that Medina was the first to defend probabilism, this characterization is best understood in light of much earlier discussions of how an agent should compare probable or endoxic opinions according to the weight given to them by competing authorities.[8] Aristotle himself contended that the reputable character of *endoxa* could admit of varying degrees.[9] The debates of late scholasticism in the fifteenth and sixteenth centuries spawned the codification of a range of views for how agents should respond to situations of moral uncertainty in the presence of conflicting probable opinions. While probabilism defended the right of the agent to act upon any probable opinion, *probabiliorism* maintained that agents were always obliged to follow the more probable opinion. Further, *equiprobabilism* maintained that the freedom to act against a law required that the probable opinions in support of and against the law were equal.

The major figures in these debates quarreled over whether the solution to cases of moral uncertainty was the identification of the degree of probability (i.e., approvability by qualified authorities) possessed by moral opinions. This intense interest in the problem of moral uncertainty in late scholasticism and early modern casuistry prompted the re-working of the traditional medieval examples of moral dilemmas into case studies for moral uncertainty. This transformation may be the cause of the neglect of the medieval period by historians of moral dilemma theory. By offering a

---

[6] See, for instance, the sixteenth-century papal pronouncements found in *Enchiridion symbolorum: Definitionum et declarationum de rebus fidei et morum*, ed. Henricus Denzinger and Adolfus Schönmetzer, SJ, 32nd edn (Herder: Freiburg im Breisgau, 1963), §§ 2103, 2175.

[7] See Robert Aleksander Maryks, *Saint Cicero and the Jesuits: The Influence of the Liberal Arts on the Adoption of Moral Probabilism* (Aldershot: Ashgate, 2008 / Rome: Jesuit Historical Institute, 2008), 127–44; and Albert R. Jonsen and Stephen Toulmin, *The Abuse of Casuistry: A History of Moral Reasoning* (Berkeley: University of California Press, 1988), 231–49.

[8] The weighing of authoritative opinions was a key issue for both moral and juridical domains throughout the medieval period, as was seen in the first chapter in the discussion of Gratian and conflicts among authorities. Consider also, for instance, the objection reported by Thomas Bradwardine, Gregory of Rimini, and Johannes Capreolus discussed above concerning whether the principle of the lesser evil could be permissibly used in situations believed to be moral dilemmas: "no one sins while acting according to a most correct judgment, the unity of saints, the canon, and the general council (*Nullus etiam faciendo secundum judicium rectissimum et commune Sanctorum, et canonis, et concilii generalis, peccat*)," in Capreolus, *Defensiones*, IV: 436, Gregory of Rimini, *Lectura*, VI: 300; Bradwardine, *De causa Dei*, 257c.

[9] See Aristotle, *Topica* 8.5 159b8–14.

sampling of moral dilemma debates from the twelfth to the fifteenth centuries, the present volume has sought to bring the medieval contributions to moral dilemma theory into view again, as they need not be occluded by the debates of high scholasticism. The rediscovery of medieval theorizing on moral dilemmas adds a new chapter to the history of moral dilemma theory.

Bibliography

PRIMARY TEXTS

(Various authors). *The Cambridge Translations of Medieval Philosophical Texts.* Volume II: *Ethics and Political Philosophy*, ed. Arthur Stephen McGrade, John Kilcullen, and Matthew Kempshall (Cambridge University Press, 2001).

(Various authors). *Chartularium Universitatis Parisiensis*, ed. Henricus Denifle, OP, 4 vols. (Paris: Delalain, 1891–9 [repr. Brussels: Culture et Civilisation, 1964]).

(Various authors). *Concilios Visigóticos e Hispano-Romanos*, ed. José Vives, Tomás Marín Martínez, and Gonzalo Martínez Díez (Barcelona-Madrid: Consejo Superior de Investigaciones Científicas, Instituto Enrique Flórez, 1963).

(Various authors). *Enchiridion symbolorum: Definitionum et declarationum de rebus fidei et morum*, ed. Henricus Denzinger and Adolfus Schönmetzer, SJ, 32nd edn (Herder: Freiburg im Breisgau, 1963).

(Various authors). *Psychologie et morale aux XIIᵉ et XIIIᵉ siècles*, ed. Odon Lottin, 6 vols. (Louvain: Abbaye du Mont César, 1942–60).

(Various authors). *Prefaces to Canon Law Books in Latin Christianity: Selected Translations, 500–1245*, ed. Robert Somerville and Bruce C. Brasington (New Haven: Yale University Press, 1998).

(Various authors). *A Source Book in Medieval Science*, ed. Edward Grant (Cambridge, MA: Harvard University Press, 1974).

Acta Sanctorum. vol. VI, tom. 5 (Antwerp, 1709 [repr. Brussels: Culture et Civilisation, 1969]).

Albericus de Rosate. *Lexicon sive dictionarium utriusque iuris* (Pavia: Michael et Bernardinus de Garaldis, 1498).

Albertus Magnus. *Opera omnia*, ed. Stephanus Borgnet, 38 vols. (Paris: Vivès, 1890–9).

Alexander of Hales. *Summa theologica*, 4 vols. (Clarae Aquae [Quaracchi]: Typographia Collegii S. Bonaventurae, 1924–48).

Glossa in quatuor libros Sententiarum Petri Lombardi, 4 vols. (Quaracchi, Florence: Collegium S. Bonaventurae, 1951–7).

Quaestiones disputatae 'antequam esset frater', 3 vols. (Quaracchi, Florence: Collegium S. Bonaventurae, 1960).

Alexander IV. "The 'De fontibus paradisi' of Alexander IV on the 'Summa theologica' of Alexander of Hales," trans. Robert Prentice, OFM, *Franciscan Studies* 5 (1945), 350–1.

Aristotle. *Ethica Nicomachea*, ed. I. Bywater (Oxford: Clarendon Press, 1920).

    The Complete Works of Aristotle: The Revised Oxford Translation, ed. Jonathan Barnes, 2 vols. (Princeton University Press, 1984).

Augustine. *Opera omnia: Patrologiae Latinae elenchus*. www.augustinus.it/latino/index.htm.

Augustinus Triumphus. *Summa de ecclesiastica potestate* (Rome: Domus Francisci de Cinquinis, 1479).

Biblia Latina cum Glossa ordinaria: Facsimile Reprint of the editio princeps, ed. Karlfried Froehlich and Margaret T. Gibson, 4 vols. (Turnhout: Brepols, 1992).

Boethius. *De topicis differentiis*, in *Patrologia Latina*, ed. J.-P. Migne, vol. lxiv (Paris: 1891).

    The Theological Tractates and the Consolation of Philosophy, trans. H. F. Stewart, E. K. Rand, and S. J. Tester (Cambridge, MA: Harvard University Press, 1973).

Bonaventure. *Opera omnia*, ed. A. C. Peltier, 15 vols. (Paris: Vivès, 1864–71).

    Opera omnia, 10 vols. (Quaracchi: Collegium S. Bonaventurae, 1882–1902).

Carolus Bovillus. *Vita*, in *Acta Sanctorum*, vol. vi, tom. 5 (Antwerp, 1709 [repr. Brussels: Culture et Civilisation, 1969]), 668–73.

Cicero. *De officiis*, trans. Walter Miller (Cambridge, MA: Harvard University Press, 1975).

Denis the Carthusian. *Opera omnia*, 42 vols. (Montreuil, Tournai, and Parkminster: Typis Cartusiae S. M. de Pratis, 1896–1935).

Descartes, René. *Oeuvres de Descartes*, ed. Charles Adam and Paul Tannery, 11 vols. (Paris: Librairie Philosophique J. Vrin, 1996).

The Digest of Justinian, ed. Theodor Mommsen and Alan Watson, 4 vols. (Philadelphia: University of Pennsylvania Press, 1985).

Durandus of St. Pourçain. *In Petri Lombardi Sententias theologicas commentariorum libri IIII*, 2 vols. (Venice: Typographia Guerraea, 1571 [repr. Ridgewood, NJ: The Gregg Press, 1964]).

Gabriel Biel. *Collectorium circa quattuor libros Sententiarum. Liber secundus*, ed. Wilfridus Werbeck and Udo Hofmann (Tübingen: J. C. B. Mohr, 1984).

Giles of Rome. *Super secundo Sententiarum* (Venice: Lucas Venetus, 1482).

Gratian. *Decretum cum apparatus* (Venice: Baptista de Tortis, 1500).

    Decretum Gratiani emendatum et notationibus illustratum unà cum glossis (Rome: 1582). Digitized at: http://digital.library.ucla.edu/canonlaw/toc.html.

    Decretum Magistri Gratiani, ed. Aemilius Friedberg, *Corpus iuris canonici*, vol. 1 (Leipzig: Tauchnitz, 1879).

    The Treatise on Laws (Decretum DD. 1–20) with the Ordinary Gloss, trans. Augustine Thompson, OP and James Gordley (Washington, DC: The Catholic University of America Press, 1993).

Gregory the Great. *Morals on the Book of Job*, 3 vols. (Oxford: John Henry Parker, 1844–50).

Moralia in Iob, ed. Marcus Adriaen, 3 vols. (Turnhout: Brepols, 1979–85).

Gregory of Rimini. *Lectura super primum et secundum Sententiarum*, ed. A. Damasus Trapp, OSA, *et al.*, 6 vols. (Berlin: Walter de Gruyter, 1979–84).

Henry of Ghent. *Opera omnia*, ser. 2 (Leuven University Press, 1979–).

Humbert of Romans. *Opera de vita regulari*, ed. Joachim Joseph Berthier, 2 vols. (Rome: Typis A. Befani, 1888–9).

Isidore of Seville. *Etymologiae sive origines*, ed. W. M. Lindsay, 2 vols. (Oxford: Clarendon Press, 1911).

The Etymologies of Isidore of Seville, trans. Stephen A. Barney, W. J. Lewis, J. A. Beach, Oliver Berghof, and Muriel Hall (Cambridge University Press, 2006).

Jerome. *Commentariorum in Mathaeum libri* IV, ed. D. Hurst and M. Adriaen, *Corpus Christianorum series Latina*, vol. LVII (Turnhout: Brepols, 1969).

Commentary on Matthew, trans. Thomas P. Scheck (Washington, DC: The Catholic University of America Press, 2008).

Johannes Capreolus. *Defensiones theologiae Divi Thomae Aquinatis*, ed. Ceslaus Paban and Thomas Pègues, 7 vols. (Turin: Alfred Cattier, 1900–08).

On the Virtues, trans. Kevin White and Romanus Cessario, OP (Washington, DC: The Catholic University of America Press, 2001).

John Cassian. *The Conferences*, trans. Boniface Ramsey (New York: Paulist Press, 1997).

Collationum, in Patrologia Latina, ed. J.-P. Migne, vol. XLIX (Paris: 1874).

John Duns Scotus. *Opera omnia* (Vatican City, 1950–).

John of Paris. *Commentaire sur les Sentences*, ed. Jean-Pierre Muller, OSB, 2 vols. (Rome: Herder, 1961–4).

Kant, Immanuel. *The Metaphysics of Morals*, trans. Mary J. Gregor (Cambridge University Press, 1996).

Practical Philosophy, trans. Mary J. Gregor (Cambridge University Press, 1996).

Religion and Rational Theology (Cambridge University Press, 1996).

Kierkegaard, Søren. *Fear and Trembling; Repetition*, trans. Howard V. Hong and Edna H. Hong (Princeton University Press, 1983).

Leibniz, Gottfried Wilhelm. *Disputatio de casibus perplexis in jure*, in *Sämtliche Schriften und Briefe* (Darmstadt: Otto Reichl Verlag, 1930), VI.1: 231–56.

Lucretius. *De rerum natura*, trans. W. H. D. Rouse and Martin Ferguson Smith (Cambridge, MA: Harvard University Press, 1975).

Mill, John Stuart. *Utilitarianism*, in *Collected Works of John Stuart Mill*, ed. J. M. Robson, vol. X (University of Toronto Press), 203–60.

Peter Abelard. "Abelard's Letter of Consolation to a Friend (*Historia calamitatem*)," ed. J. T. Muckle, CSB, *Mediaeval Studies* 12 (1950), 163–213.

The Story of Abelard's Adversities, trans. J. T. Muckle (Toronto: Pontifical Institute of Mediaeval Studies, 1964).

Peter Abelard's Ethics, ed. and trans. D. E. Luscombe (Oxford: Clarendon Press, 1971).

Peter Auriol. *Commentaria in secundum librum Sententiarum*, 2 vols. (Rome: Aloysius Zannetti, 1604–05).

Peter Lombard. *Sententiae in IV libris distinctae*, 2 vols. (Grottaferrata: Editiones Collegii S. Bonaventurae ad Claras Aquas, 1971–81).

    The Sentences, trans. Giulio Silano, 4 vols. (Toronto: Pontifical Institute of Mediaeval Studies, 2007–10).

Peter of Poitiers. *Sententiarum libri quinque*, in *Patrologia Latina*, ed. J.-P. Migne, vol. ccxi (Paris: 1855).

Peter of Tarentaise (Innocentius Quintus). *In iv librum Sententiarum commentaria*, 4 vols. (Toulouse: Academiae Tolosanae Typographum, 1649–52 [repr. Ridgewood, NJ: The Gregg Press, 1964]).

Plato. *Opera*, ed. John Burnet, 5 vols. (Oxford: Clarendon Press, 1899–1937).

    Complete Works, ed. John M. Cooper (Indianapolis, IN: Hackett Publishing, 1997).

Raymond Lull. *A Life of Ramón Lull*, trans. E. Allison Peers (London: Burns Oates and Washbourne, 1927).

    Raymundi Lulli Opera Latina, ed. Friedrich Stegmüller *et al.*, vols. i–v (Palma de Mallorca: Maioricensis Schola Lullistica, 1959–67), vols. viff. (Turnhout: Brepols, 1975–).

    Vita coaetanea, in *Opera Latina*, vol. viii, ed. Hermogenes Harada, OFM, *Corpus Christianorum continuatio mediaevalis*, vol. xxxiv (Turnhout: Brepols, 1980), 272–309.

    Selected Works of Ramon Llull (1232–1316), ed. and trans. Anthony Bonner, 2 vols. (Princeton University Press, 1985).

    Doctor Illuminatus: A Ramon Llull Reader, ed. and trans. Anthony Bonner (Princeton University Press, 1993).

Raymond of Peñafort. *Summa de poenitentia et matrimonio cum glossis Ioannis de Friburgo* (Rome: Ioannes Tallinus Bibliopolus, 1603).

Richard of Middleton. *Super quatuor libros Sententiarum*, 4 vols. (Brescia: Apud Vincentium Sabbium, 1591).

Robert Holcot. *In quatuor libros Sententiarum quaestiones* (Lyons: 1518 [repr. Frankfurt: Minerva, 1967]).

Roger Bacon. *Opera*, in *Opera quaedam hactenus inedita*, ed. J. S. Brewer, vol. i (London: Longman, 1859 [repr. New York: Kraus Reprint Ltd, 1965]).

Suárez, Francisco. *Opera omnia*, 30 vols. (Paris: Vivès, 1856–78).

    Selections from Three Works, 2 vols. (Oxford: Clarendon Press, 1944), ii: 287–8.

Thomas À Kempis. *De imitatio Christi libri quatuor*, ed. Eusebius Amort (Cologne, 1759).

Thomas Aquinas. *Opera omnia*, ed. Stanislaus Fretté and Paulus Maré, 34 vols. (Paris: Vivès, 1871–80).

    Opera omnia, 50 vols. (Rome: Ex Typographia Polyglotta / Commissio Leonina, 1882–).

    The Summa contra Gentiles, 4 vols. (London: Burns Oates and Washbourne, 1924–9).

Scriptum super libros Sententiarum, ed. P. Mandonnet and P. Maria Fabianus Moos, 4 vols. (Paris: Lethielleux, 1929–47).

In duodecim libros Metaphysicorum Aristotelis expositio, ed. M.-R. Cathala, OP and Raymundus Spiazzi, OP (Rome: Marietti, 1950).

The Disputed Questions on Truth, trans. Robert W. Mulligan, SJ, James V. McGlynn, SJ, and Robert W. Schmidt, SJ, 3 vols. (Chicago: Henry Regnery, 1952–4).

Super epistolas S. Pauli lectura, ed. Raphaelus Cai, OP, 8th edn, 2 vols. (Rome: Marietti, 1953).

De correctione fraterna, in *Quaestiones disputatae*, ed. P. Bazzi *et al.*, 9th edn, 2 vols. (Rome: Marietti, 1953).

De potentia, in *Quaestiones disputatae*, ed. P. Bazzi *et al.*, 9th edn, 2 vols. (Rome: Marietti, 1953).

On Kingship to the King of Cyprus, trans. Gerald B. Phelan, rev. I. Eschmann, OP (Toronto: Pontifical Institute of Mediaeval Studies, 1982).

An Exposition of the On the Hebdomads of Boethius, trans. Janice L. Schultz and Edward A. Sinan (Washington, DC: The Catholic University of America, 2001).

Thomas Bradwardine. *De causa Dei contra Pelagium et de virtute causarum*, ed. Henricus Savilius (London: Johannes Billius, 1618 [repr. Frankfurt am Main: Minerva GmbH, 1964]).

Thomas Le Myésier. *Electorium parvum seu Breviculum, Vollständiges Faksimile der Handschrift St. Peter perg. 92 der Badischen Landesbibliothek Karlsruhe, Kommentar zum Faksimile*, ed. Gerhard Römer and Gerhard Stamm, 2 vols. (Wiesbaden, 1988).

Breviculum seu Electorium parvum Thomae Migerii, ed. Charles Lohr, Theodor Pindl-Büchel, and Walburga Büchel, *Corpus Christianorum continuatio mediaevalis*, vol. LXXVII. *Raimundi Lulli Opera Latina, Supplementum Lullianum*, vol. 1 (Turnhout: Brepols, 1990).

Thomas of Strasbourg. *Commentaria in IIII libro Sententiarum* (Venice: Ziletti, 1564).

Wadding, Luke. *Annales Minorum seu trium ordinum a S. Francisco institutorum*, 32 vols. (Clarae Aquae [Quaracchi]: Typographia Collegii S. Bonaventurae, 1931–5).

Walter of Bruges. *Quaestiones disputatae*, ed. E. Longpré, OFM (Louvain: Institut Supérieur de Philosophie de l'Université, 1928).

William of Auxerre. *Summa aurea in quattuor libros Sententiarum* (Paris: Philippus Pigouchet, 1500 [repr. Frankfurt/Main: Minerva, 1964]).

Summa aurea, ed. Jean Ribaillier, 7 vols. (Paris: Editions du Centre National de la Recherche Scientifique, 1980–7).

Summa de officiis ecclesiasticis, ed. Franz Fischer. www.thomasinst.uni-koeln.de/sdoe/start.html.

William of Ockham. *Quodlibeta septem*, ed. Joseph C. Wey, CSB (St. Bonaventure, NY: St. Bonaventure University, 1980).

Quaestiones in librum secundum Sententiarum (Reportatio), ed. Gedeon Gál, OFM and Rega Wood (St. Bonaventure, NY: St. Bonaventure University, 1981).

Quaestiones in librum quartum Sententiarum (Reportatio), ed. Rega Wood, Gedeon Gál, OFM, and Romualdo Green, OFM (St. Bonaventure, NY: St. Bonaventure University, 1984).

Opera dubia et spuria, ed. E. M. Buytaert *et al.* (St. Bonaventure, NY: St. Bonaventure University, 1988).

Quodlibetal Questions, trans. Alfred J. Freddoso and Francis E. Kelley (New Haven: Yale University Press, 1991).

A Compendium of Ockham's Teaching, trans. Julian Davies, OFM (St. Bonaventure, NY: The Franciscan Institute, 1998).

SECONDARY LITERATURE

Adams, Marilyn McCord. "The Structure of Ockham's Moral Theory," *Franciscan Studies* 46 (1986), 1–35.

"William Ockham: Voluntarist or Naturalist?" in *Studies in Medieval Philosophy*, ed. John F. Wippel (Washington, DC: The Catholic University of America Press, 1987), 219–47.

"Ockham on Will, Nature, and Morality," in *The Cambridge Companion to Ockham*, ed. Paul Vincent Spade (Cambridge University Press, 1999), 245–72.

Armstrong, R. A. *Primary and Secondary Precepts in Thomistic Natural Law Teaching* (The Hague: Martinus Nijhoff, 1966).

Backhaus, Ralph. *Casus perplexus: Die Lösung in sich widersprüchlicher Rechtsfälle durch die klassische römische Jurisprudenz* (Munich: C. H. Beck'sche Verlagbuchhandlung, 1981).

Baldwin, John W. *The Language of Sex: Five Voices from Northern France around 1200* (University of Chicago Press, 1994).

Batllori, Miquel. *Ramon Lull i el Lul·lisme, Obra Completa*, vol. II (València: Tres i Quatre, 1993).

Baylor, Michael G. *Action and Person: Conscience in Late Scholasticism and the Young Luther* (Leiden: Brill, 1977).

Bender, OP, Ludovico. "Lesser Evil (Choice of)," in *Dictionary of Moral Theology*, ed. Francesco Roberti and Pietro Palazzini, trans. Henry J. Yannone (Westminster, MD: The Newman Press, 1962), 705–6.

Ben-Menahem, Hanina. "Leibniz on Hard Cases," *Archiv für Rechts- und Sozialphilosophie* 79 (1993), 198–215.

Blum, Paul Richard. *Philosophy of Religion in the Renaissance* (Farnham: Ashgate Publishing, 2010).

Boehner, OFM, Philotheus. "A Recent Presentation of Ockham's Philosophy," *Franciscan Studies* 9 (1949), 443–56, rep. in Boehner, 1958.

Collected Articles on Ockham, ed. Eligius M. Buytaert, OFM (St. Bonaventure, NY: The Franciscan Institute, 1958).

Bonner, Anthony. "Ramon Llull and the Dominicans," *Catalan Review* 4 (1990), 377–92.

The Art and Logic of Ramon Llull: A User's Guide (Leiden: Brill, 2007).

Bougerol, OFM, J. Guy. *Introduction to the Works of Bonaventure*, trans. José de Vinck (Paterson, NJ: St. Anthony Guild Press, 1964).

Bourke, Vernon J. "The Background of Aquinas' Synderesis Principle," in *Graceful Reason: Essays in Ancient and Medieval Philosophy Presented to Joseph Owens, CCSR* (Toronto: Pontifical Institute of Mediaeval Studies, 1983), 345–60.

Boyle, Leonard E. "The Quodlibets of St. Thomas and Pastoral Care," *The Thomist* 37 (1974), 232–56.

Bradley, Denis J. M. *Aquinas on the Twofold Human Good* (Washington, DC: The Catholic University of America, 1997).

Brady, OFM, Ignatius. "The Distinctions of Lombard's Book of Sentences and Alexander of Hales," *Franciscan Studies* 25 (1965), 90–116.

"The 'Summa Theologica' of Alexander of Hales (1924–1948)," *Archivum Franciscanum Historicum* 70 (1977), 437–47.

Brundage, James A. *Medieval Canon Law* (London: Longman, 1995).

The Medieval Origins of the Legal Profession: Canonists, Civilians, and Courts (University of Chicago Press, 2008).

Candellero, Massimo. "Un importante documento biografico Lulliano: La *Vita Coaetanea*," in *Atti del Convegno internazionale Ramon Llull, il lullismo internazionale, l'Italia. Omaggio a Miquel Batllori dell'Associazione Italiana di Studi Catalani. Napoli, Castel dell'Ovo, 30 e 31 marzo, 1 aprile 1989*, ed. Giuseppe Grilli (Naples: Istituto universitario orientale 1992), 15–33.

Cavanaugh, T. A. *Double-Effect Reasoning: Doing Good and Avoiding Evil* (Oxford: Clarendon Press, 2006).

Cessario, OP, Romanus. *A Short History of Thomism* (Washington, DC: The Catholic University of America Press, 2005).

Chenu, OP, M.-D. *Toward Understanding Saint Thomas*, trans. A.-M. Landry, OP and D. Hughes, OP (Chicago: Henry Regnery Company, 1964).

Clark, David W. "Voluntarism and Rationalism in the Ethics of Ockham," *Franciscan Studies* 31 (1971), 72–87.

"William of Ockham on Right Reason," *Speculum* 48 (1973), 13–36.

Colavechio, O. Praem., Xavier G. *Erroneous Conscience and Obligations: A Study of the Teaching from the Summa Halesiana, Saint Bonaventure, Saint Albert the Great, and Saint Thomas Aquinas* (Washington, DC: The Catholic University of America Press, 1961).

Conee, Earl. "Against Moral Dilemmas," *The Philosophical Review* 91 (1982), 87–97, reprinted in Gowans 1987.

"Why Moral Dilemmas are Impossible," *American Philosophical Quarterly* 26 (1989), 133–41.

Coolman, Boyd Taylor. *Knowing God by Experience: The Spiritual Senses in the Theology of William of Auxerre* (Washington, DC: The Catholic University of America Press, 2004).

Crowe, Michael Bertram. *The Changing Profile of the Natural Law* (The Hague: Martinus Nijhoff, 1977).

de Blic, J. "Barthélémy de Medina et les origines du probabilisme," *Ephemerides Theologicae Louvanienses* 7 (1930), 46–83.

Deferrari, Roy J., M. Inviolata Barry, CDP, and Ignatius McGuiness, OP, *A Lexicon of St. Thomas Aquinas* (Washington, DC: The Catholic University of America Press, 1948).

 A Latin–English Dictionary of St. Thomas Aquinas (Boston: St. Paul Editions, 1986).

Deman, Thomas. "Probabilisme," in *Dictionnaire de Théologie Catholique*, ed. A. Vacant, E. Mangenot, and E. Amann, 15 vols. (Paris: Librairie Letouzey et Ané, 1930–50), XIIIA: 417–619.

Donagan, Alan. *The Theory of Morality* (University of Chicago Press, 1977).

 "Consistency in Rationalist Moral Systems," *The Journal of Philosophy* 81 (1984), 291–309, repr. in Gowans 1987.

 "Moral Dilemmas, Genuine and Spurious: A Comparative Anatomy," *Ethics* 104 (1993), 7–21, reprinted in Donagan 1994 and Mason 1996.

 The Philosophical Papers of Alan Donagan, ed. J. E. Malpas, 2 vols. (University of Chicago Press, 1994).

Doolan, Gregory. "The Relation of Culture and Ignorance to Culpability in Thomas Aquinas," *The Thomist* 63 (1999), 105–24.

Doucet, OFM, Victorin. "A New Source of the 'Summa Fratris Alexandri': The Commentary on the Sentences of Alexander of Hales," *Franciscan Studies* 6 (1946), 403–17.

 "The History of the Problem of the Authenticity of the Summa," *Franciscan Studies* 7 (1947), 26–41, 274–312.

Dougherty, M. V. "Perplexity *Simpliciter* and Perplexity *Secundum Quid*: A Look at Some Contemporary Appeals to St. Thomas Aquinas," *International Philosophical Quarterly* 41 (2001), 469–80.

 "Thomas Aquinas and Divine Command Theory," *Proceedings of the American Catholic Philosophical Association* 76 (2002), 153–64.

 "Moral Dilemmas and Moral Luck: Reckoning with the Thomistic Ethical Tradition," *Proceedings of the American Catholic Philosophical Association* 78 (2004), 233–46.

 "Thomas Aquinas on the Manifold Senses of Self-Evidence," *The Review of Metaphysics* 59 (2006), 601–30.

 Pernille Harsting and Russell L. Friedman. "40 Cases of Plagiarism," *Bulletin de Philosophie Médiévale* 51 (2009), 350–91.

Evans, G. R. "Communis animi conceptio: The Self-Evident Statement," *Archivum Latinitatis Medii Aevi* 41 (1979), 123–6.

Evans, G. R. (ed.). *Mediaeval Commentaries on the Sentences of Peter Lombard*, vol. I (Leiden: Brill, 2002).

Finnis, John. *Fundamentals of Ethics* (Washington, DC: Georgetown University Press, 1983).

   Aquinas: Moral, Political, and Legal Theory (Oxford University Press, 1998).

   Moral Absolutes: Tradition, Revision, and Truth (Washington, DC: The Catholic University of America Press, 1991).

Flannery, SJ, Kevin L. *Acts Amid Precepts: The Aristotelian Logical Structure of Thomas Aquinas's Moral Theory* (Washington, DC: The Catholic University of America Press, 2001).

Fleming, Julia A. *Defending Probabilism: The Moral Theology of Juan Caramuel* (Washington, DC: Georgetown University Press, 2007).

Franklin, James. *The Science of Conjecture: Evidence and Probability before Pascal* (Baltimore: The Johns Hopkins University Press, 2001).

Freppert, OFM, Lucan. *The Basis of Morality According to William Ockham* (Chicago: Franciscan Herald Press, 1988).

Gallagher, David M. "The Role of God in the Philosophical Ethics of Thomas Aquinas," in *Was ist Philosophie im Mittelalter? Akten des X. Internationalen Kongresses für Mittelalterliche Philosophie*, ed. Jan A. Aertsen and Andreas Speer (Berlin: Walter de Gruyter, 1998), 1024–33.

Gauthier, OP, René Antoine. "Introduction au Quodlibet XII," in *Quaestiones de quolibet*, in *Opera omnia* (Rome: Commissio Leonina, 1996), XXV.2: 152–60.

Geach, Peter. *God and the Soul* (New York: Schocken Books, 1969).

Geonget, Stéphan. *La notion de perplexité à la Renaissance* (Geneva: Librairie Droz, 2006).

Gilson, Étienne. *History of Christian Philosophy in the Middle Ages* (New York: Random House, 1955).

Glare, P. G. W. (ed.). *Oxford Latin Dictionary* (Oxford: Clarendon Press, 1982).

Glorieux, P. *La littérature quodlibétique*, 2 vols. (Paris: J. Vrin, 1925–35).

González, Ana Marta. "*Depositum gladius non debet restitui furioso*: Precepts, Synderesis, and Virtues in Saint Thomas Aquinas," *The Thomist* 63 (1999), 217–40.

Gowans, Christopher W. (ed.). *Moral Dilemmas* (New York: Oxford University Press, 1987).

   "The Debate on Moral Dilemmas," in *Moral Dilemmas*, ed. Christopher W. Gowans (New York: Oxford University Press, 1987), 3–33.

   Innocence Lost: An Examination of Inescapable Moral Wrongdoing (New York: Oxford University Press, 1994).

Green, Thomas Hill. *Prolegomena to Ethics*, ed. A. C. Bradley (Oxford: Clarendon Press, 1883 [repr. Bristol: Thoemmes Press, 1997]).

Greenspan, P. S. *Practical Guilt: Moral Dilemmas, Emotions, and Social Norms* (New York: Oxford University Press, 1995).

Grisez, Germain. "The First Principle of Practical Reason: A Commentary on the *Summa Theologiae*, 1–2, Question 94, Article 2," *Natural Law Forum* 10 (1965), 168–96.

"Against Consequentialism," *American Journal of Jurisprudence* 23 (1978), 21–72, reprinted in Kaczor 2000.

Christian Moral Principles (Quincy, IL: Franciscan Press, 1983).

Difficult Moral Questions (Quincy, IL: Franciscan Press, 1997).

Hallamaa, Olli. "On the Limits of the Genre: Roger Roseth as a Reader of the *Sentences*," in *Mediaeval Commentaries on the Sentences of Peter Lombard*, vol. ii, ed. Philipp W. Rosemann (Leiden: Brill, 2010), 369–404.

Hames, Harvey J. *The Art of Conversion: Christianity and Kabbalah in the Thirteenth Century* (Leiden: Brill, 2000).

Hamesse, Jacqueline. "Theological *Quaestiones Quodlibetales*," in *Theological Quodlibeta in the Middle Ages*, ed. Christopher Schabel, 2 vols. (Leiden: Brill, 2006–07), 1: 17–48.

Hannigan, SJ, E. T. "Is It Ever Lawful to Advise the Lesser of Two Evils?" *Gregorianum* 30 (1949), 104–29.

Hare, R. M. *Moral Thinking: Its Levels, Method, and Point* (Oxford University Press, 1981).

Hartmann, Wilfried, and Kenneth Pennington (eds.). *History of Medieval Canon Law*, 11 vols. (Washington, DC: The Catholic University of America Press, 1999–).

Hill, Jr., Thomas E. "Moral Dilemmas, Gaps, and Residues: A Kantian Perspective," in *Moral Dilemmas and Moral Theory*, ed. H. E. Mason (New York: Oxford University Press, 1996), 167–98.

Respect, Pluralism, and Justice (Oxford: Clarendon Press, 2000).

Hillgarth, J. N. *Ramon Lull and Lullism in Fourteenth-Century France* (Oxford: Clarendon Press, 1971).

Hoag, Robert W. "Mill on Conflicting Moral Obligations," *Analysis* 43 (1983), 49–54.

Holopainen, Taina M. *William Ockham's Theory of the Foundations of Ethics* (Helsinki: Luther-Agricola-Society, 1991).

Honnefelder, Ludger. "The Evaluation of Goods and the Estimation of Consequences: Aquinas on the Determination of the Morally Good," in *The Ethics of Aquinas*, ed. Stephen J. Pope (Washington, DC: Georgetown University Press, 2002), 426–36.

Huber, OFM Conv., Raphael M. "Alexander of Hales, O.F.M. (*ca.* 1170–1245)," *Franciscan Studies* 5 (1945), 353–65.

Inglis, John. *Spheres of Philosophical Inquiry and the Historiography of Medieval Philosophy* (Leiden: Brill, 1998).

John, Helen James. *The Thomist Spectrum* (New York: Fordham University Press, 1966).

Johnston, Mark D. *The Spiritual Logic of Ramon Llull* (Oxford: Clarendon Press, 1987).

"Ramon Llull's Conversion to Penitence," *Mystics Quarterly* 16 (1990), 179–92.

The Evangelical Rhetoric of Ramon Llull: Lay Learning and Piety in the Christian West Around 1300 (New York: Oxford University Press, 1996).

Jonsen, Albert R., and Stephen Toulmin. *The Abuse of Casuistry: A History of Moral Reasoning* (Berkeley: University of California Press, 1988).

Jordan, Mark D. "Medieval Philosophy of the Future," in *The Past and Future of Medieval Studies*, ed. John Van Engen (South Bend, IN: University of Notre Dame Press, 1994), 148–65.

Rewritten Theology: Aquinas after His Readers (Oxford: Blackwell Publishing, 2006).

Kaczor, Christopher (ed.). *Proportionalism: For and Against* (Milwaukee, WI: Marquette University Press, 2000).

Proportionalism and the Natural Law Tradition (Washington, DC: The Catholic University of America Press, 2002).

Kantola, Ilkka. *Probability and Moral Uncertainty in Late Medieval and Early Modern Times* (Helsinki: Luther-Agricola-Society, 1994).

Kennedy, Leonard. *The Philosophy of Robert Holcot, Fourteenth-Century Skeptic* (Lewiston: The Edwin Mellen Press, 1993).

Kerr, Fergus. *After Aquinas: Versions of Thomism* (Oxford: Blackwell Publishers, 2002).

Kirk, Kenneth E. *Conscience and Its Problems: An Introduction to Casuistry* (London: Longmans, Green and Co., 1933 [repr. Louisville: Westminster John Knox Press, 1999]).

Knuuttila, Simo. *Modalities in Medieval Philosophy* (London: Routledge, 1993).

Knuuttila, Simo, and Olli Hallamaa. "Roger Roseth and Medieval Deontic Logic," *Logique & Analyse* 149 (1995), 75–87.

Kuttner, Stephan. *Kanonistische Schuldlehre von Gratian bis auf die Dekretalen Gregors IX: Systematisch auf Grund der handschriftlichen Quellen dargestellt* (Vatican City: Biblioteca Apostolica Vaticana, 1935).

"The Father of the Science of Canon Law," *The Jurist* 1 (1941), 2–19.

"Harmony from Dissonance: An Interpretation of Medieval Canon Law," *Wimmer Lecture X* (Latrobe, PA: Archabbey Press, 1960), 1–16, reprinted with additions in Kuttner 1980.

The History of Ideas and Doctrines of Canon Law in the Middle Ages (London: Variorum Reprints, 1980).

"Research on Gratian: Acta and Agenda," in *Proceedings of the Seventh International Congress of Medieval Canon Law* (Vatican City: Biblioteca Apostolica Vaticana, 1988), 3–26, reprinted with additions in Kuttner 1990.

Studies in the History of Medieval Canon Law (Aldershot: Ashgate Variorum, 1990).

Landau, Peter. "The Development of Law," in *The New Cambridge Medieval History*, vol. IV, part 1, ed. David Luscombe and Jonathan Riley-Smith (Cambridge University Press, 2004), 113–47.

"Gratian and the *Decretum Gratiani*," in *The History of Medieval Canon Law in the Classical Period, 1140–1234: From Gratian to the Decretals of Pope Gregory IX*, ed. Wilfried Hartmann and Kenneth Pennington (Washington, DC: The Catholic University of America Press, 2008), 22–54.

Landgraf, Artur Michael. "Der '*Casus perplexus*' in der Frühscholastik," *Collectanea Franciscana* 29 (1959), 74–86.

Langston, Douglas. "The Spark of Conscience: Bonaventure's View of Conscience and Synderesis," *Franciscan Studies* 53 (1993), 79–95.

Conscience and Other Virtues (University Park, PA: Pennsylvania State University Press, 2001).

Lemmon, E. J. "Moral Dilemmas," *The Philosophical Review* 70 (1962), 139–58, reprinted in part in Gowans 1987.

Lewis, Charlton T., and Charles Short. *A Latin Dictionary* (Oxford: Clarendon Press, 1962).

Liddell, Henry George, *et al. A Greek–English Lexicon* (Oxford: Clarendon Press, 1996).

Lohr, Charles H. "Metaphysics," in *The Cambridge History of Renaissance Philosophy*, ed. Charles B. Schmitt *et al.* (Cambridge University Press, 1988), 537–638.

Luscombe, D. E. *The School of Peter Abelard: The Influence of Abelard's Thought in the Early Scholastic Period* (Cambridge University Press, 1970).

MacIntyre, Alasdair. "Moral Dilemmas," *Philosophy and Phenomenological Research* 50 (1990), 367–82, reprinted with revisions in MacIntyre 1996.

Selected Essays, 2 vols. (Cambridge University Press, 1996).

Mahoney, Edward P. "The Accomplishment of Jean Capreolus, O.P.," *The Thomist* 68 (2004), 601–32.

Mahoney, John. *The Making of Moral Theology: A Study of the Roman Catholic Tradition* (Oxford: Clarendon Press, 1987).

Mäkinen, Virpi. "Rights and Duties in Late Scholastic Discussion on Extreme Necessity," in *Transformations in Medieval and Early-Modern Rights Discourse*, ed. Virpi Mäkinen and Petter Korkman (Dordrecht: Springer, 2006), 37–62.

Mangan, SJ, Joseph. "An Historical Analysis of the Principle of Double Effect," *Theological Studies* 10 (1949), 41–61.

Mann, William E. "Jephthah's Plight: Moral Dilemmas and Theism," *Philosophical Perspectives* 5 (1991), 617–47.

Marcus, Ruth Barcan. "Moral Dilemmas and Consistency," *The Journal of Philosophy* 77 (1980), 121–36, reprinted in Gowans 1987.

Marenbon, John. *Early Medieval Philosophy (480–1150): An Introduction*, rev. edn (London: Routledge, 1991).

Later Medieval Philosophy (1150–1350): An Introduction (London: Routledge, 1993).

Maritain, Jacques. *Integral Humanism*, trans. Joseph W. Evans (South Bend, IN: University of Notre Dame Press, 1973).

Martorell, Llabrés. "La conversión del Bto. Ramón Llull, en sus aspectos histórico, sicológico y teológico," *Estudios Lulianos* 12 (1968), 161–73.

Maryks, Robert Aleksander. *Saint Cicero and the Jesuits: The Influence of the Liberal Arts on the Adoption of Moral Probabilism* (Aldershot: Ashgate, 2008 / Rome: Jesuit Historical Institute, 2008).

Mason, H. E. (ed.). *Moral Dilemmas and Moral Theory* (New York: Oxford University Press, 1996).

Maurer, Armand. *The Philosophy of William of Ockham in the Light of Its Principles* (Toronto: Pontifical Institute of Mediaeval Studies, 1999).

May, William E. "Germain Grisez on Moral Principles and Moral Norms: Natural and Christian," in *Natural Law and Moral Inquiry: Ethics, Metaphysics, and Politics in the Work of Germain Grisez*, ed. Robert P. George (Washington, DC: Georgetown University Press, 1994), 3–35.

McConnell, Terrance C. "Moral Dilemmas and Consistency in Ethics," *Canadian Journal of Philosophy* 8 (1978), 269–87, reprinted in Gowans 1987.

"Moral Residue and Dilemmas," in *Moral Dilemmas and Moral Theory*, ed. H. E. Mason (New York: Oxford University Press, 1996), 36–47.

McCool, SJ, Gerald A. *From Unity to Pluralism: The Internal Evolution of Thomism* (New York: Fordham University Press, 1992).

The Neo-Thomists (Milwaukee, WI: Marquette University Press, 2003).

McCormick, SJ, Richard A. *Ambiguity in Moral Choice* (Milwaukee, WI: Marquette University Press, 1978).

McDonnell, Kevin. "Does William of Ockham Have a Theory of Natural Law?" *Franciscan Studies* 34 (1974), 383–92.

McInerny, Daniel. *The Difficult Good: A Thomistic Approach to Moral Conflict and Human Happiness* (New York: Fordham University Press, 2006).

McInerny, Ralph. *Aquinas on Human Action* (Washington, DC: The Catholic University of America, 1992).

Müller, Sigrid. "The Ethics of John Capreolus and the 'Nominales'," *Verbum: Analecta Neolatina* 6 (2004), 301–14.

Mulligan, SJ, Robert W. "*Ratio Superior* and *Ratio Inferior*: The Historical Background," *The New Scholasticism* 29 (1955), 1–32.

"*Ratio Inferior* and *Ratio Superior* in St. Albert and St. Thomas," *The Thomist* 19 (1956), 339–67.

Nagel, Thomas. *Mortal Questions* (New York: Cambridge University Press, 1979).

Niermeyer, J. F., and C Van de Kieft. (ed.). *Mediae Latinitatis lexicon minus* (Leiden: Brill, 1993).

Noonan, Jr., John T. "Gratian Slept Here: The Changing Identity of the Father of the Systematic Study of Canon Law," *Traditio* 35 (1979), 145–72.

The Scholastic Analysis of Usury (Cambridge, MA: Harvard University Press, 1957).

Normore, C. G. "Picking and Choosing: Anselm and Ockham on Choice," *Vivarium* 36 (1998), 23–39.

Nussbaum, Martha C. *The Fragility of Goodness: Luck and Ethics in Greek Tragedy and Philosophy* (New York: Cambridge University Press, 1986).

Oberman, Heiko Augustinus. *The Harvest of Medieval Theology: Gabriel Biel and Late Medieval Nominalism*, 3rd edn (Durham, NC: The Labyrinth Press, 1983).

O'Neill, John. "'The Same Thing Therefore Ought to Be and Ought not to Be': Anselm on Conflicting Oughts," *The Heythrop Journal* 35 (1994), 312–14.

Osborne, OFM, Kenan B. "Alexander of Hales: Precursor and Promoter of Franciscan Theology," in *The History of Franciscan Theology*, ed. Kenan B. Osborne, OFM (St. Bonaventure, NY: The Franciscan Institute, 1994 [repr. 2007]), 1–38.

Osborne, Jr., Thomas M. "Ockham as a Divine-Command Theorist," *Religious Studies* 41 (2005), 1–22.

Pelzer, August. "Les 51 articles de Guillaume Occam censurés, en Avignon, en 1326," *Revue d'histoire ecclésiastique* 18 (1922), 240–70.

Pennington, Kenneth. "Johannes Teutonicus," in *Dictionary of the Middle Ages*, vol. vii, ed. Joseph R. Strayer (New York: Charles Scribner's Sons, 1986), 121–2.

"Medieval Canonists: A Bio-Bibliographical Listing," http://faculty.cua.edu/pennington/biobibl.htm.

Perler, Dominik. "Does God Deceive Us? Skeptical Hypotheses in Late Medieval Epistemology," in *Rethinking the History of Skepticism: The Missing Medieval Background*, ed. Henrik Lagerlund (Leiden: Brill, 2010), 171–92.

Pinckaers, OP, Servais. *The Sources of Christian Ethics*, trans. Mary Thomas Noble, OP (Washington, DC: The Catholic University of America Press, 1995).

"La défense, par Capreolus, de la doctrine de Saint Thomas sur les vertus," in *Jean Capreolus en son temps (1380–1444)*, ed. Guy Bedouelle, Romanus Cessario, and Kevin White (Paris: Les Éditions du Cerf, 1997), 177–92.

"Capreolus's Defense of St. Thomas's Teaching on the Virtues," in John Capreolus, *On the Virtues* (Washington, DC: The Catholic University of America Press, 2001), xi–xxvi.

"Capreolus's Defense of Aquinas: A Medieval Debate about the Virtues and Gifts," in *The Pinckaers Reader: Renewing Thomistic Moral Theology*, ed. John Berkman and Craig Steven Titus (Washington, DC: The Catholic University of America Press, 2005), 304–20.

Porter, Jean. *Natural and Divine Law: Reclaiming the Tradition for Christian Ethics* (Grand Rapids, MI: Eerdmans, 1999).

Potts, Timothy C. *Conscience in Medieval Philosophy* (Cambridge University Press, 1980).

"Conscience," in *The Cambridge History of Later Medieval Philosophy*, ed. Norman Kretzmann, Anthony Kenny, and Jan Pinborg (Cambridge University Press, 1982), 687–704.

Power, M. Susan. *Jacques Maritain (1882–1973): Christian Democrat, and the Quest for a New Commonwealth* (Lewiston, NY: The Edwin Mellen Press, 1992).

Principe, CSB, Walter Henry. *William of Auxerre's Theology of the Hypostatic Union* (Toronto: Pontifical Institute of Mediaeval Studies, 1963).

Alexander of Hales' Theology of the Hypostatic Union (Toronto: Pontifical Institute of Mediaeval Studies, 1967).

Pring-Mill, R. D. F. "The Analogical Structure of the Lullian Art," in *Islamic Philosophy and the Classical Tradition: Essays Presented by his Friends and Pupils to Richard Walzer on his seventieth Birthday*, ed. S. M. Stern, Albert

Hourani, and Vivian Brown (Columbia, SC: University of South Carolina Press, 1973), 315–26.

"The Lullian 'Art of Finding Truth': A Medieval System of Inquiry," *Catalan Review* 4 (1990), 55–74.

Reboiras, Fernando Domínguez. "Idea y estructura de la *Vita Raymundi Lulli*," *Estudíos Lulíanos* 27 (1987), 1–20.

Ribaillier, Jean. "Guillaume D'Auxerre. La vie et l'oeuvre," in *Summa Aurea*, ed. Jean Ribaillier, 7 vols. (Paris: Editions du Centre National de la Recherche Scientifique, 1980–87), 1: 1–24.

Rosemann, Philipp W. *The Story of a Great Medieval Book: Peter Lombard's* Sentences (Peterborough: Broadview Press, 2007).

(ed.). *Mediaeval Commentaries on the Sentences of Peter Lombard*, vol. II (Leiden: Brill, 2010).

Santurri, Edmund N. *Perplexity in the Moral Life: Philosophical and Theological Considerations* (Charlottesville: University Press of Virginia, 1987).

Schenk, OP, Richard. "*Perplexus supposito quodam*: Notizen zu einem vergessenen Schlüsselbegriff thomanischer Gewissenslehre," *Recherches de Théologie et Philosophie médiévales* 57 (1990), 62–95.

Schüssler, Rudolf. "On the Anatomy of Probabilism," in *Moral Philosophy on the Threshold of Modernity*, ed. Jill Kraye and Risto Saarinen (Dordrecht: Springer Verlag, 2005), 91–113.

Shanley, OP, Brian. *The Thomist Tradition* (Dordrecht: Kluwer, 2002).

Shogimen, Takashi. *Ockham and Political Discourse in the Late Middle Ages* (Cambridge University Press, 2007).

Sinnott-Armstrong, Walter. *Moral Dilemmas* (Oxford: Blackwell, 1988).

Smith, Lesley. *The* Glossa Ordinaria*: The Making of a Medieval Bible Commentary* (Leiden: Brill, 2009).

Statman, Daniel. *Moral Dilemmas* (Amsterdam: Rodopi, 1995).

Stone, M. W. F. "The Origins of Probabilism in Late Scholastic Moral Thought: A Prolegomenon to Further Study," *Recherches de Théologie et Philosophie médiévales* 67 (2000), 114–57. [Retracted in "A Note from the Editorial Board," *Recherches de Théologie et Philosophie médiévales* 76 (2009), v–vi.]

St. Pierre, Jules A. "The Theological Thought of William of Auxerre. An Introductory Bibliography," *Recherches de théologie ancienne et médiévale* 33 (1966), 147–55.

Thesaurus Linguae Latinae, vol. X, 1, fasc. XI *pernumero-persuadeo* (Stuttgart and Leipzig: B. G. Teubner, 1998).

Thompson, John L. *Writing the Wrongs: Women of the Old Testament among Biblical Commentators from Philo through the Reformation* (New York: Oxford University Press, 2001).

Torrell, OP, Jean-Pierre. *Saint Thomas Aquinas*, trans. Robert Royal, 2 vols. (Washington, DC: The Catholic University of America Press, 1996–2003).

Tugwell, OP, Simon. "The Life and Works of Thomas Aquinas," in *Albert and Thomas: Selected Writings* (Mahwah, NJ: Paulist Press, 1988), 201–67.

Tuninetti, Luca. *Per Se Notum: Die logische Beschaffenheit des Selbstverständlichen im Denken des Thomas von Aquin* (Leiden: Brill, 1996).

Urban, Linwood. "William of Ockham's Theological Ethics," *Franciscan Studies* 33 (1973), 310–50.

Van de Wiel, Constant. *History of Canon Law* (Louvain: Peeters, 1991).

Vecchio, Silvana. "The Seven Deadly Sins between Pastoral Care and Scholastic Theology: The *Summa de vitiis* by John of Rupella," in *In the Garden of Evil: The Vices and Culture in the Middle Ages*, ed. Richard Newhauser (Toronto: The Pontifical Institute of Mediaeval Studies, 2005), 104–27.

Vega, Amador. *Ramon Llull and the Secret of Life*, trans. James W. Heisig (New York: The Crossroad Publishing Company, 2002).

von Schulte, Johann Friedrich. *Die Geschichte der Quellen und Literatur des Canonischen Rechts*, 3 vols. (Stuttgart: Ferdinand Enke, 1875–80 [repr. Union, NJ: The Lawbook Exchange, 2000]).

von Wright, Georg Henrik. *An Essay in Deontic Logic and the General Theory of Action* (Amsterdam: North-Holland Publishing Company, 1968).

Wass, OFM, Meldon C. *The Infinite God and the Summa Fratris Alexandri* (Chicago: Franciscan Herald Press, 1964).

Weber, Hubert Philipp. "The *Glossa in IV libros Sententiarum*," in *Mediaeval Commentaries on the Sentences of Peter Lombard*, ed. Philipp W. Rosemann (Leiden: Brill, 2010), 79–109.

Weigand, Rudolf. "The Development of the *Glossa ordinaria* to Gratian's Decretum," in *The History of Medieval Canon Law in the Classical Period, 1140–1234: From Gratian to the Decretals of Pope Gregory IX*, ed. Wilfried Hartmann and Kenneth Pennington (Washington, DC: The Catholic University of America Press, 2008), 55–97.

Weisheipl, OP, James A. *Friar Thomas D'Aquino: His Life, Thought, and Works*, 2nd edn (Washington, DC: The Catholic University of America Press, 1983).

Westberg, Daniel. *Right Practical Reason: Aristotle, Action, and Prudence in Aquinas* (Oxford: Clarendon Press, 1994).

White, Kevin. "The *Quodlibeta* of Thomas Aquinas in the Context of his Work," in *Theological Quodlibeta in the Middle Ages*, ed. Christopher Schabel, 2 vols. (Leiden: Brill, 2006–07), I: 49–133.

Williams, Bernard. "Ethical Consistency," in *Problems of the Self: Philosophical Papers 1956–1972* (Cambridge University Press, 1973), 166–86, reprinted in Gowans 1987.
Moral Luck: Philosophical Papers 1973–1980 (Cambridge University Press, 1982), 20–39.

Winroth, Anders. *The Making of Gratian's Decretum* (Cambridge University Press, 2000).

Wippel, John F. "Quodlibetal Questions, Chiefly in Theology Faculties," in Bernardo Bazàn *et al.*, *Les questions disputées et les questions quodlibétiques dans les facultés de théologie, de droit et de médecine* (Turnhout: Brepols, 1985), 151–222.

Wood, Rega. *Ockham on the Virtues* (West Lafayette: Purdue University Press, 1997).

Zimmerman, Michael J. "Lapses and Moral Dilemmas," *Philosophical Papers* 17 (1988), 103–12.

Zimmermann, Reinhard. *The Law of Obligations: Roman Foundations of the Civilian Tradition* (Oxford: Clarendon Press, 1990).

Index

Lightning Source UK Ltd.
Milton Keynes UK
UKOW06f1538230815

257371UK00005B/169/P